# Hanging
# Ned
# Kelly

## MICHAEL ADAMS

affirm
press

affirm
press

Published by Affirm Press in 2022
Boon Wurrung Country
28 Thistlethwaite Street
South Melbourne VIC 3205
affirmpress.com.au

10 9 8 7 6 5 4 3 2 1

A catalogue record for this
book is available from the
National Library of Australia

Title: Hanging Ned Kelly / Michael Adams, author.
ISBN: 9781922806406 (hardback)

Cover design by Luke Causby / Blue Cork
Typeset in 12/17 pt Garamond Premier Pro by Post Pre-press Group
Printed and bound in China by C&C Offset Printing Co., Ltd.

*In memory of those who suffered*

# Contents

# Author's Note

This isn't another book about Ned Kelly and his hunters – though you'll find these men in the pages that follow. Nor is it only about 11 November 1880 – though that dark day is related in detail. It isn't even mostly about the forgotten man who put the noose around the neck of our most celebrated and condemned folk hero – though Elijah Upjohn's life is chronicled as never before. *Hanging Ned Kelly* is instead about a society that thought it a good idea to have a drunken chicken thief act as 'finisher of the law' in Australia's most controversial criminal case.

Just as Ned Kelly was shaped by many influences, so Elijah Upjohn was moulded by his family, by his strivings and failings, and by the society he suffered and served. And just as the bushranger followed in the footsteps of others in his outlaw profession, in the colonies and in England, so the hangman stood on the shoulders of those who'd come before – in Melbourne and, following the fatal rope to its sources, in Sydney and across the seas in London.

These men – all referred to by the nickname 'Jack Ketch' – were often more hated than the fiends on the ends of their whips and nooses. Much of this vitriol arose from the nature of their work. More came from the bungling that regularly saw their victims die slowly on the gallows. Yet more was piled on because they were so often drunk and disorderly on the streets. What made their lot still worse was the unease the public felt when they thought the condemned were innocent, or at least unfairly convicted. But these executioners were all duly appointed functionaries of the law carrying out the dread sentence on behalf of God, Queen and Colony. They were killing to keep society safe.

Yet the hangmen were hated – and people loved hating them.

Hangmen absorbed the anger and animosity that might otherwise have been directed at their superiors: judges who passed death sentences; governors, premiers and their cabinets who confirmed these punishments; and sheriffs who hired hangmen, paid them their blood money and for decades declined to fire them for their outrages. Jack Ketch, in all his incarnations, did the dirty work so that his betters could keep their hands clean.

Newspapers poured fuel on the fire by demonising and mocking the executioners until they were hunted through the streets by violent crowds of larrikins. As one scribe asked, 'Who shall hang the hangman?' Yet the same mobs would fight for the chance to see him carry out his work. People who hated the hangman also made heroes of murderous bushrangers, snapped up copies of Australia's first gory tabloid newspaper, lapped up the absurd pronouncements about criminals made by phrenologists and turned a waxwork chamber of horrors into Melbourne's biggest tourist attraction.

*Hanging Ned Kelly* isn't an overview of these contradictions. This is a close-up look at the characters who lived in the shadows of the gallows and at many of the people who died in the noose. Elijah Upjohn, Michael Gately, William Bamford, John Castieau, Claud Farie, Philemon Sohier, Maximilian Kreitmeyer, Marcus Clarke, Alfred Deakin, 'Vagabond', the 'Maungatapu murderer', 'Tom the Devil', 'Captain Melville', the 'Hanging Doctor' and the tragic convict Weachurch were just some of the inhabitants of this world. They were people Ned Kelly would have heard about – from his family and friends, from his mentor Harry Power, from newspaper reports, from a pamphlet stolen from a murdered policeman, from gaolers and fellow gaolbirds – before he finally stood eye to eye with his own hangman.

Although he's unlikely to have known all the tales in this book, Kelly would have been familiar with many – and, from them, with everything that going to the hangman entailed. Scenes we associate with his last days and his legacy had a century's worth of Australian antecedents that aren't usually part of his story. Yet, strand by strand, they threaded the rope that went around his neck. That same noose strangled his executioner just as surely, though far more slowly, as it had his predecessors.

Unlike Ned Kelly and his fellow bushrangers, who were lionised for 'dying game' on the gallows, Elijah Upjohn and the others who occupied his 'loathsome office' were used as sin-eaters by a society trying to convince itself it was Christian and civilised.

Ned Kelly lived a short life. Theirs were longer and they spent them in hell.

## Note on hanging

It was only in the last third of the 1800s that the 'science' of hanging dictated that the knot be placed at the angle of the jaw below the left ear and that rope length be calculated based on weight. This long 'drop' was meant to be sufficient to break the neck – with a 'hangman's fracture' of the second and third cervical vertebrae – but not so great as to decapitate. In that fatal moment, the hempen noose snapping tight was also meant to close off the blood and oxygen supply to the brain. The intended 'humane' result was immediate unconsciousness and an 'instant' and 'painless' death. Even following these measures, this ideal wasn't always or even usually attained, due to everything from terrified victims having strong necks and shifting the knot in their struggles to bungling hangmen's incorrect calculations and ignorant officials using the wrong rope. But *Hanging Ned Kelly* is primarily concerned with the period of white colonisation in Australia before this imperfect process was formalised, when drops were short, knots were as likely to be placed under chins and at the backs of necks, and deaths were often apparently neither instant nor painless. While the frequent use of the gallows ought to have provided a trial-and-error guide to getting it 'right', execution by torture prevailed for more than a century – continuing even after the 'science' had been established and communicated. A brief discussion of modern studies of how people die by hanging can be found in Chapter Twenty-Seven.

## Note on sources

*Hanging Ned Kelly* is largely based on information found in historical newspaper and magazine reports accessed via the National Library of Australia's marvellous Trove database. Then, as now, journalists had differing perceptions, biases, talents and levels of commitment to tell it straight or sensationalise. They wrote for readerships who held certain expectations, and for editors with their own moral, social and political agendas. Finding 'the truth' is elusive; it's rare even to find two reports of an execution that agree on every detail.

Mindful of this, I've often related varying accounts as they were printed. These help us understand how elements of Kelly's hanging would become contested. But they also help to explain why the brutality of hangings was allowed to continue for so long. If *The Argus* said a culprit died instantly and *The Herald* claimed he struggled for five minutes, the authorities had what we'd now call 'plausible deniability', and the ability to shrug off criticism as 'fake news'. This was pervasive. Much as 'The Hangman in Trouble' would become the default headline for any given executioner's latest drunken outrage, 'death was instantaneous' was the go-to for describing gallows victims who often died much harder than that.

In addition to Australian newspapers, I've also relied on contemporary reports from UK newspapers, accessed via The British Newspaper Archive; UK and colonial Australian convict, criminal, penal, sheriff and coronial records held online and onsite at the Public Records Office of Victoria, the NSW State Archives and Libraries Tasmania; and colonial journals kept by convict ship's surgeons, Aboriginal 'protectors', colonial settlers and, particularly, Melbourne Gaol's governor John Buckley Castieau. Where I have consulted secondary material, I've endeavoured to confirm any claims by verifying the relevant primary sources.

For a full list of sources and secondary references, go to: affirmpress.com.au/publishing/hanging-ned-kelly. There you'll also find links to *Forgotten Australia* podcast episodes that enlarge on John Weachurch, Ptolemy and Bobby, Feeney and Marks and other characters and cases mentioned in *Hanging Ned Kelly*.

## Note on contents

*Hanging Ned Kelly* contains frequent references to and descriptions of murder, crime, sexual assault, child abuse, bestiality, violence, execution, torture, anatomisation, desecration of human remains, suicide, mental illness and addiction. There are also descriptions of First Nations people who have died, the terrible manner of their oppression and murders, and the desecration of their remains; of the oppression, criminalisation, torture and execution of homosexual men; and of the blithe legal attitudes to violence against women that let perpetrators walk free to reoffend.

# Prologue

## 11 November 1880

It's just before ten in the morning on Thursday 11 November 1880, and, in one of two cells on the first floor of Melbourne Gaol's New Wing, the convicted man awaits his appointment with the gallows. Just outside his door is a balcony that spans the narrow northern corridor. Into the wooden platform is built a drop, whose trapdoors are kept closed by a bolt attached to a lever in a box like a railway switch. Above, spanning the corridor, is a huge wooden beam. Coiled around it is an ugly rope as thick as a man's thumb. The hanging length reaches the platform with eight feet to spare and ends in a running slip noose.

In a few minutes the condemned man's arms will be pinioned – strapped – behind his back at the elbows; he'll be led to the drop as the priests pray for his soul; the noose will be fitted with the knot behind his left ear; the white cap on his head will be lowered to cover his face; the lever will be pulled to open the trapdoor; and he'll be 'launched into eternity'.

The convicted man might be given to wonder: was it always going to come to this? Was he fated by a criminal father transported to Tasmania? Fated by a system that brutalised him as a boy? Fated by the police who treated him like filth? Fated by the reckless slaughter he committed that put him in this gaol? Can he really do this? What comes after?

But what's done is done. Now this has to be done. Such is life. Such is fame. Such is death.

Outside the gaol's bluestone walls, the streets are crowded with thousands of men, women and children. They don't want today's execution to go ahead, especially those young ruffians of the 'larrikin fraternity'. Inside, below the platform, a few dozen witnesses are gathered. They gaze up at the gallows and at the drop through which the condemned man will plummet. Along with these police, warders and doctors, there are reporters with their notebooks, ready to capture every detail of how a man behaves *in extremis*.

The gaol's governor, the sheriff, his deputy and the surgeon climb the stairs to the first floor. When the city's post office clock strikes ten, the ritual's final legal formalities begin as the sheriff hands the governor a warrant and demands the body of the doomed prisoner.

This is it. Time for the convicted man to go to work on the condemned man in the cell on the other side of the balcony.

All eyes are on the convicted man as he steps out onto the stage. Leather strap in hand, he pads across the balcony, glaring down at the witnesses, who recoil at his repulsive visage. He's old, huge and hulking, and looks every inch the brutal executioner – right down to the pus-filled bump on his big nose.

The convicted man – this drunken shoveler of shit, this ridiculous quack doctor, this miserable chicken thief – must now pinion his first condemned man.

Melbourne's new hangman, Elijah Upjohn, stands face to face with his first victim, the bushranger Ned Kelly.

# CHAPTER ONE

# Strung Up Down Under

When the First Fleeters began the colonisation of First Nations land in 1788, they brought with them more than seeds and livestock, muskets and smallpox. They imported the law and lore of hangmen and hangings. How culprits were strung up, who performed the executions, the way these men were selected and supervised, what became of the dead bodies, and the language used to describe the whole process – all this had evolved over centuries.

Every man and woman who stepped from the First Fleet – free and convict, of high and low class, educated and unschooled – was steeped in the culture of capital punishment. The primacy of hanging in British society was neatly expressed in the satirical story of a shipwreck survivor who feared he had washed up on an island of heathen savages, only to fall to his knees and give thanks when he saw a gallows because he knew he was in a civilised land.

The British had embraced this method of execution more than the people of any other nation. Where the Union Jack and the Christian cross went, the scaffold and noose were sure to follow.

The long rope from Ned Kelly's neck stretched back across the oceans and centuries to 1196 and the first recorded English hanging at Tyburn, London's chief place of execution, where malefactors were strung from tree branches. This victim was the prototypical hirsute self-proclaimed saviour of the poor who had been wounded during a siege and then captured.

William Fitz Osbert, aka Longbeard, led an uprising against King Richard I, aka Lionheart, and for this treason was sentenced to death. After Longbeard was hanged in chains, his followers proclaimed him a martyr and made off with the gibbet, the chains and even blood they scraped from the road, regarding these as relics with miraculous powers. Seven hundred years later, similar scenes would play out in places on the other side of the world called Glenrowan and Melbourne.

Some 50,000 people were put to death at Tyburn over its centuries of operation. Terrified victims were 'turned off' a ladder or cart, some pissing and shitting as they struggled and strangled for up to forty-five minutes. Others were quartered while alive. Some were posthumously beheaded and burned. Corpses were left to rot on ropes. Murderers not hanged in chains were anatomised – that is, dissected after death – to ensure they were dead and as an additional posthumous punishment. What was left of killers was buried in unconsecrated ground, their bodily defilement meaning they wouldn't be resurrected on Judgement Day – considered a fate worse than death.

Although the English were Christians who followed a saviour who'd turned the other cheek before himself being executed on a Roman gallows, they nevertheless used religion to justify putting men and women to death. One of the Ten Commandments may have been 'Thou shalt not kill', but Genesis 9:6 also conveniently instructed, 'Whoever sheds human blood, by humans shall their blood be shed.' Yet many who died in agony at Tyburn were expiating far lesser sins than murder.

Tyburn took on an industrial dimension with the erection of a permanent gallows in 1571. The 'Tyburn Tree' comprised three posts supporting three beams that formed a triangle, so up to twenty-four people could be hanged at once. For gentlefolk, though, being strangled amid the rabble was no way to go, and they were able to pay or plead for a less painful exit via the headsman and his axe.

~

London's first known public executioner was Cratwell, who from 1534 to 1538 was a 'cunning butcher in quartering of men'. The first infamous hangman-cum-headsman was Thomas Derrick. When he was convicted of rape, the Earl of Essex gave him a stark choice: hang or be hanged. Derrick saved his own neck by doing violence to 3000 other necks during his career. Essex would regret his choice, at least for a bloody minute, when in 1601 he went to the block and it took Derrick three chops to separate his head from his body.

Jack Ketch was London's most notorious executioner. He held the role from 1663, when the first newspapers were being published, and became infamous for who he killed and how. In 1678, Protestant priest Titus Oates discovered a plot by papists to assassinate Charles II: at least twenty-two of the Catholic conspirators were hanged for treason. A broadside titled *The Plotters Ballad; being Jack Ketch's Incomparable Receipt for the Cure of Traytorous Recusants and Wholesome Physick for a Popish Contagion* – celebrated one of these executions and the man who performed it. This merrie account began with the victim arriving at the gallows and confessing, 'I am Sick of A Traytorous Disease.' Jack Ketch, axe in one hand and rope in the other, replies, 'Here's your Cure, Sir.'

Jack Ketch was paid three guineas per victim. Traditional perks included the used rope and the condemned's clothing, both of which could be sold to morbid or superstitious folk. Jack made more money offering painless exits. But customer service wasn't guaranteed, as Lord William Russell discovered when he went to the block in 1683 and Jack's first axe blow missed his neck and hacked open his shoulder. Lord Russell was heard to roar, 'Dog, did I give you ten guineas to use me so inhumanly?' He should've kept his coins. Jack hit him twice more – and then finished the job by sawing off his head with a knife. Spectators were appalled. Rumour had it the executioner was drunk or had deliberately inflicted suffering.

Jack – or someone claiming to be him – published *The Apologie of John Ketch, Esq.* to protest: 'It is not fit that so Publick a Person as the Executioner of Justice should lye under the scandal of untrue Reports, and be unjustly Expos'd to popular Clamour.' Jack admitted he'd been a little distracted but denied being a drunken bungling sadist. Instead, he blamed Lord Russell for refusing to wear a hood or restrain his hands; it didn't do for a man to see what was coming and be able to move.

Jack Ketch was also public flagellator, and his most famous corporal punishment illustrated the irreversible risk posed by its capital cousin. Turned out Titus Oates had fabricated the 'Popish Plot'. For perjuries that had seen so many hang, he was whipped through the London streets on successive days by the hangman. A valuable service, no doubt, but after the hacking of Lord Russell, it might've been prudent to give Jack the sack as executioner.

Yet he kept his job. In 1685, the Duke of Monmouth faced the block. He paid Jack six guineas, saying, 'Pray do your business well. Don't serve me as you did my Lord Russell.' Jack did him even worse. He brought the axe down three times and still the Duke was far from dead. The executioner exclaimed: 'God damn me I can do no more ... my heart fails me!' The sheriff ordered him to keep going and Jack rained down another five blows. Still the Duke's head was attached. As it was up to the sheriff, as enforcer of the English law, to see that death warrants were carried out, this one used a knife to finish the job. Spectators were so angry that Jack had to flee for his life.

For all of that, he still wasn't fired. When Jack *was* imprisoned in January 1686, it was for 'affronting' a sheriff. His assistant, Paskah Rose, took over as public executioner. Paskah lasted four months before he was hanged for robbery – by Jack in a triumphant but short-lived comeback before he died in November that year.

Jack Ketch was dead. Long live Jack Ketch.

Jack the man had gone to the grave, but Jack the myth lived on as a figure of fear and fun. He was the supporting villain in the Punch & Judy puppet shows popular in England from the 1660s; poet laureate John Dryden satirically celebrated this 'excellent physician' who delivered a 'fine dry kind of death'. Such was his infamy that, for hundreds of years, 'Jack Ketch' – with all the implications of drunken sadism, ghastly bungling and gallows humour – became the universal nickname for hangmen in England and her colonies.

From 1747, hanging became England's official method of execution. Tyburn executions were held eight times a year and were one of London's most popular mass entertainments. The condemned's three-mile cart journey from Newgate Prison to the Tyburn Tree could take three hours, through streets jammed with people eager to gaze on the prisoner, have a chat and share a joke, or raise a toast at inns where publicans offered free grog to the doomed men and women. Yet it could also be furious rather than festive. Felons convicted of heinous crimes got no last drinks on the house. Their ride was a torture, with the public jeering and pelting them with rocks, garbage or the human and animal shit then so abundant in the streets.

At Tyburn, watched by thousands, the condemned stood on the cart as the noose was affixed to the 'tree'. He or she had a chance to make a last speech that might even resemble what had already been printed in the souvenir programs being sold in the crowd. When the victim was turned off the cart, those who'd paid to be closest got their money's worth as they savoured the death croaks.

William Hogarth's *The Idle 'Prentice Executed at Tyburn* depicted a fictional Tyburn hanging based on this reality. In his picture, a chaotic crowd surges around the cart taking the prisoner to his doom, as he sits wearing his white cap against his coffin with the preacher exhorting him to repent. Spectators line a wall and many more pack a huge grandstand. A pieman calls his produce, a pickpocket works his trade, a mother with babe in arms spruiks copies of the speech to come. In the background, the Tyburn Tree awaits – as does the current 'Jack Ketch', draped across one of its branches, calmly puffing on his pipe.

Euphemisms were used to soften hanging – with the poetic 'launched into eternity' the clear favourite – but the reality of death in the noose was understood to some degree. In 1774, anatomy professor Dr Alexander Munro explained to gallows enthusiast James Boswell that:

> the man who is hanged suffers a great deal; that he is not at once stupefied by the shock ... a man is suffocated by hanging in a rope just as by having his respiration stopped by having a pillow pressed on the face ... For some time after a man is thrown over he is sensible and is conscious that he is hanging.

Hanging was death by torture. But the end could come quicker if the condemned paid the hangman to pull down on his legs. Forger Dr William Dodd was afforded this luxury in 1777. His case was famous for far more than that. The execution of this popular preacher was carried out despite 23,000 people signing a petition. Dr Samuel Johnson led the campaign – and famously ghostwrote Dodd's final sermon in Newgate. When the brilliance of the words led to authorship being questioned, Johnson protected their secret with his oft-quoted drollery: 'Depend upon it Sir, when a man knows he is to be hanged in a fortnight, it concentrates his mind wonderfully.' Dr Dodd's procession and crowd was one of the biggest in Tyburn's history. One newspaper said 40,000 people turned out and a single stand took box office of £100.

Hanging was a money-spinner but it couldn't compete with London's real estate market. Tyburn became too valuable to be devoted to scraggings and was last used in November 1783. This victim died hard: the 'noose of the halter having slipped to the back part of his neck, it was longer than usual before he was dead'. From then on London's main place for executions was outside Newgate Prison, where a new gallows with a drop had been built. Yet the fall and the ropes remained so short that many victims still strangled. The 'science' of hanging – knot placement, length of rope and drop based on weight – was still a century away.

The move to Newgate ended the tradition of the procession, the 'fury of innovation' angering Dr Johnson:

> No, Sir, it is not an improvement: they object that the old method drew together a number of spectators. Sir, executions are intended to draw spectators. If they do not draw spectators, they don't answer their purpose. The old method was most satisfactory to all parties: the public was gratified by a procession: the criminal was supported by it. Why is all this to be swept away?

Dr Johnson needn't have been ropeable. Newgate executions still attracted huge crowds and hanging became more embedded in the culture as villains were castigated – and celebrated – in broadsides, chap books and bawdy ballads. *The Newgate Calendar*, a massive regularly updated compendium of lives ended in the noose, was one of the most popular books in print. One edition had a frontispiece showing a mother giving the tome to her young son so he wouldn't end up like the man hanging on the gibbet outside their window.

But by the 1770s, many who'd neglected their *Newgate Calendar* lessons actually owed their lives to England's overenthusiasm for capital punishment. In 1688 there had been fifty crimes punishable by death but the number of capital crimes had expanded dramatically under what was later dubbed the 'Bloody Code'; by 1815 there would be 200. In addition to treason, murder, arson, theft and forgery, a felon could theoretically have a date with Jack Ketch for stealing from a rabbit warren;

being out at night with a blackened face; impersonating a pensioner; and keeping company with gypsies for a month. Yet this proliferation of capital punishments made juries less likely to convict, and judges more likely to commute sentences to transportation to the American colonies.

But the 1775 Revolutionary War had paused the exportation of evildoers, and the increasing numbers of unhanged convicts were incarcerated in floating prison hulks. In 1783, with the war lost, England at first didn't take no for an answer and thrice tried stealth transportation of convicts to America. The first two voyages ended in mutiny; the third was turned back by the United States, and its human cargo dumped in Honduras.

A new solution was needed.

~

Thomas Barrett was one of 775 or so convicts on the First Fleet when it sailed on 13 May 1787. Five years earlier, aged about twenty-three, he'd stolen a watch from a house in London. His death sentence was commuted to life transportation, and in April 1784 Barrett had been aboard the *Mercury*, the second attempt at shipping convicts to America as 'indentured servants'. During the mutiny, he saved the captain from having his ears cut off. When Barrett and the other rebels were caught, the judge made special mention of this mercy in commuting his second death sentence to life.

After three years on a hulk, Barrett was bound for Botany Bay on the *Charlotte* – and in trouble when the ship was anchored off Rio. He and two accomplices were caught forging coins to buy produce from visiting Portuguese traders. Ship surgeon John White was amazed by the intricacy of the work. Seeking to put Barrett's talents to good use, when the *Charlotte* reached Botany Bay on 20 January, the doctor commissioned him to turn a flattened silver pan into an engraved medal. The depiction of this historical arrival – the *Charlotte* riding a swell beneath the night sky – was the first piece of colonial art produced in Australia.

Six days later, on 26 January 1788, Captain Arthur Phillip founded European settlement at Port Jackson. The next day, male convicts began coming ashore, a process whose conclusion coincided with the first divine service being held on 3 February. The Union Jack and the Christian cross had been raised. A gallows couldn't be far off.

Phillip warned as much on 7 February, when, the morning after the women were landed and white civilisation proper got underway with a thunderstruck orgy, everyone was gathered so the documents establishing the colony could be read. The newly minted governor laid down the law of the new land by using a striking example. Back home chickens were plentiful and stealing one wouldn't get you necked. But in this harsh new land, fowls were vital to survival. Anyone stealing a bird – or anything – would be hanged.

This was at odds with Phillip's previous view on capital punishment. He had been against the death penalty – except in cases of murder and sodomy – and he was no fan of hanging. His proposed solution for Botany Bay? Confine the killer or the buggerer 'till an opportunity offered of delivering him as a prisoner to the natives of New Zealand, and let them eat him'.

In view of this, Governor Phillip may have found hanging men for petty crimes difficult to deal with. Certainly, he blinked when Australia's first criminal court was convened four days later. One convict was given 150 lashes for striking a marine. A second was sentenced to fifty lashes for thieving firewood – though this was remitted. A third man, who'd stolen bread, was chained for a week on a harbour island called *Mat-e-wan-ya* or *Mattewai*. Known and cherished by the Eora people, this bush-covered pyramid rose seventy-five feet above the water and had been used for thousands of years for fishing and leisure. Now it was the first place the white invaders used for the internal exile of their reoffenders – the prison within the prison – and was lent the nautical term 'Pinchgut', which, in time, would be conflated with how banished convicts felt as they survived on half-rations.

Floggings and exile were harsh but preferable to hanging. Yet Phillip's mercy went unrewarded. On 18 February, three convicts were tried for stealing and each was sentenced to 150 lashes. Other offenders tested the governor's patience and the colony seemed on the precipice of anarchy.

On 27 February, Australia's first death sentences were handed down. Thomas Barrett, Henry Lovell and Joseph Hall were to be hanged at six o'clock that evening for stealing bread, pork and peas from the public store. Australia's first gallows was like early Tyburn, a rope from a 'fatal tree'. Phillip ordered all convicts mustered and the condemned trio was brought forth. Lovell and Hall were respited and would live to see another day – if only that, because they were ordered hanged at this same place and time tomorrow. No mercy was extended to Thomas Barrett, petty thief, *Mercury* mutineer, saviour of ears, gifted forger and Australia's first colonial artist.

First Fleeters recorded accounts of this first hanging that varied as much as they overlapped. Surgeon Arthur Bowes Smyth, for instance, dated the hanging to 26 February. He labelled Barrett a 'most vile Character' but recorded he confessed on the gallows. So did White, who said the doomed man admitted to living a wicked life, that he'd been led astray by evil company and that he deserved what he was about to get. This was all important and good. It meant this first capital punishment, though it was to be primitive, was ticking the right boxes: crime, trial, sentence, confession, exhortation to the crowd. All that was missing was the hangman.

While the First Fleet had left England equipped with everything needed for a new society, no one had been designated the public executioner. Maybe they really thought they'd export villains to New Zealand. So a convict was hastily persuaded to play hangman. But then he got cold feet. Provost Marshal Henry Brewer threatened him severely. Major Robert Ross said the marines would shoot him. Only then, according to Smyth, could he 'be prevail'd upon to execute his office'. But that wasn't what surgeon George Bouchier Worgan recorded: 'The Man who had agreed to execute this Office, failed so much in his Duty, (either from Timidity or Feeling) in the Execution of Barrett, that, our Sheriff, was under the disagreeable Necessity of mounting the Ladder Himself, in order to fix the Halter.'

Marine Ralph Clark also noted Brewer as performing the next part of the process, putting a handkerchief over Barrett's head, which was the moment he 'turned as white as a sheet ... soon after the Ladder was pulled from under him and he Launched into the other world without a gron.' Surgeon White used the term 'launched into eternity'.

If Barrett didn't 'gron', it was likely because the rope was so tight around his vocal cords, not because he died quickly and painlessly. He was, as was customary, left to hang for an hour. He was then cut down and buried in an unmarked grave.

It was hoped the convicts had learned a valuable lesson. But Captain of Marines Watkin Tench – who dated the hanging to 28 February – didn't see any redemptive quality to the man's death, describing Barrett as 'an old and desperate offender, who died with that hardy spirit which too often is found in the worst and most abandoned class of men'. The shorthand for this – already in use in England – was 'he died game'.

Those conflicting journal entries, with their euphemistic 'launching' imagery, downplaying of suffering and accounts of penitence and defiance, through to sheriff–hangman tension, the obstinate belief in the death penalty as deterrent and the unholy disposal of the dead, anticipated much that would be found in future newspapers as the Australian colonies carved out their own history of capital punishment.

'Jack Ketch' entered Australian letters that day. In his journal, Worgan mused of the convict's refusal, writing: 'so here was an Opportunity of establishing a Jack Ketch, who, should in all future Executions either Hang or Be Hanged'.

No doubt the next twenty-four hours sharpened the minds of Lovell and Hall wonderfully. Then they were taken in the rain to the gallows and pardoned on the condition they be banished to the harbour island. This commutation raised another question that would endure. It wasn't found in journals but likely crossed the mind of many. Why were some spared for the same crime for which others paid with their lives? Did the mercy shown to Lovell and Hall essentially mean Barrett's death had been legal murder?

Hopes that Barrett's hanging would be a deterrent were quickly dashed. On 29 February, four more condemned men were brought to the tree. Three were shown mercy. That left flour thief James Freeman, whose surname was about to take on a more bitter irony.

Born in Herefordshire around 1768, Freeman as a youth fell in with a gang of thieves. While his older accomplices were hanged, his death sentence was commuted to transportation for seven years. Now, with the noose around his neck, Phillip offered him the same devil's bargain that Essex had extended to Derrick two centuries earlier: Freeman could hang or be the colony's hangman for the rest of his term. Surgeon John White noted that, 'after some little pause, he reluctantly accepted'. Australia had its first Jack Ketch.

Freeman executed his first man in May and would see off another three convicts that year. This 'deterrent' didn't stop six marines from stealing from the public stores and being hanged in 1789. Later that year, Freeman faced a task that would be the death of one of his successors: he had to hang a woman.

When Ann Davis – alias Judith Jones – was sentenced to the fatal tree for stealing clothes, she startled the court with a reason she should not swing. Collins recorded: 'On receiving sentence to die, she pleaded being quick with child.' Scragging a woman was one thing; hanging a pregnant woman was beyond the pale. A jury of the 'discreetest' mothers from the convict ranks was empanelled to decide the state of her womb. Examination complete, the forewoman, as Tench recorded, 'a grave personage between sixty and seventy years old', delivered the verdict: 'Gentlemen! She is as much with child as I am.'

Before Ann Davis hanged, she confessed to her crimes, and, in keeping with another of Tyburn's traditions, she went to the gallows drunk. As seaman Jacob Nagle recorded in his journal: 'She was hung led to the gallos by Two Wimen So Much intoxicated in Liquor that She Could not Stand with Out holding hur up it was dreadful to see her going Out of the World in Such a Senceless Shocking Manner.' Collins put it coldly: 'She died generally reviled and unpitied by the people of her own description.'

Maybe that was so, but hanging her seemed to take its toll on Freeman, who, shortly afterwards, was caught inebriated and insolent out of his hut after curfew. He was sentenced to 100 lashes and his grog ration was suspended. Australia had its first drunken and disorderly Jack Ketch.

But hangmen were hard to find and Freeman kept his job – as would his successors, be they drunk, disorderly or far, far worse.

# CHAPTER TWO

# Harbour Views, Sydney News and Hangman Hughes

Governor Arthur Phillip believed Sydney had 'with out exception the finest Harbour in the World'. The first thing to sully that view – the town's first skyscraper – was a hanged murderer rotting in chains. Yet this supposedly ghastly warning – the first man-made object visible inside the harbour to thousands of people about to land at Port Jackson – only showed how a hanging-hardened populace received such displays less as moral education and more as morbid entertainment.

White-on-white murders were rare in early Sydney. Of the thirty-six people who went to the gallows in the first decade of colonisation, only three were white settlers who had slain their fellow man. Two of those crimes were committed in 1796.

After Hawkesbury settler John Fenlow was hanged for murdering a servant, his body underwent anatomisation. What made it novel for Sydney folk was that the dissected corpse was put on public view. As David Collins recorded: 'The hospital was filled with people, men, women, and children, to the number of several hundreds; none of whom appeared moved with pity for his fate, or in the least degree admonished by the sad spectacle before their eyes.' If his crowd estimate was right, it was a sizeable proportion of the 4000 or so white people then in Sydney.

But Francis Morgan was seen by *everyone*. As an assassin who had cold-bloodedly accepted half a pint of rum to bash a settler's brains, he'd been judged deserving of an even harsher posthumous punishment. Governor John Hunter ordered a scaffold built atop Mattewai. There Morgan was hanged in chains, and there bits of him would remain. 'General' Joseph Holt – leader of the 1798 Irish rebellion – reached Sydney in January 1800 and wrote: 'Just at day-light, we entered Sydney Heads ... we sailed by Pinchgut Island. The first remarkable object I saw was the skeleton of a man, Morgan by name, on a gibbet.'

Collins noted that the Europeans were 'inclined to make a jest of it'. Not so the Eora people, Morgan's decomposing body becoming 'an object of more terror to the natives than to the white people'. So much so that they would no longer go near what had been their 'favourite place of resort'. Sydney's best location had been ruined for its owners. The gibbet was there as late as 1803.

By then the colony had a new way to savour capital punishment. Australia got its first newspaper in March 1803, when George Howe, a London printer-turned-thief who'd been reprieved from the noose and transported, launched *The Sydney Gazette and New South Wales Advertiser*. While the first issue's four printed sheets were mostly advertising and notices, the paper contained one big local story that would end at the gallows.

Fifteen Irish convicts had fled the Castle Hill settlement to become bushrangers and had set about raiding houses and farms. At one property, they fired a pistol at a servant's face, rendering him a 'ghastly spectacle', and, at another, 'they gave loose to sensuality, equally brutal and unmanly'. When George Howe went to print with his inaugural issue, the desperadoes were being pursued by a posse. This first breaking true-crime story had it all – rebellion, violence, rape and the promise of hangings.

The 'licentious banditti' were soon caught and to face justice. If their crimes really had been so violent, there was nothing of it in the next *Gazette* update, which described men who'd stormed properties but stolen little more than food, and had treated settlers and servants well. But these escapees hadn't needed to shoot, maim and rape to incur the extreme punishment. All but one were capitally convicted. The newspaper reported of one trial: 'The evidence being closed, the Court after some minutes deliberation, returned a verdict – all Guilty – Death!'

Patrick Macdermot, Patrick Gannan and Francis Simpson were first for the gallows. While the procession had been abolished in England, the condemned trio had a long journey, first by boat upriver to Parramatta, and then by cart to Castle Hill, so they could hang near the scene of their crimes, watched by a large crowd of soldiers, settlers and mustered convicts. The Reverend Samuel Marsden fervently urged the men to repent. At eleven o'clock the governor's reprieve arrived for Macdermot. He descended the cart before the executioner drove it away to leave Simpson and Gannan hanging.

The *Gazette* story now had an ending that was, if not happy, then at least spiritually gratifying. Readers learned that Simpson had been penitent since his arrest, whereas Gannan had treated his imminent execution as a joke – until the last moment, when he heeded the minister and died contrite. Except that wasn't right! Though George Howe, who produced his newspaper under primitive conditions, didn't have time to reset his main article, he was able to include a correction. It turned out *Gannan* had 'behaved himself with a penitence becoming his situation', while *Simpson* had 'died truly impenitent and hardened'.

So Australia's first newspaper's first issues contained the first unfolding capital crime story, the first sensationalism, the first mistaken reporting and the first editorial correction. George Howe had in every respect pioneered gallows journalism.

Buried in a later issue was a little notice that ten of the Irish escapees had been reprieved. What became of the other two wasn't reported. But later that year the *Gazette* carried the most incredible escape from execution since, well, perhaps, the Resurrection. Joseph Samuels, a convicted robber who was also implicated in the first murder of a police constable in Australia, went to the gallows alongside another man in Sydney. When they were turned off their cart, the other man began to strangle. Yet Samuels hit the ground, suffering only a sprained ankle. His rope had somehow broken.

With the other man still struggling, Samuels was strung up again with a new rope. This one unravelled at the knot and he again hit the ground alive. With the large crowd calling for him to be pardoned, Samuels was launched a third time, and once more survived because the rope snapped. The sheriff might have had charge of the colony's gaols and be responsible for carrying out justice, but ultimately he answered to the Governor and to God. Taking no chances, he hastened to find Governor Phillip Gidley King, who, in his wisdom, commuted the prisoner's sentence in light of the 'extraordinary circumstances'.

Whether a gallows story ended in a miserable strangling or a miraculous salvation, the *Gazette*'s coverage meant no one need miss what'd happened during the most recent enactment of the dread punishment. Such articles were a public service that reassured readers justice was being done. But they were more than that. These were entertaining dramas with the highest stakes for an endlessly renewable cast of characters who might just surprise in how they died game, died easy, died hard or didn't die at all.

Joseph Samuels excepted, culprits only got to play their roles once. The colonial Jack Ketch was a more enduring figure on the stage. But while familiar to the public who attended executions, he was initially a phantom in the press, referred to in passing and usually not by name. Later he'd become a personality in his own right, though this visibility would bring nothing but infamy.

~

Australia's longest-serving early executioner experienced many of the problems that would plague his successors. Thomas Hughes was born in Warwickshire around 1779. A small man of dark complexion, with hazel eyes and brown hair, his claimed occupation was blacksmith when he was found guilty of an unspecified crime and sentenced to transportation for life in March 1801.

After arriving in Sydney in August the following year, Hughes was convicted of stealing and sentenced to a flogging and time in a gaol gang. Not long afterwards, he was sent up to Newcastle – a new place of internal exile – as a repeat offender. There he was enlisted as public flogger and trusted enough to be made a constable.

Hughes was good at his work, and in January 1811 was selected to be sent down as Sydney's new hangman. But the sailors on the ship meant to take him wouldn't allow him to board – and threatened him with injury if the issue was forced. Newcastle's commander advised headquarters: 'I thought it better considering the temper they were in to delay his going for one day.' Hughes's successors would know similar ostracism and threats but have less considerate superiors.

Hughes made his debut a month after arriving in Sydney. James Hutchison, a notorious bushranger and escapee already twice reprieved from death sentences, ran out of luck when he and mate James Ratty had been nabbed stealing material from a shop. The duo was an early example of bushrangers dying game, making jokes as they gave the hangman instructions 'respecting the adjustment of the apparatus'. Presumably this meant the placement of the knot, which still varied depending on the hangman. Hutchison and Ratty held hands and were 'launched off in that posture'. The *Gazette* didn't record their struggles. Hughes hanged about two dozen people in his first five years on the job. But it was double that in the next half-decade. This would include a peak of a dozen in a week. So much for deterrence.

While Hughes wasn't named in the *Gazette*'s hanging articles, he was identified as the public executioner in the newspaper's returns of government expenses, with his salary listed as being £25. This was the same as principal lumberyard clerks and various work gang overseers. But those men worked six days a week to earn their keep, while Hughes was only called on occasionally.

This very disparity had been considered by Adam Smith in *The Wealth of Nations*: 'The most detestable of all employments, that of public executioner is, in proportion to the quantity of work done, better paid than any common trade whatever.' The great economist was being a little facetious as the hangman's compensation was remuneration also for the ostracism and opprobrium that came with his occupation. Others might work harder for longer hours, but they wouldn't be refused a pint of porter in a tavern or be pelted with stones in the street.

Despite being an outcast, Hughes met Susannah Smith in 1814 and the following year they had a daughter. The Reverend Samuel Marsden married the couple in 1816, and two years later Hughes received his conditional pardon. While the *Gazette* didn't report the hangman's personal life, its hanging accounts provided vivid insight into his professional vicissitudes.

In February 1816, William Langford and Thomas Hill tried to cheat Hughes by slashing their arms on the morning they were to be hanged on a gallows platform that had now replaced the cart method. After a surgeon attended the men, Langford confessed the highway robbery for which he was about to die, but said he didn't feel guilty about that. What did trouble him was the murder he'd committed five years ago in England. With that off his chest, Langford asked Hughes to give him plenty of rope for a quick and painless death. Meanwhile, his offsider Hill had lost so much blood he could barely stand, and had to be helped to the stage.

Nooses placed, Hughes opened the drop. Hill reportedly died fast. Langford at the last second leapt from the platform, seemingly to ensure his neck was broken, but he only succeeding in displacing the noose. The

*Gazette* reported that his body and limbs were 'a long time affected by strong muscular motion', accepting that such convulsions weren't a sign of life and suffering but merely the firings of nerves, and thus of no more concern than a headless chicken flapping senselessly around a yard.

How that traumatic morning affected Hughes mentally, emotionally and spiritually can only be guessed. But being a hangman could also be physically dangerous. In December 1818 he had to execute Peter Aldamos, who'd stabbed a constable dead and, after his conviction, confessed to two other murders. Going to the gallows, he made a final request: could Hughes untie his hands and instead bind his feet? The hangman refused. Thwarted, but wanting the world to know his cunning, Aldamos produced a razor he'd hidden in his bandaged hair and revealed his plan to execute his executioner. Hughes had the final say: the killer 'left the world an instant after'.

As much as the hangman was hated, readers might've cheered that outcome. Perhaps not in December 1820, though, when Hughes was called on to do the unthinkable in colonial Australia. After convict John Kirby and a mate absconded from Newcastle, they were apprehended by local Awabakal people, who passed word to the authorities. As police approached, Kirby stabbed a celebrated leader named Burigon, which caused the death of this 'kind, useful chief' two weeks later. The white men stood trial for his murder in Sydney. Aboriginal people weren't legally able to give evidence, but whites testified that Kirby hadn't been provoked. The jury acquitted the mate but Kirby became the first settler known to have been legally executed for murdering an Indigenous person.

This hanging didn't result in *Gazette* commentary. That might've been because the victim was a 'good' Aboriginal person, the malefactor a 'bad' convict and the evidence beyond doubt. It might also have been because space was limited; Kirby's death could only be noted in a column recording the executions of eleven other men the previous week.

The 1820s were turbulent for Hughes. His wife died in March 1820. Then he married a convict transportee named Mary Brown. But Hughes couldn't get lodgings because of his profession, setting this problem out in mid-1824 in a 'humble memorial' to Governor Thomas Brisbane, in which he asked for a land grant so he could build a house for his family. He was told 'that there was no Vacant Land in the town at the time'. Such difficulties would also be experienced by his successors. Denied private and public lodgings, they'd be at the mercy of the mob.

Hughes was attacked by three men in January 1825. *The Australian* reported that the 'finisher of the law' had been beaten in a 'dreadful manner' and lay in the Sydney hospital in a 'dangerous state'. The ruffians weren't apprehended – if, indeed, any effort was made to find them. Hughes pulled through. But by then he'd lost custody of his daughter, who'd been placed in the Female Orphan School. His efforts to get her back would prove unsuccessful.

The government wouldn't protect Hughes's person but it ensured he could keep up with the ever-increasing number of men who needed hanging by giving him a helper. 'Old Tom' – real name Thomas Worrall, born in Northampton in 1776 – was a shepherd convicted twice of sheep stealing. From about 1814 he used his time in gaol constructively as hangman for the town of Warwick, and continued in this role between prison stints. But he was out of a job in 1821, when his third ovine crime resulted in a death sentence, which was commuted to transportation for life. Old Tom arrived in Sydney in December that year. As a lifer, he'd be kept in a cramped cell, but he was also back in business earning a shilling a day as assistant to Jack Ketch.

By the mid-1820s, the fruits of the labour done by Hughes and Old Tom were of increasing interest to those colonial notables who'd embraced phrenology. This 'mental science' – based on the theories of German doctor Franz Joseph Gall and his countryman and collaborator Johann Kaspar Spurzheim – held that character was located in a few dozen regions of the brain, whose development or lack thereof changed the shape of the skull, which could then be measured and interpreted by reference to facial features and cranial bumps.

Two of phrenology's big areas of study were inherent criminality (were low types all but fated for prison and the gallows?) and racial superiority (were non-white people naturally inferior to Europeans?). In view of the former assumption, phrenologists were against capital punishment. This was more or less because culprits were not really to blame for their wicked ways, and because public executions degraded the public – meaning impressionable people might get a case of the bumps and themselves turn to crime after being exposed to the horrors of hanging.

The racial inferiority angle was why, in April 1816, after Governor Macquarie sanctioned the massacre of at least fourteen Dharawal people near Appin, ordering corpses be hanged to instil terror, the warrior Carnambaygal's head was cut off and the skull ended up with George Steuart Mackenzie in Edinburgh. The celebrated craniologist prized the specimen, making it a centrepiece in his museum and a focal point of his 1820 book *Illustrations of Phrenology*, one of the earliest English-language texts about the 'science'.

Phrenology's ability to 'predict' criminality was bolstered in 1826, when surgeon George Thomson of the convict transport *England* got London phrenologist James De Ville to assess all the prisoners aboard before the ship sailed for Sydney. De Ville identified the most dangerous men and pointed out one Robert Hughes as particularly concerning. As it turned out, the headcase Hughes planned a mutiny before reaching the fatal shore, which was thwarted partly because he and other phreno-logically profiled miscreants had been under surveillance. Upon the *England* arriving in Sydney in mid-September 1826, with no casualties reported, for which Thomson thanked phrenology, colonial gentlemen were enthralled. They would soon have a chance to advance the science themselves.

In mid-October Sydney witnessed a massive execution procession that started from the gaol at 6am. Soldiers, armed constables and javelin-men, under the command of police and military officials on horseback, led three carts that conveyed Hughes and Old Tom, the Catholic priest John Joseph Therry and five doomed men wearing nooses around their necks as they rode with their five coffins. The carts were flanked and followed by yet more soldiers and constables. George Street was packed as this capital punishment cavalcade headed out west, first for a triple execution at Burwood, to be followed by a double at Parramatta. The most notorious of the condemned men, bushranger Thomas Mustin, tugged at the nooses of the others in his cart, asking 'how they liked it'.

At Burwood, with mustered prisoners and road-gang convicts watching, Mustin was determined to die game. *The Monitor* recorded: 'On arriving at the foot of the gallows, he ran up the ladder, and enquiring which was his place, jumped upon the scaffold to see if "all was right".' But according to the *Gazette*, he then turned serious and sombre, telling those watching 'to take example by his end, and to attribute whatever of boldness they might have observed in his demeanour, to an anxiety to meet his fate, not to any unconcern about it'.

Mustin was out of the world at 10am – but he wasn't gone from it entirely. His body was conveyed to Mr Leak, the potter of the brickfields, who used plaster of Paris to make a cast of the head, under the direction of Dr Ivory, surgeon with the military hospital.

Creating such a thing was a gruesome business. You had to remove the hair and beard, lather the head in grease, apply a plaster to the front half, then another to the back. But once these moulds were joined, multiple casts could be made and sold, and any number of people could study a telltale head at leisure. Gents who were likely interested in seeing Mustin's cast included notables-turned-phrenologists such as the Supreme Court justice Barron Field, the surgeon William Bland and the explorer and surveyor-general John Oxley.

As George Thomson, surgeon on the *England*, had written in a letter a week before Mustin was hanged: 'All the authorities have become phrenologists.'

# CHAPTER THREE

# The Bloody Code in Action

Australia was the *per capita* hanging capital of the world during the reign of hangman Thomas Hughes. In 1829 in New South Wales – population 36,500 – fifty-two men went to the gallows. That year in the United Kingdom – population 13 million – seventy-four people were put to death. The following year, New South Wales hanged fifty – just one less than in all of England and Wales combined. Some were murderers. Most were burglars or cattle thieves.

The *Gazette*, *The Monitor* and *The Australian* offered detailed reports, some information based on posthumously released prison records. The age, nationality, religion, facial description and physique of the culprit were usually given. There'd sometimes be commentary about family background, phrenological features and assumed strength. A review of the crime, trial and evidence might be provided, with popular doubts about guilt balanced against what had been disclosed in court. Readers got a summary of how a man had conducted himself while chained in the condemned cell, with special attention paid to his penitence and prayerfulness, and his willingness to at last confess. How he slept on the last night was recorded, as was what he had for breakfast.

A condemned man who'd been keep in solitary during his trial usually handled hearing the death warrant without trouble, but the moment of truth came when his leg irons were struck off and the executioner rendered him helpless with the pinions. Then the procession through the gaol's corridors or town streets: clergymen, under-sheriff, gaoler and various gaol officials, the hangman bringing up the rear. In the yard or field would tower the scaffold, beneath which was placed the coffin. How firmly a man ascended the gallows was closely observed. All around would be soldiers, sometimes with fixed bayonets, and spectators, comprising mustered convicts and crowds of the morbidly curious. Audience sizes were noted. There were final prayers, a chance for penitence and a last confession or speech as the noose was placed. Then the cap was lowered, the drop opened, the man fell and his struggles began – and ended after some seconds or many minutes.

The structure of the story rarely changed, but there was usually some fresh dramatic angle. Some men really seemed innocent. Others openly confessed their perfidy. They died easy, died hard, died game. Post-mortem facial distortions were recorded, phrenological observations offered and bleak final resting places on the anatomist's table or murderer's unmarked grave noted.

The hangman himself was usually invisible. But when he bungled, he became a story.

*The Australian* was disturbed in August 1826, when a culprit's 'agonies appeared long and painful; and between seven and eight minutes had slowly expired, ere the body ceased to exhibit symptoms of animation. This unnecessary prolongation of punishment, at the view of which humanity shudders, was thought to originate in the executioner's negligence.'

Eight months later, Hughes bungled again when turning off four penitent prisoners, whose struggles were 'long and violent'. Worse, the executioner was 'said to have been intoxicated'. A 'general feeling of horror and commiseration' at this torture 'pervaded the sheriff and spectators ... long after the limbs of the ill-fated wretches had ceased to quiver'. If their agonies were caused by culpable negligence, *The Australian* argued, the executioner should be punished or discharged.

Yet was it really a problem? The sheriff might've pointed to the *Gazette* – which had also been there but had written nothing of criminals convulsing courtesy of a drunken hangman – and said the rival radical newspapers were exaggerating or inventing. If there was no problem, there was no need to solve it.

Bungling torture on the gallows also took subtler forms. In September 1827, a trio who murdered a soldier during a mutiny at Norfolk Island were to hang in Sydney. When the ringleader, Gough – a 'West Indian Mulatto' – had been found guilty, he'd thanked God and the jury, saying he'd rather die than be sent back to Norfolk. Led to the scaffold, he kissed his coffin and the rope. Then came the pause. *The Australian* noted: 'After being kept for some moments in a state of suspense, extremely painful to the feeling part of those looking on, owing to the awkward manner of the finisher of the law, the drop was finally let fall.' No doubt the delay – and what came next – was far more painful for the doomed men. But it was a good day for Dr William Bland, who got Gough's head, a mixed-race murderer being considered a 'fine subject for the observation of the Phrenologist'.

The hanging of an Aboriginal person was considered a fine subject for observation because it didn't happen frequently. This was in small measure due to arguments about whether the original Australian inhabitants understood English law or were even subject to it. But the infrequency of Indigenous hangings was because whites – despite the anomaly of the hanging of Burigon's murderer – could kill black people almost without fear of legal repercussion.

Two examples illustrate why relatively few Aboriginal people went to the lawful executioner. In July 1826, *The Monitor* reported that a 'Major M— took home a score or two of sculls [*sic*] of the Aborigines slaughtered in the late war. Of course the poor fellows to whose shoulders these said sculls once appertained, were not worthy of a Coroner's Inquest, either before pending or subsequent to martial law.' Two months later, *The Australian* reported that after a 'brisk conflict' at Hunter's River, a party was out hunting the 'sable gentry' so they 'may be taught to understand that wanton aggression cannot be persevered in with impunity; that if the hangman's rope is not long enough, or strong enough, a bullet will answer all the purposes, and a soldier's bayonet prove a good substitute for Jack Ketch.'

It wasn't surprising, then, that a large crowd turned out in Sydney on New Year's Eve 1827 to see an Aboriginal man named 'Tommy' – aka 'Jackey Jackey' – hanged alongside four whites. He'd been convicted of murder, which he denied in a mixture of his own language and English, and was now to feel the power of Christian law. At the scaffold, he didn't appear to understand what was happening, until his arms were pinioned and he started to struggle. Then Tommy's face was pitiful as he said, '*Murry me jerran*,' which the *Gazette* translated as: 'I am exceedingly afraid.' With a melancholy glance at the gallows, he said, 'in a tone of deep feeling, which it was impossible to hear without strong emotion, "Bail more walk about," meaning that his wanderings were all over now.' As a final insult, prominent ministers and priests on the platform bickered loudly about saving his soul.

Tommy's body was handed over for anatomisation. Given *The Australian* had reported the recent exportation of twenty Aboriginal skulls to England, it's likely he became a prize for some distant phrenologist.

~

Concerns about Thomas Hughes continued. In March 1828, during a triple hanging, William Smith hit the ground, stunned, beneath his snapped rope. Seemingly mindful of what'd happened in 1803 with

Joseph Samuels, the sheriff went to find the governor. Smith sat on his coffin, beneath the dangling bodies, the reverend reciting prayers all over again, until the sheriff returned with the bad news. The law was to take its course. Yet Smith couldn't die until the dead men had dangled for an hour. So he sat for what must've seemed an eternity. Then, as the *Gazette* had it, 'his earthly sufferings speedily terminated'.

But the paper was perturbed that this bungle was 'the second or third accident of the kind that has occurred within the last two or three years'. The problem, it believed, was that the hangman had not used the right 'species of cord or rope' to 'ensure the speedy destruction of life'. The paper hoped it 'will never again occur in this Country'.

By this time, Hughes had been hanging men for over fifteen years – and Old Tom had been in the trade nearly as long. Both served at the pleasure of the sheriff and the governor. They knew their business. Or should have. Yet Hughes and Old Tom kept their jobs. Why?

The standard argument was that it was a tough role to fill. Yet this often appeared to be excuse for official entropy. The other likely reason was simply that no one very much cared. Executions were meant to be 'speedy' but they were also supposed to be a deterrent, so it might even be desirable for the odd wretch to die in agony at the hands of an incompetent or intoxicated Jack Ketch. Perhaps the cruelty was the point.

If this was so, it may have had a trickle-down effect, as future hangmen lived in Sydney in 1828. One would soon serve this town, while another was to set the tone in as-yet-unimagined Melbourne. Knowing that Hughes and Old Tom had kept their jobs no matter what might've led these men to conclude that being a boozer and a bungler was no barrier to being Jack Ketch.

~

Being Jack Ketch was still a dangerous job. Near the end of August 1830, Hughes had another close call. *The Australian* reported that as the hangman went to work on seventeen-year-old bushranger John Tiernan, the ruffian smashed him with an elbow and then kicked him from the platform. The executioner fell twelve feet to the ground, the lad jumping down to kick the 'object of his hatred'.

Once Tiernan was subdued and back on the scaffold, Hughes cautiously roped him while Father John Therry urged the lad prove his penitence by kissing his executioner. Tiernan settled for a handshake. Then he engaged in several delaying tactics, including shifting the knot at his neck – which did buy him a few more minutes, though they were spent struggling at the end of the rope. The experience left Hughes, according to *The Australian*, 'very unwell [and] much bruised'. The hangman 'could scarcely stand to perform his last deadly operations; he has a violent mark on his left breast, where Tiernan struck him with his elbow; he declares, had he not broken the fall by seizing hold of the rope, he conceives the injury would have been fatal'.

Yet perhaps it didn't happen that way at all. In *The Monitor*'s version, Tiernan, when asked if he had any last words, shouted, 'Yes, we must go together!' as he grabbed Hughes and jumped. He was left hanging while the hangman suffered a busted arm.

The *Gazette* had yet another take: they'd fallen seven feet and Hughes had refused to carry on, until convinced 'after very great persuasion and entreaty on the part of the Under Sheriff; who certainly would have been placed in a very disagreeable situation'.

A letter writer to *The Monitor* offered a fourth version. He said it'd been the sheriff's fault in the first place. He'd hurried Hughes into harrying Tiernan while he was still praying. Then the doomed fellow had lashed out: 'Being a passionate man, he involuntarily gave him an angry push, and the platform being narrow, the executioner to save himself from falling, grasped the culprit, by which means both fell to the ground, and both were hurt, but no bones were broken.' In this account, Tiernan made his apologies and was then ushered from the world. It was a hangman drama that showed again how different writers could bear very different witness to the same execution.

In any event, Tiernan was soon overshadowed by Bold Jack Donohue. His exploits contributed to the government's new *Bushranging Act*, which, by drastically expanding police powers, increased popular resentment towards the authorities and made outlaws seem more heroic.

Bold Jack dodged hangman Hughes's noose by dying game in a shootout with soldiers in early September 1830. He became the first such figure immortalised as a folk legend, celebrated in ballads that would form the basis for 'The Wild Colonial Boy'. Such songs were reportedly banned in taverns. But another form of immortality seemed to meet with approval. *The Monitor* reported: 'We have lately seen a plaister-of-Paris cast of the late bushranger Donohue, manufactured by Morteon the potter, on Brickfield-hill. It is well done.'

Phrenology's popularity was increasing. But there were doubters, such as a *Gazette* scribe who'd penned a bitterly satirical letter purporting to be written by a London merchant advocating 'free trade in skulls, black and white, red and raw'. This mockery described the money to be made in England from 'the new sect that has sprung up amongst us, variously called Phrenologists, Craniologists, and Bumpologists'. These people, the letter said, 'run mad to get skulls of heathens from every country under the canopy'. The 'merchant' instructed his recipient to ensure that the heads of savages were plenty dented with 'heights and hollows' to fetch the best price.

> From the natives we turn to another excellent class of fellows, your prisoners. I beg you will strive to obtain, and transmit as many skulls as you can, of bushranger, robbers, burglars, murderers, and villains of every grade, class and complexion; the developement [*sic*] of their skulls will speak worlds of wonders. Do not fear detection; give to

the skulls you send the names of Howe, Brown, Geary, Brady, Septon, Williams, Kane, Kelly, &c. and we will prove them to have been the actual brain boxes of such men.

But a few years hence, the *Gazette*, in charting a sustained attempt to discredit phrenology back in 1820, explained how such attacks had only strengthened its appeal:

> It became evident, however, to all that the science was not in the least injured by the exposition. It rather contributed to give its multifarious proofs a firmer hold, and a higher reputation ... People, some fifty years hence, may laugh at our madness, in the same was that we sneer at the tea-pot fortunes of the old hags ...

Despite the evidence against it, phrenology had unshakeable believers among men of medicine, science and the law, and it was held to be educational while also providing a measure of entertainment. In this, it was just like hanging. With the Bloody Code in action in New South Wales, there'd be no shortage of fresh brain boxes for the bumpologists.

When ten surviving members of the bushranging Ribbon Gang – so called because their rebel convict leader, Ralph Entwistle, wore a 'profusion of white streamers about his head' – faced trial in Bathurst on 30 October, hangman Hughes was already on his way from Sydney 'with a three-bushel sack of official ropes'. His pre-emptive departure didn't only signal the verdict but was also because the new Act prescribed bushrangers go to the gallows within two days of sentencing. The Ribbon Gang were all found guilty and hanged. It was the biggest bulk execution to date, and the bodies were left on the ropes for a day to ensure that bushranging never happened again.

~

Just as bushrangers became ever more famous as antiheroes, thanks to newspapers willing to detail their doomed bravado, so Thomas Hughes gradually became a minor personality in proceedings – one who might even be touched by emotion.

In December 1829, called on to execute an old drinking buddy, the hangman at first refused his duty, then changed his mind and went about it sadly: 'when thrusting the fatal noose over the head of his ancient boon acquaintance, Jack's grim features glistened through a tear.'

Hughes's eye might not have been trickling just because he was upset. By the early 1830s the hangman was having trouble seeing. His superiors were aware of his condition. They didn't only keep him working, they actually added to his duties. But Hughes wasn't just going blind. He was going off the rails.

In March 1832 – the same month Hughes and Old Tom were put in charge of subjecting perjurers to the novel degradation of the pillory in the middle of Sydney – the hangman and his assistant had a blazing row. *The Sydney Herald* reported that Hughes had blasted his helper, saying he 'knew no more of his business than a donkey'. Old Tom angrily replied that he'd been in the hanging business for seven years back in Warwick, and wouldn't be snubbed by the likes of Hughes.

Lapping it up, the *Herald* said the dispute looked like it 'would have terminated in a trip to Garden Island', which was where men went to duel. But it didn't come to that. 'Fortunately some friends stepped in,' the paper mocked, 'and the life of one or perhaps both of these valuable members of society were saved.'

The *Herald* was even more gleeful in October 1833, when Hughes almost gave himself a dose of his own medicine over a *romantic* dispute with his helper:

Who would have thought it – On Thursday the finisher of the law, alias Jack Ketch, having been cut out of the affection of a fair one, by his assistant Tom,

35

attempted to slip his wind by suspending himself according to the newest fashion introduced by himself. Having provided himself with rope and soap, and a three legged stool, he retired to the privacy of his apartment, and mounting the rostrum, affixed the fatal cord to a beam, and slipping his head into the noose, kicked the stool from under him and dangled in mid air. A friend calling at the moment, and observing his critical situation, cut him down, and with the assistance of half a pint, soon restored Jack to his equilibrium.

Hughes being so romantically despondent that he tried to kill himself was fine comic fodder, and anticipated decades of similar newspaper stories about the woes of hangmen. The executioner-as-criminal was also good for a laugh, and that same month Hughes obliged when he was charged with stealing gems. The *Gazette* reassured readers that even if he went to gaol, he'd still carry out his duties, though the paper admitted there was 'something of a farce' in this.

Soon afterwards the hangman was back in court on *the* charge that would most often be brought against his successors: Hughes had been found lying drunk in the street the previous night. He asked for forgiveness and mercy but the magistrate said something along the lines of, 'You've never let anyone off!' Hughes couldn't afford to pay the fine and so 'was ordered to shew himself in the stocks to the gaze of an admiring public for one hour'.

Just the previous month Hughes had worked the pillory on a weeping woman for two hours, during which time, *The Monitor* reported, 'some of the mob expressed their love for Mr John Ketch ... by a few hoots and hisses, and by the enunciation of a few vulgar epithets'. Though there's no record of how Hughes was received by the crowd – or whether Old Tom supervised his shame – if his own pillorying went ahead, it would have constituted an extraordinary degradation.

How long would Sydney tolerate a bumbling, thieving, blind and blind drunk hangman who'd tried to neck himself and wound up sentenced to his own stocks? The answer: as long as he wanted to continue.

But perhaps being pilloried was the last straw for Hughes. In mid-January 1834, Sheriff Thomas Macquoid, Esquire, wrote to the colonial secretary, enclosing the hangman's request that he be allowed to retire. Macquoid noted: '[Hughes] has for some time been unable to perform his duty in a proper manner from the gradual decay of his sight ... It would however be dangerous to trust him longer.'

Here was an opportunity for reform. But perhaps that was too much to expect from a sheriff who'd let Hughes hang men when he was going blind.

How to choose the new Jack Ketch?

In London in 1829, after their hangman died, young cobbler William Calcraft applied for the job. This man, who supplemented his income by selling pies at executions, had a few months earlier helped out with a double hanging. His application letter was polite and compelling. But he had a rival – a fellow with experience in military executions. London's aldermen elected Calcraft, who, over the next forty-five years, would be paid well and enjoy a good reputation as mild-mannered family man and consummate capital punishment professional. Calcraft would also work in a system that seemed fairer in who it hanged. In 1832 England had begun dismantling the Bloody Code, reducing the number of hanging offences by two-thirds. People were no longer executed for theft, counterfeiting or most forgery offences.

Sydney's new hangman wasn't chosen as carefully, and there the Bloody Code was still in full effect. Sheriff Macquoid selected a man named Alexander Green, 'formerly employed as scourger at Hyde Park Barracks', who had 'tendered his services for an office rather difficult to get properly filled'. This was the policy that would prevail. Finding a hangman was hard – best to go with who you could get.

Green's appointment was authorised on 7 February 1834. With *The Australian* reporting that the 'new Jack Ketch is at present taking his degrees', he was likely being shown the ropes by Hughes and Old Tom three days later, when a couple of murderers went to the scaffold. The *Gazette* reported: 'The usual quantum of mental torture having been inflicted on the sufferers and spectators by the bungling and delay of the executioner, the drop fell and launched its victims.' One of the men died only after 'some minutes of intense agony'.

As far as it went, Thomas Hughes, around fifty-five now and pretty much used up, was able to retire gracefully and even got a £27 annual pension. We don't know how he looked back on the ghosts of his career but we know he didn't have long to reflect on the hundreds of men he'd seen out of this world. Hughes joined them in October 1835. His passing went unnoticed by the press of the colony he'd served for a quarter of a century as the finisher of their law.

During his long career, Hughes had gone from shadow on the scaffold to someone whose private and public failings were newsworthy. While this minor fame might've seemed harmless fun at the expense of the loathsome hangman, his successors' celebrity would lead to their being so hated that they'd be hunted.

Jack Ketch was dead. Long live Jack Ketch.

∼

Alexander Green was born in 1802 in Holland. He was five-foot-four or so, with blue eyes, fair hair and a pale, pock-marked face. In England he'd worked as a circus tumbler, but Green's life was turned upside down when he was convicted of stealing fabric in Shrewsbury in January 1824 and sentenced to transportation for life. He arrived in Sydney in July that year. Just days later, back in England, an appeal resulted in a pardon conditional on him remaining in the colony for seven years.

After working briefly for Reverend Marsden, Green by early 1826 was a probationary flagellator at Hyde Park Barracks. In the middle of the year, he put his hand up to wield the whip at Port Stephens. There, in April 1827, he was made an honorary constable, only to be dismissed two months later for his part in a drunken assault. Not that this hurt his flogging career, as he was back at Hyde Park Barracks in 1829. Green was next lashing men in the Hunter Valley but deserted his post in late 1833. He wrote to the colonial secretary in January 1834 asking for his last salary and claiming he'd only fled because he feared for his life.

Would the job of hangman come with less backlash? Green likely thought he'd have a more peaceful life if his 'customers' weren't alive to seek revenge. Upon learning that a freed man had volunteered to be the colony's new Jack Ketch, *The Australian* remarked: 'So much for taste.'

Green – who was on the same one shilling and sixpence daily rate as Hughes – was immediately in worse trouble than was on record for his predecessor. The *Gazette* painted an unpretty picture on April Fool's Day:

We are obliged again to point out to the Sheriff a gross instance of irregularity on the part of a person named Green, who passed along the street yesterday afternoon, with two men in irons, all of them in a beastly state of intoxication. Green (who is a scourger, and principal finisher of the law) was occasionally thrashing his prisoners with a stick ... They seemed insensible to pain, and perhaps even put up with it from necessity. Even when at the gaol door, they turned away to enter a Tavern. Is this the sort of person in whose charge it is proper to place offenders in irons? Surely the Sheriff will make an example of this man?

Sheriff Macquoid could've fired Green and set up a system in which a man like Calcraft would be well paid and protected. Doing so might have set a precedent for other colonies to follow – and might have spared them many of the horrors inflicted by, and on, the hangmen to come.

Instead Green was 'dismissed' for a month.

Then he went back to work.

CHAPTER FOUR

# Death Masks, Melbourne's First Cop Killer and Lashes for Elijah Upjohn

D r Robert Wardell was a big name in New South Wales as the colony's fiercest champion of free speech. After co-founding *The Australian* in 1824, he'd often been in the news himself, defying governors Brisbane and Darling, which saw him in two pistol duels with the latter's proxies. The doctor became the story for the last time in September 1834, when he challenged some absconded convicts on his Petersham estate and a rogue named John Jenkins shot him dead.

*The Australian*'s representative sped to the scene and found the former editor's bloody body dumped beneath a tree. What followed was a sensation, not least because Jenkins physically attacked his co-accused in court, and then gave a gallows speech that set a new standard in dying game: 'Good morning my lads, as I have not much time to spare I shall only just tell you that I shot the Doctor for your benefit; he was a tyrant, and if any of you should ever take [to] the bush, I hope you will kill every bloody tyrant you come across.'

Jenkins wouldn't have the last say. A cast of his head was made, and

*The Australian* published a letter from 'Philophrenologist', who offered the usual sort of observations, including that it showed 'a lamentable deficiency in the parts allotted to the reasoning faculties; but this deficiency was amply made up by the great size of the animal portion'. In other words, Jenkins had a beastly brain ruled by passions.

The editor's note thanked Philophrenologist, agreeing with his conclusions and saying the paper would always receive correspondence on the subject. It added this chilling note: 'This Colony presents the very best possible school for the Phrenologist, and any person with leisure and ability might probably be enabled to do great service to the lovers of science, at much less expense of time and means, than in any other part of the world.'

It's hard to interpret this as meaning anything other than that New South Wales – executing more people annually than England, and slaughtering Aboriginal people arbitrarily – could supply a lot of heads. You might make money. Just like the satirical *Gazette* letter had suggested a few years earlier.

A Jenkins likeness in lithograph – made from a courtroom sketch and showing 'the profile and full face of this notorious character' – was put on display by bookseller Mr McGarvie. Sydney's true-crime enthusiasts might've seen it when seeking a copy of *The Autobiography of Jack Ketch*. This fictional work from London – 'illustrated with fourteen humorous plates' – got solid publicity in May 1835, when the *Gazette* published an excerpt in which the old rascal depicted himself as a force of nature to be embraced rather than feared.

The Jack Ketch of imagination was amusing. The incarnation in Sydney was appalling. In April 1836, Green assaulted a well-known laundry operator and was bailed on £20 in sureties. The moment he was free, Green went to the woman's house and used his 'usual threatening language'. She gave an affidavit saying she feared for her life. As he couldn't find his sureties and a new bail, he was committed to gaol. His court appearance gave the *Gazette* the chance to indulge in another common theme in the reporting of hangmen: 'The man Green is well fitted for this office, judging from his countenance, for if ever the whole evil passions of man could be concentrated into one face, he is the man who may rejoice in it. What a skull for a phrenologist!'

Alexander Green was an abusive, violent drunkard, and it's likely only a fraction of his transgressions reached court and thus the newspapers. His occupation and his links to the sheriffs, gaolers and constabulary would've prevented many from pressing charges. But this worked both ways. Frequent abuse and attacks he suffered would've gone unreported unless he made official complaints. For instance, in December 1836, when Green was charged with stealing a hat, he said he'd only knocked it from a man's head while trying to escape a mob. 'Green said he could not walk the streets without being hooted or stones thrown at him,' the *Gazette* reported.

In June 1837, the danger Green posed was stark. Locked up for drunkenness and in a delirium, he made a noose from a piece of cord and tried to strangle his cellmate. The *Gazette* recounted: 'The constables keeping watch hearing a noisy sputtering sound, peeped forth, and found Sullivan kicking out, and foaming at the mouth, evidently at the last gasp.' But there was no punishment for this psychotic attempted murder – then a hanging offence – and instead Green only faced charges of being drunk and trespassing. The magistrate threatened him with the stocks and then set him free.

Rather than removing Green, the colonial government had bumped up his pay to three shillings and threepence a day, and it was soon paying him more to do less. In 1838, following England's example, the law in New South Wales was changed so that only the gravest offences – usually those occasioning or intending violence – were punishable by death.

The Bloody Code was no more. In the first five months of the year, Green turned off just four men. Then, on winter's eve, he made history by finishing the first murderer sent up from that far-off new settlement called Melbourne.

~

In May 1835, John Batman sailed into Port Phillip, ventured up the Yarra and wrote in his journal: 'This will be the place for a village.' He was in the position to establish this settlement because he'd made his name, fame and fortune in Van Diemen's Land by killing Aboriginal people in the 'Black War' and hunting the bushranger Matthew Brady so he could be handed over to the hangman.

At Port Phillip, Batman drew up a 'treaty' with the Kulin Nation owners and paid blankets, knives, tomahawks and so on for their Country. But Sydney considered this Crown land and the government regarded his party as squatters, which also went for John Pascoe Fawkner and other settlers. Governor Richard Bourke declared Batman's treaty null and void. But, as a realist, he recommended legitimising the occupation.

In April 1836 London agreed, authorised private settlement and directed that 'the Aborigines should be placed under a zealous and effective protection'. By then, settler John Wedge had already written to the government to report that Aboriginal people were being attacked at Portland Bay and other whaling stations. In one incident, four men and a girl had been shot and seriously wounded as they lay in their hut. In another, Aboriginal men had been shot and women abducted. Wedge lamented 'such acts of aggression on a harmless and unoffending race of men' who'd been nothing but friendly and helpful. He feared that 'unless some measures be adopted to protect the natives, a spirit of hostility will be created against the whites, which in all probability will lead to a state of warfare between them and the Aborigines'.

Governor Bourke proclaimed that anyone guilty of such attacks would be brought to Sydney to face justice. He despatched police magistrate George Stewart to Port Phillip to investigate. In June 1836, this investigator concluded that the ship's captain responsible for the attack and abductions had been killed by natives, while the whaler who'd gone on the shooting spree was out of the reach of the law.

Stewart took the opportunity to report on the riverside settlement. 'Bearbrass' comprised thirteen crude buildings, with just 177 white adults in the entire district. But Stewart's account – of sheep numbers, of agricultural potential, of wheat already grown – was promising enough for Bourke to send Captain William Lonsdale to assume the police magistrate role and act as de facto superintendent.

Lonsdale arrived in Bearbrass in September, accompanied by three constables and a convict named Edward Steel, who was to serve as flagellator. The police were lowly paid, didn't wear uniforms and weren't the cream of any crop. Drunkenness and corruption were problems from the outset: two would soon be dismissed for intoxication, and the third lost his job for taking a bribe. Steel also had run-ins with the law but kept his office.

Fortunately, most early crimes were relatively minor: drunkenness, assaults, thefts, assigned convicts absconding or refusing work. Such miscreants were usually fined or flogged because the only lock-up was an insecure slab hut on Batman's land. This primitive gaol was where contracted servants who disobeyed their masters might be sent for a month or two. Steel himself did a short stint there, for stealing bricks.

Without a Bearbrass superior court, serious offenders and any necessary witnesses had to be sent by sea to stand trial in Sydney. It was costly and time-consuming. But it had to be done when, in October 1836, Geelong convict shepherd John Whitehead tied Indigenous man Curawine – aka Kurrakoin – to a tree, shot him dead and then threw him in a river. There was no attempt to recover the victim's body, and some witnesses – including a likely accomplice – were able to flee.

In March 1837 – around the same time Governor Bourke visited Bearbrass ahead of naming it Melbourne, after the English prime minister – Whitehead went on trial up in Sydney. Witnesses testified he'd committed the murder but told the court he'd been afraid the victim was trying to summon other Aboriginal people. Whitehead was acquitted, 'with a caution from the Judge about how he comported himself towards the Aborigines for the future; as, if he had been convicted by the Jury, he would inevitably have suffered the utmost penalty of the law'.

It was a big 'if'. In the decade ahead – despite credible evidence of murders and massacres – only one white man from Port Phillip would be convicted of violence against Indigenous people. He served just two months for manslaughter.

The first white-on-white murders were far more zealously investigated. Around the time Whitehead went free, young convict George Comerford absconded from Penrith and set himself on a course for Port Phillip and colonial infamy.

Using a false name and claiming he was colonial-born and free, Comerford got work with settler Charles Ebden as he drove his sheep south from the Murray River. The youth fell in with Joseph Dignum – an older escapee using a similar ruse – and they allied themselves with servant John Smith. In May the trio held up Ebden at gunpoint, stole a horse, supplies and firearms and took off. Out in the bush, they linked up with six other absconders. They all set out for Portland Bay.

They weren't a happy band of bushrangers. Dignum, Comerford and another man known as 'the Shoemaker' axed and shot their companions while they slept and then burned the bodies. Shortly afterwards, Dignum and Comerford murdered the Shoemaker and dumped him in a water-hole. The deadly duo then had a brief bushranging career that consisted chiefly of using their pistols to harass Ebden's servants for supplies and horses. Fleeing north, they were caught near the Murrumbidgee River in June 1837.

Comerford made a self-serving confession and turned 'approver' against Dignum. The Sydney authorities were sceptical about his story of mass murder. The only way to know for sure was for Comerford to take police to the crime scenes. So he was sent down to Melbourne in the charge of constable William Partington. That he reportedly tried to escape custody at Twofold Bay should've put everyone on guard.

In Melbourne in mid-December, the Sydney policeman was joined by local lawmen: Sergeant Isaac Chinn, Constable Matthew Tomkin and a soldier named McDonald. The quartet set out with their prisoner for the scene of the crimes. Ten days later they found some remains of the six men, just as Comerford had described. But before they reached the Shoemaker's grave, they realised they hadn't brought sufficient rations and would have to turn back for Melbourne.

On the morning of 30 December, they forgot their tea when they broke camp. While Partington and McDonald went back for the precious brew stuff, Chinn and Tomkin continued on. Foolishly, they'd taken off their mass-murdering prisoner's handcuffs so he could lead a pack horse. When they stopped, Comerford grabbed the sergeant's musket and mortally wounded Tomkin before escaping into the bush.

Reaching his old stamping grounds, Comerford bailed up shepherds, boasted of his deeds and bragged about his plan for more murders. But on New Year's Day four brave convict servants overpowered the fugitive and handed him over to the somewhat disgraced constabulary.

Right as this drama was playing out, John Pascoe Fawkner was putting the finishing touches on the first issue of Melbourne's first newspaper. Far more primitive than even the early *Sydney Gazette*, the 1 January 1838 issue of *The Melbourne Advertiser* comprised four handwritten sheets, mostly of advertising and notices. But Fawkner had one actual news scoop:

A report had reached Melbourne that Cummerfield the Murderer who was sent from Sydney to point out where the 7 men were said to be murdered has Killed the Two Constables and One Soldier who had him in charge and is now at large in the Bush well mounted and Armed. A party of Volunteers are gone in pursuit.

As with *The Sydney Gazette*'s first issue, Fawkner's errors sensationalised the story. But the errata in the *Advertiser*'s following issue didn't correct these mistakes, though they did acknowledge the killer's name was 'Cummerford'. In his follow-up, Fawkner offered background to the story and reported that the police party had confirmed the claims of mass murder when they found '1 to two Bushels of human bones calcined – some human Teeth and also hair was found unburnt and a quantity of Shoenails and Buttons from the Clothes of the murdered Men'.

Comerford was sent back to Sydney. On 29 May he pleaded guilty to the murder of Tomkin. But in doing so, he now couldn't give evidence against Dignum, who'd be sent to Norfolk Island for fifteen years on robbery charges.

When Comerford went to the gallows the day after his trial, all the Sydney newspapers remarked on how mild-mannered this young mass murderer appeared. According to *The Australian*: 'He was not afraid to die – indeed he looked forward to the day which was to launch him into eternity, as a release from a state of misery.'

Alexander Green went about his work watched by a large audience that included 'several of the more respectable inhabitants of the town'. If Comerford struggled, it wasn't reported. *The Commercial Journal and Advertiser* 'borrowed' a poetic variation on 'launched into eternity' that the *Gazette* had already used twice two years earlier for other hangings: 'the drop fell and the soul of the murderer ascended to its maker'.

Nearly six months later, Green and Old Tom had the historic task of hanging the seven men convicted of the massacre of at least 28 Wirrayaraay people at Myall Creek. *The Monitor* made the hangings seem painless: 'In the midst of their prayers, the bolt was withdrawn, the floor fell from under their feet, and they descended till brought up by the fatal rope.' But Sydney gent JH Bannatyne wrote a letter to a friend in England: 'I have just returned from seeing the seven men all launched into eternity at the same moment it was an awful sight and has made me feel quite sick – I shall never forget it.'

~

Few men forgot a flogging. So the wisdom went. On Christmas Eve 1839, Elijah Upjohn, Ned Kelly's future executioner, was about to get a reminder of how the cat-o'-nine-tails rendered your back like so much raw meat.

Elijah was seventeen years old, and he stood out from the crowd of convicts in Van Diemen's Land because he was already six-feet tall with still an inch or two to grow. Otherwise he was unremarkable in appearance: a sallow complexion, hazel eyes in a longish face, fleshy features framed by brown hair that tended to long.

On his arrival in Hobart in the middle of the year, Elijah had been transferred to the Launceston Barracks and then assigned to the Van Diemen's Land Company, a huge farming operation trying to tame the north-west of the island for sheep, and doing so by killing a lot of thylacines. During this, his first southern summer, Elijah was expected to work sixty-two hours a week. But he'd failed and been charged with 'gross neglect of duty'.

Now, on 24 December, Elijah was sentenced to the unwelcome early Christmas present of twenty-four lashes. Despite his youth, he knew what to expect. That was because he'd first endured this torture when he was just a small child back in Shaftesbury.

Shaftesbury, in Dorset, known for its buttons and beer, had been helping England get done up and undone for centuries. It'd also long been home to the Upjohn clan. But the period before Elijah Upjohn was born saw the town hit hard by the economic depression that followed the end of the Napoleonic Wars, by the coldest and wettest crop-destroying decade in a century, and by the Corn Laws that then drove up the price of food. More misery and starvation came during 1816's disastrous 'Year without Summer', caused by Mount Tambora exploding in far-off Indonesia and its ash, smoke and dust encircling the globe to cause disastrous climate change.

Things were tough all over, but Shaftesbury's agrarian and cottage industries were to suffer more harshly because neither factories nor the railways reached the town. Beer and buttons from elsewhere were cheaper to make and transport. Many who could emigrate from Shaftesbury did so: two Upjohns who went to the United States became hugely rich and famous in the fields of pharmaceuticals and architecture.

Henry Upjohn wasn't a man of such means. Born around 1786, he worked as a labourer until he was twenty-one. Then he enlisted in the 2nd Foot Soldiers in 1807 and later claimed to have played an important role in the Peninsular War. Despite a few conduct hiccups, Henry was promoted to sergeant. He served until 1815, likely losing his job when the end of the Napoleonic Wars resulted in mass demobilisation. Henry got work as a gardener – a precarious job in times of rapid climate change.

Henry married button-maker Elizabeth Burridge in 1819. They had a daughter in 1820 and named her Elizabeth. In May the following year, Henry was convicted of inciting a man to break open a shop and was sentenced to six months in prison. His and Elizabeth's first son was born in late 1822, his baptism recorded on 1 January 1823.

They named the boy Elijah, which was filled with portent, the Biblical miracle worker having raised the dead and himself ascended to heaven, body and soul. This Old Testament figure was so revered that some of Jesus's disciples believed their saviour was the reincarnated Elijah. A big difference between these messengers from God? Christ forgave trespassers. Elijah killed his enemies.

Henry and Elizabeth had another mouth to feed when son Robert was born in 1825. But around this time Henry was charged with not maintaining his dependants and sentenced to a month in gaol with hard labour – which can hardly have made their lot any easier. Then, in January 1826, Elijah, not yet five years old, became the 'man' of the family permanently, when his father was arrested for breaking into a barn and stealing two sack bags and four bushels of wheat. Whether Henry had been trying to keep his wife and children from starving made no difference to the magistrate, who in March sentenced him to seven years' transportation to Van Diemen's Land. Elizabeth – who'd later call herself a widow – was left to fend for herself and their three children.

Elijah helped out by working as a labourer. In April 1834 – by then eleven – he was arrested for stealing a pair of trousers. A pawnbroker told the Dorset court that the boy had sold the pants to him for one shilling. Yet this witness was visibly drunk – he admitted to having partaken of three or four pints of the local product – and was ordered to withdraw. But Elijah wasn't off the hook and others testified against him. Found guilty, he got three months with hard labour and was sentenced to be flogged – twice. Elijah then stood just four-foot-ten, which made such punishments even harsher. How it affected him might be seen in his prison behaviour record: he was 'disorderly'.

Elijah had been out of trouble for three years when his sister died in October 1837. Just weeks later he got a six-week sentence with hard labour for stealing 'tame rabbits'. The boy was again listed as disorderly and was again flogged. In May 1838, it was third time unlucky when he was convicted for stealing shoes. Elijah, now sixteen years old, was sentenced to seven years' transportation.

Like father, like son.

After nine months in gaol and on the hulk *Leviathan*, on 17 March 1839, Elijah and 239 other prisoners sailed from Portsmouth aboard the *Marquis of Hastings*. According to the ship's surgeon, they were in a 'tolerable state of health'. It was plain sailing at first. They crossed the equator a month into the voyage and continued to enjoy fine, dry weather. The men were kept on deck as much as possible to benefit from the fresh air and sunshine.

Things got dicier when the *Marquis of Hastings* was around the Cape of Good Hope and churning east, just above the Roaring Forties. The weather turned wet, windy and cold, and men got sick. Elijah was treated for scurvy. He recovered but four others didn't.

When the weather allowed, the surgeon and crew got the men on deck in smaller groups so they could move around. Down below, a school was established, and about forty previously illiterate prisoners could write and read 'tolerably well' when the ship arrived in Hobart in mid-July 1839. Elijah may have benefited from this education. His English prison record said of him, 'Reads' – which meant he couldn't write – while his Van Diemen's Land record specified that he was capable of both.

Not that it did him any good on Christmas Eve 1839, when he was to feel the lash. But being flayed then did have an upside. Christmas Day and Boxing Day were public holidays. So Elijah would have some time to heal before going back to work. Just a few days after that, it'd be the start of the 1840s. Halfway through the decade he'd be free.

But that was a long way off. Between now and then – and despite cuts from the cat across his back – Elijah would remain disorderly. Offence after offence, every available space in his conduct record would fill up with tiny, spidery reports.

~

Up in Sydney, Alexander Green was now a married hangman. The unlucky woman was a convict widow named Alien 'Ellen' Robertson. Sentenced to seven years for stealing, she'd arrived in December 1837 with her two children, and become his bride the following October.

Green didn't enjoy domestic bliss for long, as by January 1840 he was living with another woman in Castlereagh Street when they were arrested for being in possession of stolen food. Part of his claim to innocence was that his lady friend had brought some of the goods from their last abode. *The Commercial Journal* described him in court as 'that most revolting and hateful looking agent of death'. The *Gazette* fretted facetiously: 'What will become of him if he is committed to the Sydney Gaol?'

Unfortunately for Ellen, her husband's charge was dismissed. So they were back under the same roof in September 1840 when, after a boozy breakfast, he beat her with a pot stick until it broke – and then he laid in the boot. Ellen's daughter Margaret tried to protect her mother and hurled insults at her stepfather. When the constables arrived, Ellen was 'insensible'; she'd be under medical care for weeks.

Green was bailed and went to trial for assault in late November. Ellen refused to testify, saying he'd been sufficiently punished and that he'd otherwise behaved well to her and the children. But Margaret was compelled to give evidence about the assault. Green tried to dismiss it as a 'drunken spree' between husband and wife, after which he'd lost his temper because Margaret had called him 'an howdacious hangman'. At this time, 'hangman' was such a deadly insult it had led to at least one murder. But the jury surely wondered why Green, of all people, would take offence. He *was* the hangman – and the hangman was now going to prison for six months.

Even then, Green didn't lose his job. In fact, he was right back where he was needed – in Sydney Gaol.

On 16 March 1841, an immense crowd gathered to see what would prove to be the city's last mass hanging. On the scaffold were six members of the 'Jew Boy Gang', later given this name because their leader was Edward Davis, aka 'Teddy the Jew'. But these bushrangers were famous for more than his Judaism. With their courteous speech, repudiation of violence except in self-defence, honour in keeping promises to return borrowed horses, and supposed practice of giving some of their plunder to servants, the Jew Boy Gang might have been modelled on Robin

Hood and his Merry Men. But there were other things about this flash young mob – prominent tattoos, flamboyant clothes and bridles decorated with ribbons – that made them early incarnations of the species that would later be known as 'larrikins'.

Things went wrong in December 1840, when they went to Scone and split into teams to rob two stores. During one of these raids, one group was fired on by a young clerk, and gang member John Shea shot the fellow dead. The gang escaped to the bush. Davis, who hadn't been with Shea's team when the man was killed, reportedly said: 'I would give £1000 that this had not happened.' Police magistrate Denny Day – who'd apprehended the Myall Creek murderers – and his posse caught them after a gunfight that left Davis wounded.

Shea was tried for murder – and the rest of the gang as accessories. Davis's defence was that he hadn't been present so could hardly have 'aided and abetted'. They were all found guilty and sentenced to death. Davis's popularity as a gentleman bandit resulted in an appeal for mercy, but it was denied. The men reportedly died fast. *The Monitor* hoped 'their fate will have a beneficial effect, in deterring others from adopting the same lawless course'.

But in Melbourne, fate was writing the future of another flash larrikin bushranger even as the town was erecting its first gallows.

# CHAPTER FIVE

# Melbourne's First Hangings

Melbourne promised new lives to white settlers. But it was a place of mean streets.

In winter, Elizabeth and Swanston streets became raging rivers after heavy rains. Flinders Street was a swamp and Collins Street often a bog. During the frequent floods, muddy holes would swallow up dogs, pigs, horses and other beasts, only for them to reappear as rotting carcasses when the waters dried up. Getting around in the summer was dangerous too, because there were no horse cabs: pedestrians were at constant risk of being trampled by furious riders galloping on their horses.

Even amid such harsh conditions, and an economic downturn, settlers kept coming to the Port Phillip district. Its population reached 12,000 by 1842, and Melbourne now comprised a hundred or so brick and timber dwellings and businesses.

Among those seeking a new start was a young Anglo-Irish barrister, Redmond Barry, who made the town his home in November 1839; he was escaping being made *persona non grata* in Sydney after having an affair with a married woman. There wasn't major legal work for him yet because Melbourne didn't have a Supreme Court, but Barry would be put in charge of a special court conducted in a hotel billiards room that heard small debt cases.

The influx of people included many Irish bounty immigrants. Two of their number were James and Mary Quinn, who arrived in July 1841 and started their new lives on a little rented farm close to the village of Brunswick. Their daughter Ellen, then nine years old, would in a decade marry one of a less welcome breed of immigrant to the district: expiree convicts from the other side of Bass Strait. As Ellen was getting used to her new home, this future husband, John 'Red' Kelly, was crossing the ocean on a convict ship from Dublin to Van Diemen's Land, sentenced to seven years' transportation for stealing a couple of pigs.

~

By the early 1840s, the frontier war that John Wedge had feared was a reality. Settlers shot dispossessed Aboriginal people, who attacked settlers, who conducted reprisal massacres. Port Fairy squatters would in 1842 write to Superintendent Charles La Trobe asking for protection. His reply left no doubt that he considered some of them guilty of atrocities: he'd just received a report that whites had murdered three Aboriginal women and a child while they slept, and he asked the settlers to provide any information they had on the culprits. The squatters replied to say they were offended by the inference that they knew anything.

There had been even worse slaughters. In March and April 1840, at least sixty-one but likely many more Jardwadjali men, women and children are reckoned to have been murdered in what became known as the Fighting Hills and Fighting Waterhole massacres. But the killing of whites continued to command more attention. In May that year an overseer named Patrick Codd – privately described by La Trobe as a wanton murderer of black people – was beaten to death by Aboriginal people on a station at Mount Rouse. In the days that followed, settlers killed three or four Indigenous people in general retaliation, and were said to be 'determined to exterminate the offending hostile tribe'. But the culprit remained at large – for now – though the gallows was on the horizon.

From April 1841, Melbourne could conduct its own major criminal cases in its new but modest brick Supreme Court. Those awaiting trial were now incarcerated in the cramped Eastern Watchhouse, part of the town's recently built but already inadequate gaol. Cases were heard by the first resident judge, John Walpole Willis, an erratic contrarian who had been removed from Canadian and Jamaican colonial positions; Sydney's exasperated leaders had all but exiled him to Melbourne. These trials would now be covered by three newspapers. John Pascoe Fawkner's primitive pioneering newspaper had morphed into *The Port Phillip Patriot and Melbourne Advertiser*, and had as its competition *The Port Phillip Gazette* and *The Port Phillip Herald*.

The recently deceased John Batman's dark deeds in the Van Diemen's Land 'Black War' haunted the Port Phillip district in late 1841. The conflict he'd helped prosecute had been meant to rid the island of Aboriginal people. As a 'humane' alternative to total extermination, a 'conciliator' named George Augustus Robinson was employed to convince survivors to go to the Wybalenna mission, on Flinders Island, for their own 'protection'. There, more than one hundred people were to die of sickness awaiting a promised return to their homeland.

In 1838 Robinson was made Chief Protector of Aborigines for the Port Phillip District, and soon after received Sydney's sanction to take a 'family' of fifteen or sixteen Wybalenna survivors to the mainland to help him 'conciliate' the natives under his jurisdiction. Once they were landed, the government denied them anything like full rations, and in October 1840 cut them loose entirely.

Nearly a year later, two of these men – Tunnerminnerwait, known as 'Jack', and Maulboyheenner, called 'Bob' – and three of the women – Truganini, Planobeena and Pyterruner – struck out from

Melbourne on what would've been called a bushranging spree if they were white. They stole guns, raided stations and had shootouts with settlers.

In October 1841, Tunnerminnerwait and Maulboyheenner killed two whalers. The motive was never definitive: it may have been a case of mistaken identity, the men thinking they were shooting at a white man and his son whose house they'd robbed hours ago; it may have been in retaliation for what the whalers had done to the women of the gang, or more generally directed at their class of violent mariner who'd previously abused and/or abducted them; it may have been a payback for what whites had done in Van Diemen's Land and were still doing in Port Phillip, which Tunnerminnerwait had knowledge of because he'd recently assisted Robinson in investigating what became known as the Convincing Ground Massacre.

After a manhunt, the five displaced Tasmanian Aboriginal people were arrested. The men were charged with the murders, and the women as accomplices.

Before they went to trial, though, Judge Willis heard the case of Sanford George Bolden. The prisoner had allegedly shot and wounded an Aboriginal man and left him clinging to a log in a waterhole while he went to get more ammunition. When Bolden returned, he shot his victim dead, the body slipping beneath the surface. There were witnesses to this. But as the corpse wasn't recovered, Bolden's only charge was shooting with intent to murder.

Bolden's defence was conducted by Redmond Barry, who argued the Aboriginal people had been troublesome and thieving, while Judge Willis was so incensed the case had been brought at all that he directed the jury to acquit. Disturbingly, he said such shootings were justifiable because anyone, white or black, trespassing on someone else's property was fair game. It was a bitterly ironic opinion, given what was happening to the continent's Indigenous people, whose land had been, and still was being, stolen. Willis's statement caused consternation not for that reason but because he seemed to be endorsing vigilantism.

Two weeks later, on 20 December 1841, Willis presided in the trial of the five Aboriginal bushrangers. The case against them relied on circumstantial evidence about the murder of the whalers. Barry, who was Standing Counsel for Aborigines, conducted their defence, arguing that the accused weren't subject to English law, that the case should be heard by a jury comprised half of Aboriginal men, and that if any charge was proved, then the Black War depredations were strong grounds for mitigation of any capital sentence. Protector Robinson testified to the good characters of the prisoners: he told the court how Truganini had once saved him from drowning, for instance.

The jury acquitted the women and convicted the men. But it did so with a recommendation of mercy 'on account of general good character and the peculiar circumstance under which they are placed'. Judge Willis did not agree. He donned a black cap over his white wig – symbolic of the seriousness of what he was about to do – and then passed the death sentences.

But there was still hope. While Port Phillip remained part of New South Wales, any capital case would ultimately be decided by the Executive Council in Sydney. The council – which comprised the governor and his cabinet – was to review the case notes and then issue a reprieve or send down the death warrant. This process would take about a month.

Many expected Tunnerminnerwait and Maulboyheenner to be shown mercy. James Dredge, formerly an assistant protector, wrote in his diary: 'It was generally supposed that this recommendation would have averted the forfeiture of their lives, but the last mail from Sydney brought their Death Warrants.'

The *Gazette* was appalled, raising its voice generally against capital punishment, saying it specifically shouldn't apply to the 'savage', who knew no better, and criticising Willis for 'contradictory decisions' in setting a white man free before the Crown's attempted murder case was complete, and then straight after sentencing black men to hang despite the jury's recommendation to mercy.

The *Gazette* was at least pleased the sheriff had trouble finding a hangman, believing this spoke well of the character of a district where most people were free settlers. But when the offer was put to convicted felons, *The Herald* claimed, eighteen men applied, all wanting the reward of £10 and a ticket of leave. The paper reported: 'the successful aspirant for the new office was a "lifer" of the name of Davis [*sic*]'.

～

John Davies was about forty-five. He stood five-foot-four, had light hair, grey eyes, a face marred by a couple of scars and a beard of 'carroty whiskers'. Davies had been convicted of stealing sheep in England in March 1832. Though it was his first offence, he was transported for life and forced to leave behind a wife and two daughters. After being put to work in Sydney as a saddler and harness maker with the Ordnance Department, he was transferred to Port Phillip in 1840 to be the gaol messenger and occasional turnkey.

A gallows was erected on a green field near where the massive new Melbourne Gaol was being built on the Eastern Hill. This structure comprised two upright poles about twenty feet in height, with a cross-beam between them to which ropes were attached. About six feet below the stage was a plank two feet wide that was fastened to one post with a hinge and supported on the other side by a prop.

The journalist Edmund Finn, aka 'Garryowen', later recalled in 'The Chronicles of Early Melbourne': 'It was a "killing" contrivance of the roughest and most inhuman kind ... This remarkable invention was reached by two short ladders as unstable as itself, and when mounted carefully afforded standing room for the criminals and the executioner. Nothing could well be imagined more scanty and insecure.'

From before daylight on the morning of 20 January 1842, people streamed towards the gallows. They came on foot, in carts and on horseback. The *Gazette* said they 'numbered upwards of three thousand souls'. *The Herald* reckoned 'between four and five thousand'. The turnout was enormous, given the settlement's small population.

A Tyburn carnival mood prevailed, with 'more the appearance of a race-course than a scene of death'. The *Gazette* told readers that 'the greatest levity was betrayed, and the women, who made by far the greatest proportion, had dressed themselves for the occasion.' Men wore their finery and pranced about on horses. A large number of children were also in the crowd. These people swarmed the walls of the gaol under construction. Some jumped on the coffins that awaited the condemned at the foot of the gibbet. Everyone was 'anxiously awaiting the awful scene about to be enacted as if it were a bull-bait or prize-ring'. The exception was a small group of Indigenous people, who watched solemnly from nearby trees.

While the procession hadn't been seen in London for more than half a century, the Aboriginal prisoners were taken from the gaol in a cart guarded by sheriff's officers, constables and mounted police. Surging spectators were frustrated that the condemned men were shielded behind curtains. The audience was so dense around the gallows that soldiers had to clear space at bayonet point before Tunnerminnerwait and Maulboyheenner could step into view. Then, with their arms pinioned, they had to climb the rickety ladders by clinging to the rungs with their chins and knees, so that they were 'partly dragged and partly pushed up to the slaughter'.

On the little platform, Tunnerminnerwait seemed imperturbable but Maulboyheenner shook and moaned in terror. Twenty minutes of prayers were met with crowd cries of 'Cut it short'.

Davies affixed the ropes, climbed back to the ground and the ladders were removed. When the signal was given, he and his fellow convict helper, John Styleman, hauled on the rope connected to the prop. That end of the plank merely fell a couple of feet. The *Gazette* reported: 'There was a dead pause, and a cry of shame from the crowd.' Maulboyheenner gave a start 'indicative of repressed terror', while Tunnerminnerwait shook with fear, 'which increased the horror of the sight'.

The hangmen pulled the prop again, and now the platform fell. Tunnerminnerwait died almost instantaneously – or, as Davies put it, 'he hung beautiful'. But Maulboyheenner's knot became displaced, which, *The Gazette* said, 'rendered his struggle more lasting than his partner's'.

Dredge wrote in his diary that 'the unhappy victims were bunglingly and cruelly consigned to their fate. Jack seemed to leave the world without a struggle, as if the bitterness of death had been long passed. Not so Bob, his fine athletic frame was dreadfully convulsed, it was an awful sight.'

Who was to blame for this cruelty? *The Herald* reported Davies said the gallows was so insecure that 'the least violence on the part of the criminals would have thrown him from the scaffold'. Garryowen later wrote that the clerk of works who'd devised the ridiculous gallows bore most responsibility, and should've faced more than a simple reprimand. But he also recorded the reality of the hangman's unspoken role when such things happened: 'Loud and long were the execrations vented upon the botching hangman (though he was not so much to blame), who only grinned horribly a ghastly smile'.

Once the bodies had hung an hour, they were cut down, put into their coffins and buried outside the cemetery. Only then did the crowd disperse, to drink and talk about what they'd witnessed. Dredge wrote: 'Such an affecting, appalling, disgusting, execrable scene my eyes never saw – God forbid they should ere behold the like again.'

But Melbourne was just getting started. There were white bushrangers about.

# CHAPTER SIX

# Wanted: A Hangman

While the convict escapee George Comerford was too blood-thirsty to be romanticised as a bushranger, and the dispossessed Aboriginal men Tunnerminnerwait and Maulboyheenner were the wrong race and colour, Melbourne's next highwaymen were just right. Ned Kelly would draw direct inspiration from later outlaws such as Ben Hall and Mad Dan Morgan, but there's a good chance he'd heard tell of Jepps & Co, whose last days were packed with bushranger thrills.

Dan Jepps, John Williams, Martin Fogarty and Charles Ellis were 'white and free'. But these contracted servants got on the wrong side of the law when they absconded from their employers. They made themselves candidates for the gallows when they used guns to start bailing up road travellers south-east of Melbourne in late April 1842. Next they took to raiding stations, helping themselves to money, jewellery and weapons, and dining at the tables of their victims and quaffing their champagne. Fogarty even wore a scarlet and gold Austrian Hussars uniform – complete with sword – that was part of their plunder.

The gang had dash and flash. But they were also drunk and dangerous. Fogarty, Williams and Ellis threatened to shoot defence-less captives – and they hatched a plan to assassinate Judge Willis as he went about his regular Monday morning business at Merri Creek. The more sober-minded Jepps stopped them from killing settlers, and argued against their plot to settle the judge.

At first the gang had little to worry about from the law. By the time official parties were chasing them in Dandenong, they were twenty miles north at Plenty River, where they committed nine robberies in a day. When a rider reached Melbourne with this news, two gentlemen had themselves deputised and were joined by three other respectable vigilantes. 'The Fighting Five' rode out of town to hunt down the bushrangers.

That morning the outlaws had raided another station, bailing up the owner and five men, and stuck around to help themselves to a breakfast of roast duck. As the Fighting Five rode up, Jepps cried, 'To your arms, men – to arms!' and the bushrangers unleashed a volley of gunfire from outside the hut. Three retreated inside but Williams was cut off and had to hole up in a nearby storeroom.

As vigilante Henry Fowler crept up on the hut, he was shot through the face and went down with a horrific wound. His comrade Oliver Gourlay stormed the storeroom, dodging a bullet from Williams, knocking a loaded pistol from the bushranger's other hand and getting inside his defences. Gourlay stuck his pistol in the villain's mouth and pulled the trigger. It misfired. As they struggled, Williams shot Gourlay in the side, but the gent's innards were saved when the ball deflected off a gunpowder flask in his pocket. Just as Williams put a pistol to Gourlay's head, posse member Peter Snodgrass burst through the door and fired his rifle.

This bullet glanced off the bushranger's head and inflicted a scalp wound on Gourlay. Williams was down but not out, and raised himself up and reached for his pistol with the cry: 'If I'm going to die, I'll die game!'

Snodgrass swung his rifle and broke its stock over the outlaw's head. Moments later, posse member Robert Chamberlain ran in and shot the bushranger through the heart.

Reinforcements arrived in the form of Constable George Vinge, other police and a band of recently robbed settlers hellbent on payback. These men held a council of war to discuss rushing the hut or burning out the desperadoes. But well-known Melbourne horse-trader 'Hopping Jack' Ewart used a lull in the gunfire to parley with the bushrangers in the hope of finding a peaceful way to end the siege. Fogarty gave himself up around 11am. Jepps and Ellis refused to budge because they knew they were for the gallows if they surrendered – which was one of the downsides to capital punishment in such desperate and deadly situations.

Hopping Jack and another fellow risked their own necks by going into the hut to convince the men to give up. They eventually agreed. But it seemed their real plan was suicide by constable.

Jepps came out first and 'coolly stood beside the hut lighting his pipe with bank notes'. Then he approached Constable Vinge, saying: 'Gentlemen, rather than being taken to Melbourne and made a public show of on the gallows, shoot me.' Jepps was instead handcuffed to Fogarty. When Ellis surrendered, he took a swing at a policeman, which led to someone shouting, 'Shoot him!' But Constable Vinge cried, 'No!' and knocked Ellis down. La Trobe was relieved the bushrangers had been caught so promptly. The superintendent feared they had many more sympathisers who'd been set to join the gang.

Jepps, Ellis and Fogarty were charged with highway robbery and shooting with intent to kill. Judge Willis was ridiculously keen to hang these men. Before the trial he even asked the Executive Council in Sydney to skip their case review. They refused this unseemly request. During the trial, Willis's courtroom speeches were heavily biased. The trio was found guilty and he sentenced them to hang.

While Melbourne waited on Sydney's confirmation, several settlers petitioned for Jepps to be spared because he'd saved them from being shot by his mates. Jepps now also had an unlikely supporter in Willis, who had learned he'd prevented his assassination. The Executive Council wasn't moved to mercy.

Melbourne didn't want another horrifically bungled execution. The astronomical sum of £60 was spent on a sturdy new gallows, erected under the direction of the sheriff, and John Davies, who'd again be assisted by John Styleman, rehearsed by hanging a straw effigy.

On the morning of 28 June, the *Gazette* reckoned 1000 people turned out, the *Patriot* said it was twice that number and Garryowen believed it to be 7000. The condemned trio wasn't screened from public view as they sat on their coffins in a cart with four clergymen.

On the platform, Jepps gave a penitent speech that began: 'Fellow Christians! You see before you three young men in the prime of health and strength about to suffer on the scaffold for the crime of bushranging. I trust you will take warning by our untimely fate, and avoid those crimes which have brought us to this end.'

When Davies had to repeatedly adjust the nooses. Jepps took pity on him, saying, 'God bless you and your poor soul.'

Then the hangman descended. And everyone waited ... and waited while the reverend read the burial service, *The Herald* remarking that 'their excruciating sufferings in this dreadful state of suspense, were obvious to the bystanders'.

As was sometimes pre-arranged, so that victims wouldn't know the exact moment they would hang, when the reverend got to 'In the midst of life we are in death', Davies pulled the bolt. Ellis died instantly, Jepps shook for a few seconds and Fogarty convulsed for three minutes because the knot had shifted. Even so Davies and everyone else had done their work well enough. But now, according to Garryowen, the hangman showed 'outrageous indecency' by pulling the clothes from the corpses in full view of the crowd.

Jepps, Fogarty and Ellis were buried outside the cemetery, near Tunnerminnerwait and Maulboyheenner. The ghosts of these white and black men, Garryowen would report, were often seen fighting after dark – though he put these spirit sightings down to people imbibing too freely of spirits.

~

During the time Jepps & Co. had been awaiting trial, Judge Willis had courted more controversy by ordering a man convicted of stealing clothes valued at ten shillings to gaol for a month, and at the end of his sentence to be tied to a cart in public, where he would receive fifty lashes. His Honour's reasoning for this degrading flogging was that 'imprisonment seemed to have but little effect in intimidating parties from the commission of those petty thefts which were so numerous and frequent in the town'.

Melbourne's hangman refused to do the scourging. His reasoning was unassailable: 'If I hang a man, that's an end of it, but if I flog him, he might meet me in a dark lane one night and duff me up by way of repaying the compliment.' This was paraphrased in the *Gazette* under the headline: 'Logic of a Jack Ketch!' This refusal – and New South Wales governor George Gipps ratifying the punishment too late – spared the man's back.

But future Melbourne hangmen would take up the cat-o'-nine-tails and this would make them more monstrous to the public – and put targets on their own backs.

~

One more man would hang in 1842, this execution performed by John Styleman, who had officially taken over the job. More than two years after the brutal overseer Patrick Codd had been killed for his Frontier War atrocities, an Indigenous man named Figara Alkepurata – known as 'Roger' – was tried for the crime despite there being no white man who spoke his dialect sufficiently to provide proper interpretation. The

Crown's case comprised dubious evidence from the dead man's mates, which the jury believed over claims the accused hadn't been in the area at the time of the murder.

Willis sentenced Figara Alkepurata to hang, and recommended it be done near the scene of the crime to instil terror in the Aboriginal population. La Trobe told Sydney he didn't think that was a good idea. He also requested clemency. Privately, La Trobe would write that he'd learned Codd's behaviour was 'criminal in the highest possible degree', and that by his death 'the sly murder of many of that race was avenged'.

Sydney sent down the death warrant.

On the morning of 5 September, Figara Alkepurata was subjected to the procession and pinioning and then led up the platform – only for a halt to be called to the hanging. The sheriff – who by law had to be present – had either slept in or forgotten to come. The condemned Aboriginal man sat amid 'grinning, excited, merry-looking faces' for about fifteen minutes before the tardy official finally arrived, 'puffing and blowing, and breathlessly tokened the proceedings to be resumed'.

Styleman went about his work. The *Patriot* reported that Figara Alkepurata went through the drop and was still for a second. Then 'suddenly his body exhibited the most dreadful convulsions, his whole muscular system was in agitation ... When his struggle had ceased, his legs were drawn up to his neck, showing the violent nature of the dreadful struggle for life in which he had been engaged.'

～

Melbourne wouldn't have another execution for nearly five years. Not for mercy's sake but because Judge Willis's erratic ways saw him recalled in mid-1843. But the legality of his dismissal was murky, and until it was resolved in London no further death sentences were carried out in the Port Phillip district. At least, this was the reason given by Garryowen.

The temporary pause was likely also due to penny pinching.

After having to fight to be paid just half his fee – because, as it turned out, La Trobe hadn't Sydney's authority to dangle a £10 carrot – and get his ticket-of-leave, John Davies was to work as a cobbler. John Styleman also got his ticket and melted away. After them, the position of hangman would go unfilled. The gallows remained standing because the administration was too cheap to pay the £5 it would have cost to dismantle and remove it. But by the end of 1842, the press had shamed the government into breaking it down.

From December 1844, if Willis's replacement – resident judge Roger Therry – handed down a death sentence, there was no hangman and no gallows to carry it out. In April the next year, when Peter Stratton was convicted of attempted murder, *The Geelong Advertiser* said that with 'no man in the Province being so debased as to take the office', Sydney spared the condemned man's life to save the expense of sending down an executioner and building a new gallows. Stratton was transported to Van Diemen's Land for life.

'Wanted: A Hangman' – so read the headline in *The Australian* in June 1845, when it was reported that an executioner was to be recruited for Melbourne. An offer was made to prisoners at Hyde Park Barracks, but 'there was no candidate for the disgusting office'. When the word was put out elsewhere, seven free men applied for the job. Yet no one was appointed.

So when Thomas Ware was sentenced to hang for murder in Melbourne in February 1846, it perhaps shouldn't have been, as *The Gazette* reported, 'to the astonishment of the spectators' that 'there was a broad grin upon his face'. Making a mockery of the law, he too was off to Van Diemen's Land.

How could Port Phillip have a place in the British empire – let alone strive for separation from New South Wales – if it didn't have its own hangman and its own gallows?

That things were about to change was signalled in June 1846, when the government released its budget estimates for the following year. There – amid the salaries for the post and harbour masters, the clerks and coroners – was the line item: 'Executioner at 2s 6d per diem.'

A permanent hangman was coming and he'd be paid £45/12/6 per year. But who would take the role of Jack Ketch?

# CHAPTER SEVEN

# The Hangman Cometh

On Sunday 10 January 1847, the iron paddle steamer *Shamrock* reached Melbourne from Sydney. Twenty-six respectable passengers disembarked at Queens Wharf; the cargo unloaded included cases of wine, hogsheads of brandy, kegs of tobacco, bags of coffee and the champion horse Petrel, which would be a draw in the upcoming Melbourne races.

What wasn't noted in the 'Shipping Intelligence' columns was that the *Shamrock* had conveyed another important passenger. Propriety would have demanded he be kept under guard and out of sight, lest the other voyagers feel the chill of death dance along their spines.

John Constable Harris – known as Jack – was born in December 1790 in Kent. He stood five-foot-nine and in his younger years had a fair complexion, brown hair and hazel eyes. Little is known of his early life. He claimed to have served for nine years in the 'Indian wars', which probably meant the West and East Indies campaigns of 1804–11.

In March 1815, in Sussex, Jack Harris was convicted of stealing clothes and sentenced to six months. In May 1816, recruited to the West Kent Militia, he was pinched trying to steal a parcel of fifty shoes, though at his trial he managed to talk his way out of a possible death sentence and walked free. But Harris's luck didn't last. In October that year, at East Farleigh, he stole a jacket, a pair of trousers and a few other articles. This time he got a year with hard labour. After serving this sentence, Harris was at liberty for less than six months when he was convicted of an unspecified crime in March 1818 in Sussex. The third-time loser was to be transported for life to New South Wales.

Harris spent four months on a hulk and the next six on a gruelling summer-to-summer voyage aboard the *General Stuart*, during which the 250 convicts aboard were underfed and harshly treated. The ship arrived in Sydney on New Year's Eve, and its convicts were shortly after dispersed to Parramatta, Windsor, Liverpool and Bringelly.

Jack was one of three John Harrises aboard the *General Stuart*, so it's not clear where he was sent. But in August 1819 he was identifiable by his ironic middle name when he was convicted of an unspecified offence and sentenced to Newcastle for one year. This penal settlement was then reserved for recidivists, and conditions there were harsher than in Sydney. Around the anniversary of his arrival, Harris was given fifty lashes 'for repeatedly refusing his Govt Work'. By January 1821 he was back in Sydney before the bench for another offence that sent him back to Newcastle for another six months.

On his return to Sydney, Harris was one of the army of convicts working at the Old Lumber Yard near Bridge Street. Soon after, he had a new master in wool pioneer John Macarthur, until he absconded in January 1823. *The Sydney Gazette* told readers he was thirty-two and had dark flaxen hair and a dark ruddy complexion. He was now a 'nutbrown', his changed appearance the result of slaving in the sun for the past four years.

By this time there were hundreds or even thousands of men like him at large. Escaping wasn't too difficult if you'd been assigned to settlers and not kept in leg irons. Staying alive was harder. You could try to live off the land and avoid being killed by Aboriginal people. You might find work with a sympathetic settler. But if you turned to crime and got caught, you risked a date with hangman Hughes.

How Harris got by isn't known. In November 1823 he was back in custody. This time he was sent to Port Macquarie, which had replaced Newcastle as a harsh place of internal exile. Three years later, Harris was back in Sydney and working for another esteemed colonial master, George Druitt, until he absconded again. In April 1829 he was convicted of running away from his gang, sentenced to fifty lashes and returned to government work at Parramatta.

After this, Harris appears to have become better behaved. This may have been how the old lag came to be Melbourne's first permanent hangman. A few days after his arrival in the southern settlement, *The Argus* would announce him as 'the Sydney Jack Ketch, who has for some time held the office of finisher of the law'. But this wasn't correct: Alexander Green still occupied that role, even after being sentenced to one year for yet another serious assault on a woman. Yet Old Tom had died in July 1846, making it probable Jack Harris briefly pocketed the one shilling per day as Green's helper. As *The Port Phillip Herald* would soon report, the new man 'had never officiated by himself before, but only as an assistant'.

However he got the job, Jack Harris was now Jack Ketch. While he was still a life prisoner of the Crown, this new town could offer new life to an old soldier, gaolbird and convict. All he had to do was kill for it.

And Jack would be doing that soon enough.

~

Since 1839, Scottish settler Andrew Beveridge had enjoyed much success twenty-five miles north of Melbourne. He'd established a sheep run and the Hunters Rest Inn at Mercer's Vale. The pub was informally known as 'Beveridge's' and the town that grew up around it would later be given its founder's name. In 1846, two of his sons and their business partners took a large swathe of Wemba Wemba land near the Murray River and stocked it with sheep and cattle. At first, relations with the traditional owners were peaceful. But Andrew Beveridge Junior was speared one Sunday morning in August 1846 by a group of Aboriginal men he'd accused of stealing sheep.

The culprits remained at large for two months until they were identified by a man who claimed the dying settler had used his last breath to tell him their names. No matter that Beveridge had died alone – and before this 'witness' had arrived in the district. Acting on this information, Corporal William Johnson – the man who'd hunted down Maulboyheenner and Tunnerminnerwait five years earlier – went undercover as a settler with some cronies, and together they lured a large party of Aboriginal men across the river on the pretext of a peaceful feast. Once everyone was settled, Johnson and his men lassoed three suspects and threatened the others with swords, forcing them to retreat.

That night an army of Aboriginal men launched a ferocious attack on the settlers' hut in an attempt to free their brothers. At least two warriors were shot dead by white men who narrowly escaped with their lives. Their Aboriginal captives – known as Ptolemy, Bobby and Bullet-eye – were brought down to Melbourne and presumed guilty by the press, who also praised their captors as heroes.

While the three awaited trial, Port Phillip shuddered at another terrible murder. In November, a young Irish bounty immigrant, Jeremiah Connell, was drinking at Mr Veitch's Inn at Buninyong when he got into an argument with a man named Tom Buckley. They were blustering about the Protestant William of Orange taking back the English throne from the Catholic James II back around the time of the original Jack Ketch. Connell was an Irish Catholic adherent of the popular rural movement known as Ribbonism; Tom was an Ulster Protestant, an Orangeman. During their argument, Connell, Ribbonman and self-confessed boisterous drunk who suffered blackouts, was heard to shout: 'I will never be satisfied until I have the blood of an Orangeman on my soul!'

Sectarian fighting words like these had been heard a lot recently in Melbourne. Hatreds had boiled over in the middle of 1846, when hundreds of Catholics besieged a Protestant hotel in the middle of town. Fists and bullets flew, with a few combatants and bystanders seriously wounded. When only Orangemen were prosecuted, *The Argus* protested that former mayor and current magistrate Henry Moor had facilitated these 'Popish riots' and then let the real criminals go free. The paper even printed a poem calling for Orangemen to sharpen their blades and load their guns because the law had abandoned them.

This was the atmosphere in which Connell went on his drunken tirade. Tom Buckley didn't want fisticuffs, but a fellow drinker named Robert Cameron was up for a fight. They took it outside, stripped to the waist and traded blows as the inn's crowd cheered them on. Connell knocked Cameron to the ground. Then he hit him again, crying, 'I am a papist!' One of the innkeeper's servants, Edward Martin, roared that he was a very cowardly Catholic to hit a lad when he was down. The crowd gave Connell a beating, with Martin one of his attackers.

Over the next few hours, the pulped papist licked his wounds, drank more booze and mulled his revenge. Then he burst into the inn's kitchen to exact it. Martin was sitting at a table reading a newspaper. There were more than a dozen other men in the room, and three or four attacked him. Connell grabbed a poker, lashed out and tried to escape. Caught in the bar, he was beaten savagely, tied up and dumped in the yard. He managed to free himself, then hid out on a nearby sheep station.

Waking up the next morning with the usual hangover and shame, Connell couldn't remember much but was bruised enough to believe he'd come off worse off than anyone else. So he was surprised to be arrested. Edward Martin was dying. In his frenzy, Connell had caved in the man's head.

On 15 December 1846, Connell was tried in the Supreme Court, the case heard by new resident judge William à Beckett. Connell couldn't afford a barrister and no one would stand for him, so he conducted his own defence. Under the law, an accused person could not give sworn testimony, the fact of the charge rendering them not competent, but he could question witnesses and make an unsworn statement. Connell did this pretty well to establish that he'd been drunk, had been beaten and had lashed out in self-defence and without premeditation. À Beckett gave the jury the option of a manslaughter verdict but they found Connell guilty of murder.

Despite the sectarian street war that had taken place just blocks away six months earlier, His Honour professed dismay at what had led to this crime: 'Gracious heavens! That religious dissensions should give rise to murder! By whatever name they call themselves, whether Protestant, Catholic, or Orangemen, they should remember they are Christians, but it would appear that murder is committed in the name of Christ! – in the name of the Devil, I should say!' Then he sentenced Connell to death in the name of that same God.

The next day, Ptolemy, Bobby and Bullet-eye faced the judge for Andrew Beveridge's murder. However, the three men didn't understand English at all and there was no interpreter available. À Beckett said they couldn't be tried immediately and Redmond Barry offered the hope protectors might 'improve' the men sufficiently to understand the charges by their next court appearance.

When the Executive Council in Sydney reviewed the Connell case and decided to let the law take its course, Melbourne could no longer be without a hangman.

~

Jack Harris's arrival hadn't been in the shipping columns but his presence was announced in all the papers a few days later. *The Argus* made its

'Sydney's Jack Ketch' mistake, and mocked his 'fashionable arrival'. The *Patriot* said he'd been sent down because the Crown couldn't get a free man to take the 'repulsive office'. The *Gazette* headlined its little article 'Arrival of an Executioner' and *The Herald* commented that his appointment 'we regret to add, is permanent'.

By now Harris was approaching sixty and hardly fit the monstrous image of the executioner. A young gaol turnkey named John Castieau would later recall that 'hair white as snow, together with a pair of silver-mounted spectacles, made [Harris] look like a very nice pious old gentleman.'

Melbourne must have seemed very modest to Jack Harris. The roads hadn't yet been macadamised and there still weren't horse cabs, so most people got around on foot. To reach the other side of the Yarra – its waters now sullied by the run-off from boiling-down works, where fat was rendered from animal carcasses for tallow – meant using the rickety wooden bridge or paying for a punt. But while the town was primitive compared to Sydney, it had something lip-smackingly in its favour. Melbourne might have been home to just 11,000 whites but it had nearly 100 public houses. As the *Gazette* calculated, when you discounted women and children, 'every 33 full grown men have a public house for their own use'. And, under the terms of his employment, Jack would be able to visit all of them if he wished, even though he was still a prisoner of the Crown serving a life sentence.

Jack Harris was to be a free man *and* a gaoled convict. Under the terms of his employment, he'd reside in the recently opened Melbourne Gaol and be able to roam the town each day, so long as he returned to his quarters by six o'clock at night. In addition to his two shillings and sixpence a day, he'd get third-class rations that included tea and tobacco. With a bed, a roof, food and makings for his pipe taken care of, Jack's salary would keep him in a *lot* of colonial beer. This had to feel like paradise for an old lag.

But Jack would start earning his money and freedom soon enough. The day after he got to Melbourne, Jeremiah Connell's death warrant turned up in the overland mail. The Executive Council had set his execution for 27 January 1847.

~

Connell's hanging would be carried out inside Melbourne Gaol. But his death wouldn't be private. A new gallows was being built in the treadmill yard. When finished, it would rise forty feet, so the upper third towered over the walls. People outside would see the condemned man on the platform. When Jack pulled the bolt, Connell would fall, and according to Garryowen, 'about three-fourths of him would disappear, leaving only the white calicoed face, shoulders and breast to be seen by outsiders'.

Sectarian tensions flared again when an outraged *The Herald* reported that four Irish Catholic prisoners had been singled out by a malicious Protestant turnkey and ordered to build the gallows to hang a fellow Ribbonman. When they refused, they were each sentenced to fifty lashes by visiting magistrates in the secret 'star chamber' system that determined punishments for convicts who offended in gaol.

But *The Argus* slammed *The Herald* as a pro-papist propaganda sheet trying to stir up trouble, claiming only one of the four prisoners was actually an Irish Catholic. Besides, they weren't erecting the gibbet, which was the work of a contractor being paid £35, but merely clearing lumber left over from the old scaffold. Yet *The Argus* shared its rival's outrage that flogging – 'a revolting species of punishment, which is a remnant of the evil effects of our by-gone connection with the convict Colony of New South Wales' – was set to disgrace Melbourne. Even the condemned man weighed in, with a last request that the four men be spared the lash.

In a letter to *The Herald*, Garryowen, under the name 'Verax', wrote an impassioned argument against flogging, saying there had only been three instances thereof in the past seven years. The most notorious victim of such punishment, a violent robber who'd threatened to harm fellow prisoners, had only received thirty lashes. If these men were to be flogged for refusing to erect a gibbet, what was stopping the government from compelling convicts to act as hangmen under threat of the lash?

As Connell's hanging drew near, he took consolation from Catholic priest John Therry – a veteran of many Sydney hangings – who'd arrived in Melbourne a few months earlier. When Therry had come to New South Wales in 1820, he'd brought rosary beads blessed by the Pope himself, and he now allowed Connell to pray with them.

In the early morning light on 27 January, men, women and children threaded their way through Melbourne's streets to crowd around the gaol and gaze up at the gibbet. The papers reported a turnout of 2000 – about one in six people then living in the city.

At 7.30am Connell was taken from his cell to have his leg irons removed by the gaol blacksmith. Jack Harris pinioned Connell's arms behind him at the elbow. The condemned's nerve held – perhaps because he had Therry's rosary beads in his right hand. At 8.30 a gaoler led Connell from the cell block. He was followed by Therry, gaol governor George Wintle and the new hangman, Harris.

The finisher of the law climbed the scaffold ladder first. Gazing down at the sea of faces and across Melbourne, Jack Harris perhaps felt like he'd not only been raised high but made mighty. Here he was, an old lag, holding the power of life and death in his hands before thousands of spellbound people.

Connell was next up, responding to litanies chanted by Therry, who was right behind him. Upon seeing the doomed man, the crowd let out a 'loud hoarse burst of commiseration'. Connell turned to Therry and asked for the rosary to be put around his neck. This done, he stepped towards the front of the scaffold.

'Good people!' he said in a loud, clear voice. 'I never intended to kill that man. I am sorry from the bottom of my heart, and feel regret more at killing him than I do for losing my own life. I am perfectly resigned to my fate, and hope the Lord will grant me a favourable judgement.'

Connell spoke like a preacher at a pulpit; some spectators even responded with 'Amen'. He then embraced the gaoler, shook hands with Therry and even with Harris. The hangman lowered the white cap over Connell's face and adjusted the noose.

The execution was unfolding perfectly. Found guilty after a fair trial, treated well in gaol and offered the comforts of his faith, he had confessed his wrongdoing on the gallows and was conducting himself like a God-fearing gentleman.

Harris pulled the rope that removed the bolt which opened the trap that dropped Connell. But his neck didn't break. *The Herald* reported:

For eight minutes he must have undergone the most excruciating torture, from the fact of the overthickness of the rope and the knot shifting to his chin. He did not struggle much, as least externally, but his inward suffering must have been dreadful; in fact, his hard smothered breathing was distinctly audible to every person in the yard, who appeared shocked at the conflict between life and death. The unfortunate man was strangled and not hanged, and if the drop fall had not been so extremely great as it was, the agonising scene would, in all probability, have been protracted for half an hour.

Garryowen would later write: 'One of the newspaper representatives, becoming very indignant at Harris's bungling, told the old fellow a bit of his mind as he leaped from the ladder and looked up at the swinging corpse.'

Harris took the criticism 'very coolly', and told the reporter to mind his own business. Garryowen paraphrased the hangman saying something like, 'Perfection in any art isn't attained at once, and I will take care and do it better next time.'

How much responsibility really rested on Harris's shoulders? The rope had been the wrong type – which the *Port Phillip Gazette* also noted – and the new hangman was inexperienced. Were these issues his fault? Gaol governor Wintle had been present at all the executions in 1842. Deputy sheriff Alastair Mackenzie had been in his job for five years. They'd had plenty of time since the warrant arrived from Sydney to obtain a rope fit for purpose, and to ensure the new hangman knew what he was doing. But Harris's bosses hadn't done these things.

Not that they had to worry about taking the blame, though, because in the heat of the moment the vast crowd would focus any bad feelings on Jack Ketch. Their hands would stay clean, no matter how badly he did their dirty work.

Jack Harris might've been used as a sin-eating monster, but that wasn't the way he saw himself. He believed he was a public servant faithfully executing his duty. He even felt it was his place to write a memo to the sheriff that day confirming he'd hanged Connell, signing the document in the officialese of the time: 'I have the honour to be, Sir, John Harris, Obedient Servant.'

~

Executing Connell inside Melbourne Gaol created an insider class. Back in 1842, reporters had stood around the public gallows like everyone else. From now on, they'd depend on the authorities for access. *The Port Phillip Gazette* ended its article: 'The attention of the sheriff was very courteous to the reporters of the press in offering them what their convenience required.' With newsmen needing this favour, how wise would it be for them to criticise the sheriff over the actions of his hangman? Decades of reporting would excoriate the finisher of the law rather than his superiors and the system he served.

Before he died, Connell was granted his request: the four prisoners were respited from their flogging. Garryowen would claim credit for this mercy, saying La Trobe had been swayed by his 'Verax' letter. Flogging wasn't to return to Melbourne – yet.

Connell had also received permission for his body to be handed over to his fellow Irish Catholics rather than be consigned to a murderer's grave. After Harris cut Connell down, the body was hurried away in a coffin by 300 of his countrymen and buried in a cemetery so he could rest in peace.

Except he couldn't. Only after Connell was in the ground did Father Therry realise he'd forgotten to retrieve his rosary. He had to plead his papist cause to Protestant officialdom before permission was granted for the grave to be dug up so the priest could claw back his blessed beads.

~

Melbourne didn't have to wait long to see whether Jack Harris would do better next time.

Ptolemy, Bobby and Bullet-eye were tried at the end of February 1847, defended by Redmond Barry. All three accused maintained they hadn't killed Andrew Beveridge. But they still didn't appear to understand the proceedings and, even if they had been able to speak English or had an adequate interpreter, they were legally not allowed to give evidence. Barry put up a spirited defence that challenged the shaky testimony given by two of Beveridge's workers. While they'd been present that morning, and seen the accused among the Aboriginal party, neither had witnessed who inflicted the fatal wounds. Barry also elicited that Beveridge had accused the Aboriginal men of stealing sheep.

Yet a crucial white witness wasn't there to give evidence. Settler James Kirby had been with the Beveridges when they'd gone up to establish their runs. He'd been part of the group that caught the suspects, and he'd shot dead at least one Indigenous warrior in the subsequent battle. Kirby later wrote a memoir in which he said Beveridge, who wore a pistol in his belt, had told the Aboriginal men he'd summarily shoot them if they stole sheep. Had this been known in court, Barry might've mounted a self-defence argument, his clients on the fatal morning having every reason to fear the white man with the gun accusing them of thievery.

Judge à Beckett directed that the jury acquit Bullet-eye because there was no evidence against him. While the recent Connell jury had been allowed a verdict of manslaughter as an option, His Honour told this one that they must either acquit or convict these men of murder. The jury didn't bother retiring, and three minutes later pronounced Ptolemy and Bobby guilty. À Beckett sentenced the men to hang.

It was two months before the death warrants for Ptolemy and Bobby arrived from Sydney. On the last day of April, as *The Patriot* reported, 'a large concourse of persons had assembled outside the New Gaol, to witness the disgusting spectacle'. The paper was predictably appalled at the number of women present, 'some of whom actually had infants in their arms, and conducted themselves on the occasion with most unbecoming levity'.

Inside the gaol, Ptolemy and Bobby were overwhelmed when Harris pinioned them, and, as *The Port Phillip Gazette* reported, 'they cried and sobbed in a manner painful to behold'. Their distress intensified when they reached the scaffold and saw their coffins. Harris had to help Ptolemy up the ladder. Bobby needed even more assistance from the clergy and protectors to ascend. Ptolemy rallied somewhat, gazing at the crowd and seeming to take a moment's pleasure in feeling the sun on his face. Bobby had to be helped to stand while Harris adjusted the ropes. Then he tried to turn his back on the crowd – and the hangman had to turn him around repeatedly.

Having set the nooses, Harris descended the ladder – only to be told he'd forgotten to lower the men's caps. He went back up, fixed his mistake, came down and drew the bolt.

Harris had ensured they had long drops. Ptolemy reportedly died almost instantly and without struggle. 'Not so with Bobby,' *The Herald* reported, 'as when the drop fell, he endeavoured as a last effort for life, to get his foot on a portion of the platform. This ... almost turned him head over heels, in consequence of which, his struggles were protracted and severe.'

*The Port Phillip Patriot* had hoped their fate would instil a 'wholesome terror into the minds of the Murray blacks, and deter them from the commission of further transgressions'. James Kirby later wrote that Bullet-eye had been kept in Melbourne and made to watch his friends die. Then he was returned to his people to spread word of the white man's justice. As Kirby recalled, the message was received and acted upon when warriors then killed shepherds by hanging them. After his son's murder, Andrew Beveridge Senior and the rest of the family moved up to the property near Swan Hill. In 1848 a 'Mr Beveridge' was reported to have 'settled' at least seven or eight Aboriginal people by leaving poisoned flour in their way.

Jack Harris had on this occasion not been the 'finisher of the law' but the finisher of a skirmish that resulted in more killings in the Frontier Wars. The murder of Andrew Beveridge Junior and the executions of Ptolemy and Bobby would soon fade into obscurity. So too would the town that became known as Beveridge – until it was revealed as the place where Australia's most infamous hanged man first entered the world.

# CHAPTER EIGHT

# Jack Ketch in His Capers

In the half-century from 1847, the Melbourne press would frequently ask why the city had to suffer their detestable hangmen. Given there were several executioners during that period – supervised by a succession of sheriffs, themselves serving successive governors, then premiers, and all of them taking their cues from England with its centuries of law, lore and tradition – there was no simple explanation.

But part of the answer surely lay with the newspapers themselves, and the love/hate relationship they established early on with their finishers of the law. While writers would wring their hands about the hangmen's debaucheries, they also couldn't help depicting them as comic figures. It was hard to stay angry at such fiends – and to sustain serious campaigns for their removal – when they were such fun to write about.

The early coverage of Jack Harris set a tone that would be maintained for decades. In mid-May 1847, *The Port Phillip Gazette* reported, under the headline, 'Jack Ketch in His Capers', that he was 'full rigged in a new uniform' when he went on a bender in New Town (later renamed Fitzroy), insulting several women by offering them money he'd earned in his new profession, apparently believing they were engaged in the world's oldest one. The hangman was then booted out of the Traveller's Rest pub and charged with being drunk and violating his curfew. The article said the offended women were prepared for his return, and 'determined, if he again insults them, to make him cut more capers than his last two victims did on the gallows'. But the authorities should 'keep this fellow in close quarters,' the newspaper wrote, 'or we think some amateur will be trying his hand upon his unfortunate neck, nor could a man be condemned for trouncing a blackguard like this for intruding upon his family, his wife and household'. To the *Gazette*, Harris was both a colourful character and a menace deserving of vigilante violence. *The Herald* was less effusive but called him a 'Bacchanalian' and 'inveterate drunkard [who] every time he can get what is termed a "slant" of Mr Wintle ... leaves his quarters at the gaol to some neighbouring tavern to regale himself'. For his drunken offences and being absent without leave, Harris was punished with a week in solitary confinement on bread and water.

Harris had probably been an alcoholic in Sydney, but as a convict his access to grog would have been limited. Now – likely reeling from the horrors he'd committed on the gallows – he had money and as many as pubs as he pleased to spend it in.

In July 1847, the *Gazette* described Harris stepping out with the 'notorious Mary Smith', a robber's wife, prostitute and brothel keeper just released from Melbourne Gaol. Describing Harris as a 'high' official enjoying an 'elevated' state, the paper painted a ribald scene:

*Master Ketch*, with great gallantry, offered the 'lady' his arm, to shew her the lions of the Town. Now, be it remembered that this worthy's services are so very indispensable, that the government allow him more 'swing' than any other poor devil under the ban of the 'broad arrow'. So Jack has full and free permission to roam about the town, on condition of returning to his crib at 6 p.m. But, alas for duty, when female blandishments are in the way! Jack, in the society of the female he had accompanied ... forgot that there was such a place as Wintle's hotel, boldly entered into a certain

Tavern in Town, and with the air of a Brummell, demanded a bed room 'for self and partner'. *Master Ketch*'s looks though being none of the most enticing, he had to go farther at the risk of faring worse.

The unlovely duo were pounced upon by a constable and hustled off to gaol. The *Gazette* reminded its readers that Harris had not long ago been behind bars 'for making fierce love to all the married women in Collingwood', and these vengeful wives were still waiting for his return so they could scald him with hot tea.

The fun continued the following morning, when Harris sobered up and fronted court. There, he very politely tried to tell the magistrate the reason he'd been running late getting back to his cell was because he'd been at the Teetotal Hall with a mind to joining the temperance movement. The arresting constable testified that the accused was 'not in a very fit state to join it, as he was nearly blind drunk'. The magistrate sentenced Harris to three days in solitary on bread and water. The *Gazette* didn't think it enough:

> The vagabond deserves a month, had he got that it might possibly have kept him for some time to come from offending the public eye with his death foreboding image. We wish the Governor of the Gaol much joy of his 'pet' and we should be obliged to him to check John's exuberant spirits a little more for the future. If he is always allowed such liberties, and gets off as easily, he will get so very 'high' in the world, that he will 'look down' on every man jack and mother's son.

The man was a disaster on the drink but he had a certain rascally charm when sober. Around this time, he was brought before Melbourne's mayor, Henry Moor, to answer the usual charge.

The hangman spun a 'long plausible lying yarn' that won Moor over enough that he let him off with a warning. Harris was surprised. He bowed, exclaiming, 'Oh, then, I thank yer ludship, and I can only say if you ever come in my way I'll try and do you a good turn.'

The astonished magistrate shot back: 'My good fellow, I shall take very good care that you shall never have the chance of turning me off, or doing me a turn either good or bad – be off about your business, and if you are brought before me again you shall have six months.'

The fun times continued and other newspapers adopted the tone. When Harris was caught roaming the city streets on a Saturday night in mid-August, the *Patriot* described him as being 'in a state decidedly approaching to the "glorious"'. Under the headline '"Jack Ketch" Again!' the *Gazette* reported that after too many 'sundry potations' he had missed the 'witching hour' and been nabbed by the constabulary while 'taking a crab-like method of reaching head-quarters – I.e. by walking backwards'. Upon being arrested, he shouted he was 'John Harris, the hangman', and told the constables not to 'lay their hands on his sacred person'. *The Argus* reported he had 'expressed a strong hope' to hang the sheriff, La Trobe and another official. The *Gazette* reckoned he'd added the mayor to his list, vowing that if he ever got a chance, he would 'tuck them up in a manner never seen even at Tyburn, and give them the benefit of a knot reserved only for special friends'. The *Gazette* protested too much when it commented: 'Really we are becoming somewhat tired of recording the vagaries of this "high" official.'

But the authorities were genuinely perplexed at how to deal with this special case. Harris's offences were minor and didn't merit harsh or lengthy punishment. While he could be imprisoned and threatened with loss of his position, he could also put his superiors in a tricky spot by refusing to do his work. Why not replace him? It was a question that would cause much angst in the coming decades.

At this time, Melbourne was even more constrained than it would be in future. For starters, the pool from which to find a local replacement was small, and it had already been reported several times that no local man would take the job. Requesting another executioner from Sydney would not reflect well on Superintendent La Trobe, or be well received by his boss, Governor Charles FitzRoy. Further, Alexander Green was still the hangman for New South Wales despite having committed far more serious crimes, making it difficult to justify the inconvenience and expense of removing Harris simply because he was a disorderly drunkard.

From a practical perspective, too, finding a new hangman would be difficult. Given it had taken years for one to be appointed to the province in the first place, even if permission was granted for a replacement it would likely take a long time. In the interim, the sheriff might have to perform the duties of Jack Ketch. That a sheriff should step up was a suggestion that would be made repeatedly in the years to come. But it was said with a hint of mockery, because such a thing was simply unthinkable.

Back in 1788, when the volunteer convict hangman got cold feet, the provost-marshal was reported to have served as Jack Ketch. However, the circumstances on that day had been urgent, and the sheriff, First Fleet sailor Henry Brewer, was certainly no 'gentleman'. The men who became Melbourne's sheriffs were a more genteel breed. Alastair Mackenzie was a good example of why – by virtue of their class, standing, ambition, tradition, *everything* – they were most unlikely to tie a noose, pull a bolt or rock the boat.

Born around 1804, Alastair Mackenzie, Esquire, was the son of a Scottish general and gentleman. As a younger man, Mackenzie held the rank of captain in the army and had been a magistrate in the Bahamas, where he'd married the daughter of the American consul. Appointed by the Queen in 1842 as Deputy Sheriff to Port Phillip, five years later Mackenzie enjoyed an annual salary of £400 and was married with two young children. Within a few years he'd be colonial treasurer, second only in importance to Governor La Trobe himself. God forbid he should taint his reputation – and risk his immortal soul – by scragging anyone in an era when it could be deadly just to call someone a 'hangman'.

So Jack Harris wasn't going to be fired – at least not this early in his career. But he did have to be punished for his latest drunken shenanigans. Magistrate Moor put him on a £40 bond and ordered him to keep the peace for six months, starting him down the road to sobriety with solitary for a fortnight on the usual diet. Moor remarked that he was curious to see the effect on Harris of this more severe sentence.

The answer came a week after Harris's liberty was restored. He got so drunk while defying curfew at the Traveller's Rest that *The Argus* said 'it became a matter of some doubt whether he was to ever return to consciousness'. The *Gazette* reported Moor remarking that Harris had given the police a lot of trouble lately, and 'His Honor the Superintendent' – that was, La Trobe – had requested a 'longer period of confinement than he has recently got'. He sentenced Harris to four months.

The hangman was furious. *The Herald* recorded him saying: 'This is very bad payment for a useful man like me.' The hangman added he had been in government service for forty-two years, before leaving the court, the *Gazette* said, 'highly indignant!'

What Harris didn't do was quit. Being in gaol on salary was better than just being in gaol – and confinement didn't prevent him from doing his job. During the coming months, he was inside with Irish ex-convict John 'Pretty Boy' Healey, who'd been charged with a savage murder in Gippsland. The dodgy police investigation had seen them put a snitch in his cell and let them get drunk so as to extract a 'confession'. They'd also placed Pretty Boy on a patch of earth one dark night, told him he was standing on the murder victim's grave and taken his shivering as a sign of guilt. At his trial two men who might've been the real culprits gave crucial testimony that helped convict Healey.

Pretty Boy went to the gallows at the end of November. Harris – having been deprived of drink for months – did his business efficiently in front of a smaller crowd, who nevertheless stood in the rain and wind to watch the murderer hang.

~

By January 1848 Harris was out. In the middle of the month *The Argus* reported he was in an 'unquestionable state of beer' on Little Bourke Street and 'vowing vengeance' on a tribe of boys who were taunting him for his 'peculiar avocations'. In court he complained that he was too well known, and it was a sad thing he could not walk the streets in peace. The boys weren't charged, while he got three days in solitary.

Alexander Green and Thomas Hughes had been victims of this type of persecution, but this was the first time Melbourne's hangman was reported as the subject of harassment. It was a minor incident but set a precedent: the hangman was fair game. In time, such attacks would escalate until they helped determine who hanged Ned Kelly.

~

Not that Jack Harris needed help to get into trouble. When sober, as John Castieau would recall, the man's pious look was matched by his reverence during Melbourne Gaol's divine services. 'He used to read the responses very audibly,' Castieau wrote, 'and took a leading part in the psalmody'. But in February 1848 at St Peter's Church – two weeks after Melbourne had been proclaimed a city in this very venue – the congregation got a taste of what Harris was like when he mixed drink and devotion.

Harris was pie-eyed, shouting 'Amen' and wielding a big stick. The sexton urged him to behave. But when the organist started playing, the hangman thumped his staff on the floor and twirled it over his head in euphoric delirium. The stick slipped from his hand and nearly brained a young choir member, before Harris retrieved it and threatened injury to the skulls of the reverend and sexton. Pulling out a well-thumbed novel, he then read to the congregation as though intoning from a prayer book.

A police sergeant was called and he collared Harris. Or, as Garryowen put it, 'After a smart tussle of cuffing and kicking, the scoundrel was dragged away, howling like a maimed gorilla, and swearing that if he had his rope with him, "he would strangle the whole lot of them, parson and all".'

The next morning, a sad and sorry Harris was in the court again before Moor. 'Really, Your Worship,' he said, 'I acknowledge my mortified sins and transgressions.'

But the curious magistrate wanted to hear the whole story – including just which tome Harris had read from in the church.

The arresting sergeant obliged: 'I took the book from him – it was Cooper's novel of the Bravo of Venice.'

The court burst into laughter. Their mirth wasn't simply at the juxtaposition of Jack Constable Harris being a fan of James Fenimore Cooper. It was because *The Bravo*'s hero, Jacopo, is forced to become an assassin by the evil Council of Three, who rule over the corrupt city of Venice. After trying to rebel, he's framed for murder and, in the final chapter, it's his head on the block as his girlfriend races to the public square with the news that he's been saved: 'Gelsomina uttered a cry of delight, and turned to throw herself upon the bosom of the reprieved. The axe glittered before her eyes, and the head of Jacopo rolled upon the stones, as if to meet her. A general movement in the living mass denoted its end.'

No wonder the court was amused. Did Jack see himself as Jacopo? Or as the axeman? Maybe both! While most readers thought *The Bravo* had an 'unhappily ever after' ending, perhaps the hangman savoured it professionally? Given how he'd railed against the city's rulers, were Messrs La Trobe, Wintle and Moor his very own Council of Three? It was all very droll.

When the laughter stopped, the magistrate sentenced Harris to six months in prison with hard labour. That gave him plenty of time to ponder *The Bravo*'s final sentences, which reveal that the true horror was not Jacopo's fate but that, after his beheading, Venice went about its business as if his life, sacrifices and death had meant nothing:

> The gay laughed, the reckless trifled, the master pursued his hidden purpose, the cantatrice and the grotesque acted their parts, and the million existed in that vacant enjoyment which distinguishes the pleasure of the thoughtless and the idle. Each lived for himself, while the state of Venice held its vicious sway, corrupting alike the ruler and the ruled, by its mockery of those sacred principles which are alone founded in truth and natural justice.

Certainly *The Argus*'s description of Harris that day was worthy of Cooper's grim denouement: 'Horrible as his occupation may appear, particularly when classed with a consciousness that in the common course of nature his days upon earth must be few, [he] makes no scruple in admitting that he glories in what he proudly terms his profession.'

Old Jack Harris might have been an irredeemable wretch with one foot in the grave, but at least he'd found meaning in life by putting other men in theirs.

∼

At the time of Jack Harris's arrival in Melbourne, there was concern that criminals were being imported wholesale into the province in the form of 'Vandemonians' – expiree convicts from Van Diemen's Land – and 'Pentonvillains' – minor offenders who'd been 'exiled' to Port Phillip after being supposedly rehabilitated in Pentonville and other English prisons.

Augustus Dansey was an example of the latter. In April 1848, this nineteen-year-old had allegedly murdered his exile mate Matthew Luck out near Williamstown. There was a hint that this was the tragic end of an intimate relationship. *The Port Phillip Gazette* said the dead man had a 'great attachment' to his alleged killer, which had 'originated in their being confined together in the same cell for a period of three years'.

Dansey was confined to Melbourne Gaol while he awaited his trial, and there his path crossed with that of the man who'd likely hang him – 'the opportunity being too tempting to allow Mr Harris to pass it over without exchanging some sweet converse'. The *Gazette* reported he'd said, 'Well, Dansey, how d'ye find yourself – don't get down upon your luck.'

The accused was cheerful, if resigned. 'Not I,' he said, 'but I suppose it'll be this.' Dansey then drew his finger across his throat and let his head flop to one side.

Like Jeremiah Connell, Dansey didn't have a lawyer and no one would stand for him. So this lad, who'd run away from home at the age of twelve, defended himself. His understanding of the law was shown when judge William à Beckett asked if he wanted to challenge any members of the jury. He replied: 'I don't know any of them, Your Honour.' The evidence was circumstantial but convincing enough for the jury to find him guilty in ten minutes.

In sentencing, à Beckett said, 'There is a possibility – I say, emphatically, a possibility – of your innocence.' He added: 'It is better, if you are innocent, that you should have been found guilty, than, being guilty, that you should have been acquitted.'

This reversed the legal tenet that it was better that nine guilty men go free than that one innocent man be hanged. The *Gazette* felt that if the accused had had representation, the verdict would have been different. À Beckett didn't recommend mercy, and the Executive Council in Sydney didn't reprieve him.

On the first morning in August, Dansey again met Harris. The reverend urged him to confess so he didn't die with a lie on his lips. The doomed man declared his innocence so believably that the clergyman was convinced another victim was 'to be sacrificed to circumstantial evidence'.

Guilty or innocent? After Harris dispatched Dansey, there might be a way, some said, to know the truth *scientifically*.

Melbourne had since at least 1839 been graced with a few gentlemen who occasionally expounded on phrenology. When Dansey was cut down, the Antarctic explorer turned customs agent John Greenlaw Foxton made a 'phrenological examination' of the head, with the 'kind permission of the Deputy Sheriff'. A few days later, 'Phreno' – likely Foxton – furnished the *Patriot* with Dansey's bumpological portrait, complete with all the measurements. The man had been burdened with too much secretiveness, destructiveness and acquisitiveness, and not enough benevolence, perception and reflection, et cetera, et cetera. It boiled down to the dead man not having the right sort of brains to avoid his fate as a murderer. Phreno concluded: 'There does not remain, there-fore, the slightest doubt on my mind, of his guilt.'

But the kicker was the phrenology movement's general *opposition* to capital punishment. Phreno criticised those who'd hang the likes of Dansey, saying that if they'd been cursed with the same brain and lack of education and moral training, they 'would, in all probability, have been hanged long ago'.

In the days that followed, *The Port Phillip Patriot* contained a vitriolic back-and-forth between Phreno and his critics. The latter didn't doubt the science of phrenology, but accused him of bringing it into disrepute with his simplistic conclusions and his desire for fame; there was even a satirical poem that had him swooning like a maiden at the prospect of swooping on a murderer's skull with his pincers. It would be weeks before the debate died down.

Unlike Dansey, phrenology wouldn't stay buried. Now that the pseudoscience had reared its bumpy head, many more Melbourne men would make names for themselves by helping themselves to the brain boxes of hanged criminals.

~

Dansey's death also helped resurrect Harris's fortunes. While preparing the gallows, he saw something buried under the yard's treadmill. Harris dug up two long, knotted ropes made from torn blankets. He reported his find to Wintle, who quickly uncovered an escape plan involving nearly two dozen prisoners. The ringleader, Richard Lovell, supposedly refused to submit to a search, and threatened to throw Wintle and a turnkey over a banister.

Justice was swift, with a star chamber comprising the mayor and two magistrates convening. The secrecy was disquieting to the *Gazette*, who reported 'the Clerk of the Gaol was not permitted to take the evidence in the case'. They sentenced the rebel prisoner to fifty lashes – with the stipulation that half a minute be allowed between each stroke of the cat-o'-nine-tails so that the suffering could really sink in.

A *Gazette* editorial headlined 'The Horrors of the Lash' said the three magistrates should be dismissed for ordering this brutal punishment for an 'imaginary offence'. The paper claimed Harris had been promised a commutation of his sentence if 'he would use his best exertions to make the punishment as severe as possible'. Unlike in 1842 and 1847, this time the flogging went ahead.

What came next was horrific. The *Gazette* reported: 'the unhappy victim's flesh was at each successive stroke of the cat torn in pieces the thickness of one's finger from his mangled back'. Lovell endured forty-five minutes of this torture, supposedly in silence, despite having bitten through his lip in agony.

Just as bitterly competitive papers would have different accounts of hangings, *The Herald* refuted everything the *Gazette* had claimed: there had been no departure from the usual record-keeping procedure, no order for thirty seconds between lashes, and the flogging had been bloodless and over in five minutes.

Either way, Harris – already hated as a hangman – can't have improved his standing in anyone's eyes by dobbing on his fellow prisoners and then whipping their leader. The exception to this, of course, was the government, who, grateful to their servant, set him free so he could stagger straight back into trouble.

By the end of August 1848, Harris was in Bourke Street in a state of 'beastly intoxication', performing an impromptu pantomime in which he imitated the agonies of his victims. A crowd of boys gathered to curse him. *The Argus* said this 'indescribably disgusting' scene forced them to ask 'why the authorities allow such a wretch to have any opportunity to insult public decency ... The man is a convict and consequently can be kept within the walls of the gaol if it is so willed.'

It was a good point. Two weeks later, Harris was rolling around drunkenly in New Town and offering to hang onlookers. Further court appearances followed. At one, Wintle told the magistrate what everyone knew: Harris drank his pay at the first opportunity and then became abusive. But Wintle – no doubt appreciative that the man had helped prevent a mass escape on his watch – offered a character reference, saying that when the hangman was sober he was a fair sort of person.

Harris then pleaded for compassion and recognition of his service: 'There are many things that I have done while holding office that the best among the whole lot of government office wouldn't dare attempt,' he argued. He got fourteen days on bread and water.

Adam Smith had written that the hangman was the best paid of the trades, based on the actual amount of work done. That was especially true for Harris: after Dansey, there wasn't another hanging in Melbourne for nearly three years, and nor had more floggings been prescribed to keep him busy. There was no reason for him to be a public man – except for his fondness of the public house and the trouble it brought him.

But Harris didn't even have to be drunk to find himself in quod. In August 1848 he was in Collingwood, outside the door of a lady friend, when a constable heard the hangman rhyming in the cause of romance. Had it been anyone else, it wouldn't have been news, but the *Gazette* had fun with an article headlined 'A Distinguished Individual in Trouble', which sampled his 'pathetic ditty', including his concluding entreaty: 'Let me in, my darling – open the door, my pet.' The constable arrested him for being out after curfew, and he spent the weekend in the watch house. In addition to having a laugh, the *Gazette* took the opportunity to query the wisdom of giving this 'loathsome wretch' early release for 'flaying a man alive'.

Such reporting kept Harris in the public eye and demonised him. No one lifted a finger when he fell over drunk in Collingwood in February 1849, flailing on the street and calling out that he was an officer of the law in need of help. Instead, the *Melbourne Daily News* reported, disgusted bystanders had been considering hanging the hangman. Of this scene, which might've resulted in deadly violence, the paper couldn't help punning that he'd 'become "elevated" by "a drop" and had met with "a fall"'. In court, Harris claimed he hadn't been drunk but had gone down after being robbed. There had to be laughter at this implausible yarn – especially when the hangman admitted that he actually remembered nothing because he'd been in a 'reprehensible state of colonial beer'.

For this, apparently his twelfth drunkenness offence, he was fined five shillings. This magistrate, however, warned Harris that he would be dismissed from his job if he got in trouble again.

Maybe Harris was actually worried. He went back to Melbourne Gaol, collected his month's pay and took off. This set off new angst, with *The Argus* railing: 'This man has been for a very long time an object of disgust, which no ordinary community would have tolerated for a moment.'

Predictably, Harris was nabbed in a pub. In court, charged with being illegally at large, he told a variation on his lie about being robbed, this time adding the exciting detail that he'd been out not on a spree but on a mission to track down his assailants. Harris got a fortnight in solitary on the usual diet. But he wasn't fired.

In April 1849 – after more than thirty years as a convict under orders – Harris was granted his ticket of leave. Now, theoretically, he could pursue another line of work. But why do that when he was being paid to do nothing? His drunken antics continued, as did attacks by boys, and by editors bellowing for his removal. On one occasion, arrested as a drunken vagrant and fined five shillings, Harris exited court telling everyone to go to hell – or, as *The Melbourne Daily News* waxed comic-lyrical, 'left the office consigning magistrates, constables, and the whole bunch of officials to a place generally supposed to be warmer than is congenial to the constitutions of the majority of mortals'.

Soon afterwards, around August 1849, Sheriff Mackenzie 'suspended' Jack Harris. Exactly why he felt empowered to act isn't known. Likely it had to do with Harris having secured his ticket-of-leave, meaning he was no longer a convict under control and this could be argued to Sydney as a reason to do away with his services. Perhaps it was also because it had been well over a year since the last hanging, and Mackenzie wanted to save £45 per year by getting rid of a redundant employee. Presumably the sheriff felt confident that he'd be able to get Harris back when he was needed.

Turned adrift, without pay or a place to stay, Harris was treated sympathetically by the proprietors of the Supreme Court Hotel, who'd surely absorbed a goodly percentage of his income over the past few years. They gave him a place to sleep in their storeroom, and fed him meals from their kitchen. Harris repaid them by stealing a gown-piece belonging to a servant girl and selling it for a couple of shillings. That got him back home to gaol for two months. He was thus on hand in November when two prisoners in Melbourne Gaol were sentenced to fifty lashes for supposedly plotting an escape. So, even while suspended, Harris was still in his role.

When he laid on the cat, Melbourne's previously outraged newspapers weren't particularly appalled by this instance of corporal punishment. Nor had they been back in January, when Harris had flogged a prisoner who'd attacked a warder. *The Argus*'s editor had then only stirred himself to say: 'It is difficult to see what else could be done, but flogging is a nasty remedy, and ought to be left to the penal colonies.' This time, instead of expressing regret, the paper instead provided a tacitly approving portrait of the suffering: 'Murray, an expiree, bore the punishment without a murmur, but Blanchard, who was not accustomed to such treatment in Pentonville Prison, writhed tremendously under the infliction.'

This was the flickering of a dark flame.

## CHAPTER NINE

# Hadn't the Chap a Nice, Quiet Tumble Down!

From June 1850, Jack Harris was gaoled for a year after impersonating a constable and stealing from a sympathetic woman who'd given him a bed for the night in Geelong. The ex-hangman was now so notorious that when direct convict transportation to the Port Phillip district was again raised as a possibility, *The Argus* made him the subject of a facetious editorial, depicting him as the 'chief anti-transportation apostle of Victoria'. Harris should be sent to London, the paper said, so they could 'really see the people that you send us'.

*The Argus* didn't yet know what London had actually already sent. Two months later, Garryowen scooped them for *The Herald* (as *The Port Phillip Herald* had by then been officially renamed) when he was the first to learn of the great blessing bestowed by Queen Victoria. With his editor out of the office, he took it upon himself to rush out a special extraordinary edition, headlined 'Glorious News! Separation at Last!!'

This was the biggest news in the history of what was to be a 'new-born Colony'. It was 11 November 1850. The story to eclipse it would come thirty years later to the day.

The year ahead would be momentous. First came the massive

celebrations in anticipation of the official establishment of the colony of Victoria – which coincided, on 16 November, with the long-awaited opening of the bluestone-and-granite Prince's Bridge over the Yarra.

Two days later there was a quieter, private celebration – not of separation but of union. In the past couple of years, up at Wallan, where Ellen Quinn's parents now rented a larger farm on the Merri Creek, she had met and fallen for expiree Vandemonian convict Red Kelly. More recently, he'd got her in the family way. They'd eloped to Melbourne and married at St Francis' Church on 18 November.

The first year of Ellen and Red's life as husband and wife coincided with huge drama. In February 1851, the Port Phillip district burned in the Black Thursday bushfires. In July, Victoria officially became a separate colony and Charles La Trobe was elevated from superintendent to lieutenant-governor. That same month payable gold was found at Clunes, and soon after that the Victorian rush began and the colony's population began to explode.

October 1851 saw the first hanging in the new colony of Victoria. By now Alastair Mackenzie was colonial treasurer, and James Simpson, Esquire, had taken over as sheriff. The colony also had a new executioner. Little is known about James Cahill, other than that he was from Sydney and a freed convict who'd never performed an execution. As this was the new man's debut, Jack Harris – despite now being a habitual thief designated by *The Argus* as the worst of the worst – was called on to supervise.

The condemned man was Patrick Kennedy, who'd killed his wife in unimaginably brutal circumstances. The accused's defence was that he was drunk and the devil made him do it. Much was made of Kennedy's fixation on 'fatalism'. He'd looked everywhere for omens, coincidences and auguries, and this had warped his mind. When the youngest of his four children – little Micky – had spoken his first words, they'd been 'Mammy dead and Daddy gone'. The boy repeated this chant over and over, and Kennedy became so terrified that he prayed the boy would die.

Then he'd murdered his wife in full view of a horrified witness.

Kennedy's insanity plea was rejected. The day he was sentenced to death, little Micky died, as if in answer to his murderer father's dark prayer. While Kennedy awaited execution, his spiritual consolers included a young seminarian named Henry James O'Farrell.

On 18 October, a crowd of just 600 to 800 people gathered outside the gaol. Lest this be taken as an improvement in taste and morals, *The Melbourne Daily News* reminded readers that a great number of men had gone to the diggings.

Kennedy ascended the gallows to be dealt with by Cahill and Harris. But even between the two of them, they still couldn't get it right. Perhaps because Sheriff Simpson was so new to the job, Wintle was the one to order them to reposition the unhappy man correctly on the drop. But the gaol boss didn't appear concerned that a thick rope was being used.

Cahill went to the bolt, Harris gave the order, Kennedy dropped and struggled terribly for three minutes. But that wasn't the worst part. The *News's* reporter – devastated by what he'd seen – recorded that Harris 'remarked to several bye standers [*sic*], in a tone of high glee, and evidently pluming himself on the profundity of his professional knowledge, "I knew he would not take more than three minutes, I said so."' According to Garryowen, Harris rubbed his hands and added: 'Hadn't the chap a nice, quiet tumble down!' Another journalist was so incensed he wanted to give Harris a kicking. The hangman was instead hauled off and tossed into a cell.

None of these details would be found in *The Argus*, which was now firmly against capital punishment. Indeed, the paper had announced a policy of reporting only the barest accounts of hangings, in part because by giving 'still further publicity to the sickening details, the Press is guilty of pandering to a vitiated taste'. Whether this policy had the intended effect is doubtful. By hiding a hanging away, people could perhaps more easily put its horrors out of their minds.

But anyone who'd heard the horror of Harris's outrage to decency could have been forgiven for thinking it would finally, *irrevocably*, exclude him from ever again serving as executioner. But he still had a future on the gallows.

So too, sadly, would Kennedy's consoler Henry James O'Farrell. In an eerie denouement to an eerie case, he didn't become a devout priest but a drunken paranoiac, who in 1868 would go to his own hangman in Sydney for shooting and wounding Prince Alfred, the Duke of Edinburgh.

~

By March 1852, Jack Harris was free and again inflicting himself on Geelong. While *The Argus* held him up as the worst of convictism, not all former lags were bad news. In fact, Geelong might do with a few more men in the mould of Elijah Upjohn.

After being whipped on Christmas Eve 1839, Upjohn didn't have a smooth time during the rest of his stay in Van Diemen's Land. He'd been punished repeatedly for misconduct, disobeying orders, insolence and disorderly conduct, for having illicit confectionery, for being absent without leave and for larceny under £5. He got sentence extensions, hard labour on the roads and more lashes.

Even so, by the start of 1844, Upjohn was a probationary passholder who could hire himself out, and the following year he had his ticket of leave. That didn't keep him out of trouble. In August 1845, thinking him a suspicious character, a trio of constables searched him on a street in Hobart. They found three counterfeit sixpences – and several items recently stolen from a local woman's home. Police searched his digs in Argyle Street and discovered a mould for counterfeiting coins and other implements used for casting, filing and polishing the fakes.

Despite this wealth of evidence, when he faced trial two months later it was for receiving jewellery, valued at six shillings, stolen from another man. Upjohn was sentenced to two years with hard labour. Making a false, frivolous and vexatious accusation against an official saw him given an extra nine months in 1847 – though this was recorded as remitted. Despite his chequered convict record, Upjohn was free to cross 'Bass's Straits' around 1849–50 to start a new life.

Upjohn's arrival coincided with Victoria undergoing an incredible transformation. By the end of 1851, he was in Geelong, the colony's second-largest town, then booming as the closest port to the goldfields. Despite being a world away from Shaftesbury, Elijah had family close by. His brother Robert, now a tailor, emigrated to Australia in October 1852 and settled in Geelong. Their cousin William Upjohn had also come to Geelong by then. Elijah and Robert's father, Henry – who'd been given his ticket of leave in Tasmania back in 1834 – would also be on the scene.

Given his background, Elijah was soon doing alright for himself, acquiring some fenced land with standing fruit trees that he then sold for £200 to a reverend. While cousin William and his wife, Charlotte, were a couple of times in trouble with the law – including destroying said fruit trees after they'd been sold to the reverend and another case in which they'd killed a man's cat by throwing it into a cesspool – Elijah appeared a reformed man. He had his own business, as a labourer and carter, and in June 1854, at St Paul's Church, Geelong, he married Ann Copp of Devonshire, England, who'd arrived in the colony a year earlier.

Now when Elijah was in court it was as a plaintiff, seeking to have a stolen cart returned, or to be paid monies he was owed for an excavation or plastering job; the ledgers that Ann kept for the business were used in evidence. Soon the couple would have their first son, Joseph Elijah.

Despite what *The Argus* said about Jack Harris, not all former convicts were a blight on Victoria.

~

While the Pentonvillains and Vandemonians had been a source of concern, what really changed villainy in Victoria was the numbers of people drawn by the gold rush. At the start of 1851, the district was home to 77,000 people. Three years later the population was 237,000.

In time, the wealth from gold would help to build 'Marvellous Melbourne', but its first effects were far from marvellous. While there were famously ostentatious displays of the fortunes made by a few diggers, hardship, poverty and suffering were far more pervasive. Lodging houses charged extortionate rates so that people could sleep cheek-by-jowl in packed rooms. On the other side of the Yarra River, a squalid canvas town had sprung up, home to 5000 people. Melbourne was under immense pressure but was still without railways, gas lamps, telegraph wires or a system for fresh water and sewage.

The law and penal system were being severely tested. Convictions and incarcerations soared exponentially. Just as Melbourne's accommodations were overflowing, so too were the Eastern and Western city gaols and the Pentridge and Richmond stockades. The colony resorted to yellow-painted hulks moored in Hobsons Bay as floating prisons. The first, the *President*, took prisoners from December 1852. The conditions were horrific: men wore heavy irons and were kept idle and isolated in tiny cells. They weren't even given hard labour to break up the monotony. Four other hulks soon came into use, their inmates forced into long days of backbreaking work on shore.

Men found their gold dreams dashed when drink led them to a judge donning the black cap. In May 1852, a Californian named James Barlow came before the new Supreme Court puisne justice Redmond Barry. The very penitent accused had been in a drunken blackout when he stabbed a stranger who'd jostled him in a crowded lodging house. This was Barry's first capital case on the other side of the bench. With his voice quavering from emotion and tears rolling down his cheeks, His Honour said he hoped Barlow would get his pardon in the next world, then sentenced him to leave this one with his neck in a noose. For all his tears, the judge wasn't disposed to be merciful.

*The Argus* remained vehemently opposed to the 'atrocious wickedness' of the death penalty, and was incensed that Barlow was to die for a drunken, unpremeditated act. A legislature that abolished the present odious system would achieve 'honorable immortality', the paper proclaimed, exhorting Barry to urge La Trobe to reprieve the condemned man.

Barlow was hanged by Cahill on 22 May.

As part of its anti–capital punishment stance, which had included reprinting English letters by Charles Dickens about the horrors of public hangings, *The Argus* the following month published a lengthy letter from a phrenologist. The writer said criminals were almost always the victims of brains so badly balanced that they were half-idiots or half-lunatics. Society was to blame for allowing people with such primitive heads to roam free, get roaring drunk and carry on like savage animals. Traditional punishments were useless. So these miscreants – whose propensity for criminal behaviour could be measured – should be pre-emptively put into facilities for their moral re-education.

*The Argus* endorsed the letter, the sentiments of which 'correspond so precisely with our own'. Crime was a disease. Phrenology was the cure.

~

Melbourne had a hangman dilemma. Cahill had met 'a fine buxom immigrant girl of no mean personal attractions', and, as Garryowen explained, 'They met, they saw, they conquered.' Their church wedding was well attended by ladies 'eager to see how a hangman could bear the tying of an ecclesiastical halter about his own neck'.

The answer appeared to be: not terribly well. Cahill soon after deserted his bride and cleared out for New Zealand. The latter detail of this piquant melodrama was confirmed in *The Herald* in October 1852, when it reported that Cahill had resigned and taken off across the Tasman, leaving authorities with the difficult task of finding a new man for the undesirable job.

Sheriff James Simpson – already about to retire – went with the devil he knew. Jack Harris, only some weeks ago sentenced to six months for stealing a rug, agreed to resume the noose in return for a remission. Like the original Jack Ketch, he'd succeeded his successor.

Harris was needed to tend to the unfortunately named John Riches. This Vandemonian had been drunk when he shot a digger mate dead on the goldfields on 7 October. At breakneck speed, Riches was arrested, charged, committed, tried, convicted, sentenced to death by Barry, and had his case reviewed by the Victorian government's own Executive Council. On 2 November, he went to the gallows. Separation really had sped the wheels of justice.

*The Argus* gave only basic details of the hanging, noting: 'We abstain from furnishing any details of the sad scene.'

~

The year 1853 got off to bad start for Jack Harris. On New Year's Day, in Richmond, he took a horse he didn't own. His defence was typically imaginative: he'd been rushing to the gaol to keep an appointment with Wintle to sign some important documents when he'd seen the horse already loose, and had mounted the steed with every intention of returning the animal.

In court, Harris cross-examined Wintle, who, rather unhelpfully, didn't recall any scheduled meeting. But the governor offered his usual character endorsement: the accused was honest and well behaved ... when sober. Jack made his usual pleas about his decades of 'service'. The jury found him guilty.

Horse stealing was a serious crime, and this was Harris's fifth appearance in the Supreme Court. Justice Barry sentenced him to four years with hard labour. It was a harsh punishment for a man now past sixty.

~

There was a new sheriff in town at the time Melbourne needed a new hangman.

Sheriff Claud Farie, Esquire, was the son of a Scottish coal baron. In 1837, aged twenty, he'd come to the colony already cashed up, and only got richer with a sheep run. The young squatter had been a leading voice when the Portland settlers had complained to La Trobe that he'd smeared them in regards to Aboriginal massacres in 1842. In December 1845, in Launceston, Farie married Jane Cox. In an odd coincidence, her grandmother was Rebecca Upjohn of Shaftesbury, making Claud distant kin-in-law to Elijah, who at that point was still doing it tough elsewhere in Van Diemen's Land.

Not long into the gold rush, Farie, his wife and their young daughter were living on a fine riverside estate in South Yarra. In November 1852, La Trobe, who had become close to Farie, appointed him sheriff. With Victoria's population and crime rate soaring, this was one of the highest positions in the colony. Farie's salary would soon be £1500 – more than one-tenth of his department's entire budget. But he did work for it.

Farie's day-to-day duties included everything from requesting the discharge of lunatics held in the gaol to the Yarra Bend Asylum, to hearing reports from surgeons as to conditions on the hulks. There was the ongoing management of hiring and dismissing staff, and the never-ending business of accounting for every penny spent, all of it in writing to the chief secretary. Farie was to be sheriff for nearly two decades and he left thousands of files that detail his work. In some respects, such as the treatment of lunatics and of female prisoners, he was progressive.

But the executioner was barely raised in Farie's correspondence. When he was mentioned, it was usually in relation to expenditure or a sentence remission. Gallows bungles weren't worthy of official note. Not when there were other messes to sort out, whether it be seeking the chief secretary's permission to fire a drunken turnkey or politely informing the same that a convict whose death sentence had been commuted to fifteen years with hard labour – the first three in irons – actually only had one leg.

Farie, soon to be elected to brief stints on the Legislative Council and the presidency of the Melbourne Club, appeared to be a hard worker. But he was also as unlikely to rock the boat as his predecessor in matters relating to hangings. Farie certainly wasn't the sort of gentleman to play Jack Ketch in a pinch. What he would do was allow the degradation of the executioner's office to become entrenched.

Yet at first Farie did appear to want practical reform, at least in who did the hangings, and he appointed a man named John Walsh as the new Jack Ketch. The sheriff also put him on the payroll as a turnkey, at the princely sum of five shillings and ninepence per day. Not much is about known Walsh except that he was said to be another expired convict from Sydney, and that he'd applied for the job several times before. Now he had his wish and was set to hang his first man.

On the same day in November 1852 that Farie had become sheriff, George Pinkerton, a well-educated nineteen-year-old from a good family, arrived in Melbourne from Liverpool in the most horrific of circumstances. Pinkerton was a junior officer aboard the filthy *Ticonderoga*, overcrowded with 795 passengers, 100 of whom died of typhus during the three-month voyage. But not everyone expired from the fever. Pinkerton – who'd already been mentally scarred by an apocalyptic vision of the last judgement – was traumatised by what he saw and heard on the ship. He'd write: 'On the passage, two drowned themselves, and one or two turned insane. You would hear their echoing through the vessel, "Oh, I'll die! I'll die!"' The *Ticonderoga* was put into quarantine at Port Nepean, where another sixty-eight people were to perish from sickness.

Pinkerton wasn't one of them: he fled from quarantine and took up work with Charles and Bridget Smith on their farm at Cheltenham. In mid-January 1853, Pinkerton – reportedly a nice, quiet, temperate fellow, if somewhat melancholy – tried to rape Bridget. He strangled her when she resisted, throttled her infant son and then shot himself in the chest.

But Pinkerton survived and went to trial for murder. Witnesses – including Charles Smith – testified to the accused's mild nature. The jury rejected his insanity plea and he was sentenced to death. A petition signed by prominent gentlemen – including the case's coroner, another surgeon and the superintendent of the Yarra Bend lunatic asylum – was presented to La Trobe seeking a more thorough investigation into Pinkerton's mental state. A stay was granted. The Executive Council heard from men who'd observed Pinkerton in custody – including the gaol's new assistant surgeon, Dr Richard Youl, and Governor Wintle – and they believed him sane.

Pinkerton went to the gallows in early April 1853. *The Argus*, 'in accordance with our custom', abstained from 'publishing any particulars'. *The Herald*, presumably Garryowen, offered a poignant observation: 'On gazing at the suspended and stiffened corpse, the thought intruded itself that such a scene was more adapted for the barbarous ages than an enlightened nineteenth century.'

Dr Youl and up-and-coming surgeon Dr Edward Barker conducted a post-mortem to examine the murderer's brain. They set the Executive Council's minds – along with their own – at ease when they declared there was no evidence that Pinkerton had been deranged. But Melburnians might have wondered about that when the traumatised murderer's final letter, written just before his hanging, was published in the newspapers, vividly describing both his hellish dream and his hellish voyage.

~

The gold rush increased John Walsh's workload, with Harris sometimes called in to help. In 1853 Victoria executed thirteen men – two more than in Melbourne's first decade. In this same year New South Wales hanged two people, South Australia executed one, and the gallows in Queensland and Western Australia went unused. In Van Diemen's Land – where there had been a love of the gibbet in the 1820s and 1830s – nine men died in the noose.

While New South Wales' and Van Diemen's Land's high hanging rates earlier in the century were attributable to a large convict population and their rulers imposing harsh justice under the Bloody Code, Victoria wasn't in either situation: it had never had direct transportation, and it hadn't even existed back when simple theft was a capital offence. True, the colony's population had surged after the discovery of gold, by now around 200,000, but this was still a tiny fraction of the United Kingdom's population of some 28 million. Yet during all of 1853, there were eleven hangings in England and Wales. Victoria – which had come to the noose last – was embracing it, while in the other colonies and 'at home' it was used ever more sparingly.

By mid-August 1853 New South Wales had passed legislation abolishing public execution, though it was yet to receive royal assent. This was a bold reform, yet to be seen even in England, despite the agitation of Charles Dickens and other luminaries. A similar move was soon afoot in Victoria, but for the time being men were still hanged for the education and entertainment of crowds. They swung for murders and attempted murders, for the rapes of women and children, and for violent bushranger robberies. Public interest remained high, especially if the characters and crimes were sensational.

Bushrangers George Melville, George Wilson and William Atkins, who'd robbed a gold escort and inflicted gunshot wounds on four troopers, were a big attraction in early October 1853. Fair weather and the notoriety of these men led to what *The Herald* reckoned was the largest ever turnout – though if he was reporting, Garryowen for once didn't provide a crowd estimate.

The hangman was reported as doing the solemn duty poorly. Atkins died fast; Wilson struggled for some time. Their mate needed special attention: 'the executioner having drawn down the legs of Melville with considerable force, he presently ceased to move'.

Melbourne businessman Charles Evans wasn't there to watch the executions, but he happened on the aftermath. He noted in his diary:

> The bodies were hidden from view by a wooden erection, a contrivance which takes a little from the horror of the exhibition. To have the last awful grapple with death set up like curiosity for the edification of a gaping multitude is a sickening contrivance unworthy of an advanced country.

Evans described going about the rest of his day, buying a nice spring cart at a saleyard for £42. But he might have suffered an apoplexy if he'd been in the market for a cheap seafood lunch. Melville's wife, who ran an oyster shop, had been allowed to retrieve her husband's body. *The Argus* reported:

> [A] few hours afterwards it might have been seen decorated with ribbons, lying in the shop window of an oyster shop, in Little Bourke-street! Disgusting brutality can scarcely be carried further. It may be fairly presumed that this act was perpetrated with the view of attracting custom to the house.

From then on, bodies were not released to families. Eventually this would be made law. While such ghastly details might have made for conversation at the Melbourne Club, they wouldn't be found in Sheriff Farie's files. Unfailingly, his execution reports to La Trobe simply confirmed that death sentences had been carried out in accordance with the law.

~

In November 1854, Walsh was off to Geelong to perform a double hanging, the first executions performed outside Melbourne. Murderers John Gunn and George Roberts drew a crowd of some 2000 – about one in ten people then living in the town. We don't know whether Elijah Upjohn was among them. If he was, he may have reflected on his criminal past and thought: 'There but for the grace of God ...' He might also have assumed that he'd never witness another hanging, because the Victorian government was awaiting royal assent to its own private executions act.

*The Geelong Advertiser* believed that couldn't come soon enough: 'It is to be hoped that ere another one takes place, the new bill that is about to pass into law will confine these necessary yet disgusting sights to those within the precincts of the gaol exclusively.'

~

The goldfields brought fortune for some and misery for others. But for Red Kelly they provided sufficient earnings that he could set himself up. He'd gone to the Bendigo diggings and with what he'd made – augmented by money from a horse-trading business with his father-in-law – he and Ellen bought a farm at Beveridge, where they could raise their new baby daughter, Annie.

At this time there was unrest on the Ballarat goldfields over the expensive licensing system. Chief gold commissioner William

Wright – formerly the New South Wales commissioner of Crown lands, who in September 1845 had ordered the mass shooting of Wiradjuri people defending their land in the Wellington district – took a softer line with white diggers defying authorities. He cautioned La Trobe's successor, Lieutenant-Governor Sir Charles Hotham, that the twice-weekly licence hunts he'd insisted upon were a mistake: the situation called for 'extreme forbearance and conciliation'.

Hotham ignored his warnings of an imminent violent battle. Instead, the governor allowed assistant commissioner Robert Rede to continue provoking miners. Rede had already vowed to teach the diggers a 'fearful lesson'.

In early 1854 Australia's first telegraph line had begun operation between Melbourne and Williamstown. By December it had reached Geelong and the first message sent to Melbourne told of the Eureka Stockade tragedy. Rede had unleashed his British soldiers: at least twenty-two diggers and five troopers had been killed.

It was most likely around this time at Beveridge that Red and Ellen Kelly had their second child, a son they named Edward. This boy's later exploits would be flashed all over Australia by telegraph – as would be his hanging under the direction of Rede.

~

Claud Farie's choice of hangman was proving every inch the Jack Ketch, fined forty shillings in January 1855 for being drunk and annoying the military stationed in the gaol. The next month, when the first of the Eureka rebels went to trial, 10,000 people gathered outside the Supreme Court – and they were elated at news of the men's acquittal. But not everyone was happy. Inside the chamber of justice there was disapproval from the law's highest officer right down to its lowest, at least according to *The Geelong Advertiser*:

Mighty was the dismay which blanched the cheeks of all the salaried officials in court, when the foreman pronounced the magic words, 'Not Guilty'. The Chief Justice shook, the Attorney-General groaned, the Sheriff sighed, the big, burley black whiskered Crown Solicitor grinned, and a fellow very much resembling Jack Ketch, from a prominent part of the Gallery treated the audience to a fearful gnashing of teeth.

At the trial of the fifth 'foreign anarchist' Jan Vannick, one of the jurors was Graham Berry, a young grocer from Prahran. When he and his fellow jurymen acquitted, *The Age* laughed that these legal defeats were doing more to embarrass the government than a year's worth of their own editorial sniping: 'What a pity that Sir Charles and Jack Ketch cannot transact this little piece of business themselves!'

The remaining rebels would also walk free. Graham Berry was to interest himself in progressive politics, becoming secretary of the Prahran Reform League, and be seen at public meetings speaking out against ruling class measures, such as the Hotham government giving £50,000 a year to the clergy. Berry, along the path to political power that would see him serve three times as Victorian premier, was also to become a critic of the death penalty.

~

In recent times, the hangman's pay had gone up to six shillings per day, necessary to keep pace with gold rush inflation. But as a measure of priorities, when government cutbacks came in April 1855, Walsh lost sixpence a day to save the state just over £9 annually.

As for Jack Harris, he wasn't being paid anything, and that would prove a problem. In June 1855 he was on Lonsdale Street, released after serving half his sentence under the labour reward system – basically good behaviour and exceeding work expectations – when he spied a chance to make a few shillings by stealing some boots from a kitchen. The footwear belonged to Mary Binns, and she chased Harris down, and roughly took him into custody. For her bravery, the prosecutor said she deserved a reward – and appointment as a detective, which her constable husband can't have liked hearing. Harris pleaded guilty and was sent back to gaol for three months, so at least he had food and board again.

On 25 July 1855, James McAllister was hanged outside Melbourne Gaol for shooting a woman he'd once lived with. He was a run-of-the-mill malefactor who attracted only 500 spectators. What they didn't know was that they'd witnessed the colony's last public execution.

But that didn't meant Melburnians would be deprived of the chance to gaze upon the faces of murderers. When McAllister was cut down, Charles Pardoe, a surgeon-dentist from Manchester, took a plaster cast of his head. Pardoe gave this relic to his business partner, Philemon Sohier, who was now to pave the path for phrenology in Australia – and his showmanship would led to Ned Kelly's death mask becoming an enduring tourist attraction.

# CHAPTER TEN

# The Professor, Lucky Harry Power and the Price Isn't Right

From Redmond Barry to Red Kelly, Jack Harris to Elijah Upjohn, all sorts of men came to Victoria and reinvented themselves. But few did it so quickly and with such flair as Philemon Sohier, who'd spin the spoils of the hangman's noose into fame and fortune.

Born to a French couple from Jersey in the Channel Islands during 1821, by twenty Sohier was living in England, teaching French at posh schools and using newspapers to advertise his private tuition to the 'nobility and gentry'. As late as 1852, he was still calling himself a professor of French in the Bath newspapers. Then he abruptly left England, running off with married woman Ellen Williams. But by the time Sohier reached Melbourne, teaching French ran a distant second to his new profession, announced in *The Argus* in March 1853:

**Phrenology.**

Le Professeur Sohier (lately from Paris, London, Bath, &c.) proposes shortly to deliver, at the Mechanics' Institution, a few entertaining and instructive Lectures on this noble science, with illustrative craniological manipulations.

When Sohier took to the stage in May, he afforded 'a good deal of amusement and information' by inviting audience members up so he could feel and measure their bumps, his pronouncements met with their grins, laughter and applause. Phrenology appeared to be a money-maker. Sohier charged 2/6 for general admission and five shillings for reserved seats.

Visitors to his headquarters – where a sign read 'Know Thyself' – spent more. Five shillings for a verbal reading and chart, double that to get it in writing, and a hefty £1 for the really deep dive. But as Sohier insisted, you weren't *spending* when you consulted him, you were *investing* in your best asset: yourself.

While phrenology had previous Port Phillip proponents, none packed the promo pizzazz of Le Professeur. In the mid-1850s he ran thousands of eye-catching and thought-provoking notices in *The Argus*. Unlike other businessmen, who relied on the same tired blurbs week after week, he'd offer numerous new and intriguing messages every day, such as: 'What is Phrenology? – The science of the Mind. If you have one, call on me.'

Melbourne in the wake of the gold rush was a time of uncertainty and excitement: prices and wages were soaring, fortunes were being made and lost, science and technology were making giant strides with such wonders as the telegraph, photograph, refrigeration and the railways. How to navigate this changing world and still satisfy the unchanging human desires for happiness and love, health and wealth? Phrenology would help with everything, from staying sober and losing weight to choosing a career and raising good children. This forerunner to psychology and self-help preached that you already had the answers; the professor would merely assist in unlocking them: he wanted you to 'find the gold mine in your brain'.

After Melbourne's last public execution, Sohier was to have much more show for his business. He gave a preview of McAllister's cast to a phrenologically inclined *Argus* journalist, who dutifully reported that the small skull showed clear deficiencies in the reflective faculties and moral sentiments, which made it likely that McAllister would 'cherish a blood purpose deliberately, and ruthlessly to carry it out'. Elsewhere in *The Argus* a notice said people could make up their own minds about the mind of this monster: 'The Public are respectfully invited to inspect the Cast of the Murderer, McAllister, Victoria Phrenological Institute, corner of Bourke and Stephen-streets. Admission Free.'

Phrenology would implant itself in the minds of Victorians, whether they were true believers or merely thought it was a bit of fun. Le Professeur found new ways to popularise the subject, and press coverage kept its principles in the public consciousness. While there were detractors in Victoria and many more abroad, the 'science' of phrenology was treated with a seriousness not afforded astrology or soothsaying. Some politicians also lent it credibility.

One such adherent was Horatio Wills: former newspaper editor, pioneering republican and member of the Legislative Council, father of the father of AFL and eventual victim in a Frontiers War clash that led to a notorious reprisal massacre – and controversy over the involvement of his son Tom. Horatio's endorsement of Sohier's bumpology read: 'Many of my intimate acquaintance have submitted their heads to his manipulation, and his summing up of character has, I feel bound to state, appeared to me truly wonderful.'

~

The arrival of Australia's first steam railway line proved irresistible to Jack Harris. From September 1854, the train was taking passengers from Flinders Street, where a weatherboard station had been built, along a couple of miles of track to Sandridge, which would later be renamed Port Melbourne.

A year after it opened, Harris, who'd been out of gaol a month, stole a passenger's carpetbag from the Sandridge railway depot. Shortly afterwards, this man was surprised to see an old ruffian wandering by with his distinctive satchel. He grabbed Harris and handed him to the constables. In court, the ex-hangman was given a ticket to Melbourne Gaol, the return portion not valid for six months.

Harris's latest incarceration coincided with Victoria's private executions law – formally known as *An Act to Regulate the Execution of Criminals* – receiving royal assent. *The Argus* was pleased at this step towards the abolition of capital punishment. Melbourne would no longer suffer the 'disgusting spectacle' in which 'crowds of the scum of both sexes of human kind are assembled, holding a kind of satanic high festival under the very gallows'.

Murderer John McCabe looked set to be the first man privately hanged. But his conviction was so dubious that a deputation to the governor saw his sentence commuted to fifteen years. *The Bendigo Advertiser* noted: 'It would have been quite impossible to brave public opinion in depriving this man of his life under the circumstances of the case.'

Yet McCabe's conviction hadn't been overturned: he was still a murderer in the eyes of the law. But young bushrangers James Condon, John Dixon and Alfred Henry Jackson were *not* killers. When they went before Redmond Barry in mid-November 1855, it was for robbing and wounding an old man.

Their trial was observed by John Buckley Castieau. Then a young Melbourne Gaol officer, he would later play a fatherly role for many doomed prisoners, including a future bushranger likely then taking baby steps up at Beveridge.

Castieau watched as the trio of just-convicted men were asked if they had anything to say as to why sentences of death should not be passed. In the diary he'd keep for decades, Castieau noted that Condon gave a 'very effective speech'. The bushranger's argument was that there was no evidence they'd shot at the old man, let alone wounded him, and he asked the judge for leniency. Judge Barry shed tears and repeatedly had to regain his composure as he sentenced the three men to hang.

Castieau was struck by how such a verdict condemned not only these men but also their families. Dixon had children, who were waiting with their mother at the gaol, which to a 'reflective mind formed a very melancholy picture'. The little ones would soon be 'made orphans by the law of man. Their future career perhaps embittered by the taunts of the vulgar as to their father's fate.' Their mother was to be left alone, 'probably dependent for subsistence on the scraps thrown from the spoils obtained by the crimes of men who had been her husband's associates and who would not while they were out of Gaol, allow the Moll of the Bloke who was scragged to starve'.

But maybe this melancholy outcome could be avoided. After all, John McCabe had just been spared, and he'd actually murdered someone. Condon, Dixon and Jackson hoped for the same mercy.

Under the new law, the gallows was shielded from view inside a narrow wooden tower. The new Act set out that the execution was to take place in the presence of the usual people – the sheriff or deputy sheriff, the gaol governor and officers, along with justices of the police and military who wanted to attend. But it also allowed for 'adult spectators as the said Sheriff or Deputy Sheriff may think fit to admit'. It was this last phrase that would regularly be used to make a mockery of the spirit of the law. From the time of Sheriff Farie, many 'private' executions became raucous crowd events.

Though nothing could been seen from outside Melbourne Gaol, a large crowd gathered anyway. They weren't all just morbidly curious. Many knew the condemned men and hoped they'd be spared, as McCabe had been. *The Herald*'s reporter circulated among the crowd and recorded the outraged comments expressed at the double standard when it became clear that the executions were to proceed.

This journalist entered the gaol as Condon, Dixon and Jackson were being handed to the hangman, 'one of the most repulsive-looking old men we ever met with'. Castieau was on duty and watched as Harris pinioned the trio. He wrote:

> The horrible white cap was then placed upon the poor wretchs [*sic*] heads and, with the minister in front reading the Burial service the procession marched to the Scaffold. The men all walked firmly & neither made any remark. In a few minutes the ropes were adjusted round their necks the bolt drawn & their souls in eternity. May God have mercy on them.

Outside on the streets, supporters heard 'a slight jerking noise' to indicate it was all over.

*The Argus* called it 'A Bad Beginning', because these men had not been murderers, and the paper restated its opposition to capital punishment. But it also said that if hangings had to happen, then private executions – 'being quietly strangled in a cell' – should act as more of a deterrent than public hangings: 'We hope that the terrors of such a fate as this will have their due effect.' Criminals would no longer be able to show the world how game they could die. 'The romance of capital punishment is gone,' *The Argus* concluded.

Maybe this was so, but the exploitation of execution was entering a new phase in Melbourne. The new Act required that a jury conduct an inquest to formally determine that the death sentence had been carried out. This would have to be signed by official witnesses. It was telling of the hangman's status that his name and signature were not to be found on these documents. The Act also stipulated that the body was not to be buried or removed from the gaol for eight hours. It was not the law's intention, but this left plenty of time for Charles Pardoe, given access by Farie, to go to work with his razors, his grease and his plaster of Paris.

Sohier displayed the death masks of Condon, Dixon and Jackson at Temperance Hall on 1 December 1855. *The Argus* reported that 'attendance was very good, and repeated plaudits testified the satisfaction of the audience with the illustrations of the science presented to them'. The new lecture show was called 'Hanging and Phrenology'.

Sohier soon had competition in Archibald Hamilton, who'd practised as a head-reader in England, Ireland and Scotland as early as 1841, using 'Casts and Busts of eminent and notorious characters'. He set up in Melbourne in mid-1856 and offered phrenological analysis for half the price of Le Professeur. Hamilton also attracted a good-sized crowd to a Mechanics Institute lecture in which he referenced the 'skulls of notorious characters', examined the heads of two living Aboriginal people to declare that they suffered a 'deficiency of conscientiousness and hope', and brought white gents up on stage so he could feel their bumps and reveal their true characters. Sohier would have to keep his shows fresh and engaging if he was to remain the city's flashiest phrenologist.

~

The next execution wasn't until April 1856, when James Ross went to the scaffold at Geelong for the murder of his infant son and of a woman trying to protect the wife he'd already brutally attacked. No one seemed sorry to see him hang, not even *The Argus*, who called him a 'wretched monster'. This was the first execution overseen by Geelong's recently appointed deputy sheriff Robert Rede, whose actions at Eureka had led to such disaster. His promotion was mocked by *Punch* as a 'token of the Governor's appreciation of his heroism, in Digger-hunting at Ballarat'.

As winter approached in Melbourne, Jack Harris stole two shirts and two pairs of trousers. In court he pleaded that he had no choice. *The Argus* reported: 'The prisoner said that stealing was the only resource open to him, as directly as he obtained employment, somebody recollected his former profession and cried out "There's Jack Ketch," and he was discharged.' Once a hangman, always a hangman. Jack was given six months.

In January 1857 John Walsh went to the home of a former gaol turnkey he claimed had insulted him with that deadly epithet 'the common hangman' – which, of course, he was. At the man's door, Walsh unleashed a torrent of abuse. The turnkey told him to get lost. Walsh left but soon returned with a large sword, threatening to 'rip his guts out'. The man ran for the police, chased by the blade-wielding executioner. When Walsh couldn't catch him, he went back to the house. There, he hit the man's heavily pregnant wife twice in the head with the sword, leaving her heavily bleeding.

Not long before, Jack Harris had been given four years for stealing a horse. Now Walsh was found guilty on three charges arising from his vicious attack, and received a total sentence of three months. It was a time when a violent assault on a woman might be considered less serious than a minor property crime. The following month, Jack Harris was caught stealing a box in Collingwood and got six months.

So it was that Melbourne's Jack Ketches were both behind bars during a particularly violent period in Victoria's history.

~

On 16 October 1856, Sergeant John McNally became the first member of the colonial Victoria Police to die in the line of duty, shot dead at the Mount Ararat goldfields by a man named William Twiggem.

Less than a week later, Melbourne was in for a greater shock when a work gang of ten convicts returning to the prison hulk *Success* tried to seize their longboat, beating to death warder Owen Owens and tossing seaman John Turner overboard to drown. A prisoner in irons named

Stevens also went over the side and was never seen again.

The first to face trial for murder was convict Frank McCallum. Known as 'Captain Melville', he'd been found guilty on three bushranging charges in 1853 and given three sentences totalling thirty-two years, which Judge Barry had ordered him to serve consecutively. Now Captain Melville conducted his own defence, arguing it'd been Stevens who'd killed Owens. In court, he revealed the brutal treatment he and his fellows suffered on the hulks:

> I was clutched by 13 able-bodied men, who dragged me, struck me, beat me with bludgeons, leaped on me, trampled me, and dragged me by the heels to a dungeon ... they hoisted me up, and fixed me, so as to leave me but on the tips of my toes, and in this position of torture they held me for five days and six nights ...

There was much, much more – suffice it to say Melville believed Norfolk Island's horrors were paradise compared with the hulks. Regardless, he was found guilty and sentenced to death. But his co-accused successfully argued the same defence, citing Stevens as the murderer. Melville's verdict was reversed and he resumed his original heavy sentence at Melbourne Gaol because it had also been established in court that he wasn't lawfully detained on the hulk, having been sentenced to do his time on the roads.

One of Melville's co-accused had been Henry Johnstone – aka Johnson – a Vandemonian ticket-of-leave man convicted on two horse stealing charges in 1855 and given eight- and five-year sentences, which at least were to be served concurrently. After he was acquitted in the Owen Owens case, Henry would do his time, be released and then get another seven years for horse stealing in 1864. By the time he escaped from Pentridge five years later, he was better known as Harry Power, and he'd soon after teach the ways of the bushranger to young Ned Kelly.

Another convict on the *Success* the day of the 'rush' would also leave a lasting impression on Victoria's future iron outlaw. In 1854 Justice Barry had given 'John Smith' a dozen years for robbery at Castlemaine. He'd first endured the hell of the hulk ship *President* before being transferred to the *Success*. But John Smith was a well-behaved prisoner and didn't have anything to do with the uprising. Once he'd served his time, Smith took to bushranging and became infamous as the very badly behaved 'Mad Dan' Morgan.

After the *Success* outrage, Melville's claims contributed to the Legislative Council appointing a select committee to investigate the colony's prison system. The man with explaining to do was John Price, Inspector-General of Penal Establishments. This notoriously cruel former commandant of Norfolk Island had been in his present position since January 1854. Newspapers now printed accounts of his abuses and cruelties at Pentridge and elsewhere. Parliamentary inquiries were still going in February 1857, when *The Age* said Price was 'utterly unfit' for his position.

No one had been hanged for Owen Owens' murder. But in mid-March William Twiggem went to the gallows for murdering the policeman – alongside Chinese digger Chu A Luk, who'd stabbed a countryman dead over a small debt at Diamond Gully. *The Argus* didn't use this double hanging to rail against capital punishment. Was it worth getting worked up about a constable killer and a homicidal celestial heathen? *The Age*'s report made it seem not. 'Twiggen [*sic*] had a determined sinister expression of countenance, and had been long pursuing a course of crime. The Chinaman was also an ill-looking specimen of his race. Even in death his features bore the stamp of unusual ferocity.' There was also no complaint from *The Argus* five days later, when Eaglehawk wife-slayer James Cornick 'struggled, as we are informed, slightly after the fall'.

But there was uproar a fortnight later, when the *Success* murder had its sequel. Convicts on hulks had been getting more restless since the murder of Owen Owens, Melville's revelations and the inquiries into John Price and the penal system. Now, sent to shore to work at Point Gellibrand, they refused their duty and demanded to see the inspector-general. Price went out to negotiate but aggravated the situation with harsh comments. A group of men rushed him, hitting him with fists, stones and a shovel. The inspector-general died the next day. This was the spur-of-the-moment assassination of the highest man in the Victorian penal system and perhaps the most hated man in Australia. In years to come, Marcus Clarke would use Price as the basis for the villainous commandant Frere in *For The Term Of His Natural Life*.

But in mid-April 1857, Judge Barry was far from impartial when fifteen convicts stood trial for Price's murder. He denied requests for defence counsel, and, as Price's biographer would write, his 'performance was that of a hanging judge, and his comments in sentencing the prisoners to death reveal that he entered upon the trials convinced of the guilt of the prisoners and of the desirability of hanging them by way of deterrent example'. Crown witnesses included the dead inspector-general's underlings, who'd fled the melee rather than help their boss, and twice- and thrice-convicted hulk prisoners, who were saving their own skins and getting remissions by giving evidence.

The accused men denied having struck Price – and related their sufferings at length. Eight men were acquitted, seven were convicted and sentenced to death by Barry in long sanctimonious homilies. Adding insult to the sense of injury, His Honour also praised Price as a humane figure, while brushing aside the prisoners' claims about brutality. The inspector-general's reputation would also be posthumously whitewashed when investigations exonerated him of any brutalities.

Jack Harris – now paid on a freelance basis – would be busier than ever. As a warm-up, on 27 April, he turned off Frederick Turner, convicted of robbery with violence on Flemington Road. This man struggled at the end of the rope for 'several minutes'. The following day, Thomas Williams, Thomas Maloney and Henry Smith were the first to hang for Price's murder. *The Herald* reported: 'The executioner Harris presented himself at the bottom of the stairs, and rapidly performed the operation of pinioning. In a few moments the unhappy men were in eternity. They were executed at the same time, and died without a struggle.'

Henry Smith might've gone fast, but *The Herald* was perturbed that he'd gone to the gallows at all:

It may be remembered that the jury strongly recommended Smith to mercy, not only because there was no evidence that he had taken a prominent part in the murder, but the fact of his having only two months to serve to entitle him to his liberty, rendered it rather improbable that he should engage in an attack which he must have well known would in all probability be attended by such fatal consequences.

At this triple hanging, *The Herald* reported, 'an unusually large number of spectators were present, probably fifty'. That Sheriff Farie had let them in – for whatever reason – seemed against the spirit of 'private' executions.

Before he hanged the next day, Francis Branigan confessed he'd been the first to attack Price – and said Williams had been the one to smash him on the head with the shovel. But he said some of the other condemned men were innocent. Branigan and Richard Bryant seemed to die instantly – but William Brown suffered longer. The seventh man, John Chesley, faced Harris alone on 30 April and died 'after an unusually protracted struggle'.

Nevertheless, Farie recognised Harris's recent workload by writing to his bosses to request that – in addition to his hangman fees – the rest of the man's sentence be remitted. What the sheriff didn't record was that he'd also given entry each day to Pardoe. Professor Sohier's new phrenology lecture, at the Mechanics Institute on 15 May, promised to be his most gripping yet. Having such famous felon heads resulted in what *The Age* reported was an 'unusually large attendance', the crowd applauding as Sohier pointed out various cranial malignancies and explained how they arose from inherent evil: 'The bad man was not the effect of his having a bad head, but the bad head was the effect of the bad man.'

~

After cheating the hangman at the Owen Owens trials, it seemed Captain Melville was going to Jack Harris after all. In late July 1857, in Melbourne Gaol, he used a sharpened spoon to wound Governor Wintle in the neck and he also did a lesser injury to a turnkey.

Before he stood trial, Melville, who'd supposedly been faking madness in the hope of escaping from an asylum, was placed in solitary confinement, where he could be observed by the gaol's medical officer, who was to assess whether he really was insane. Despite being under 'continual watch', in mid-August the prisoner used a 'handkerchief' – two feet long, reportedly his own – to strangle himself. There were rumours Melville had been murdered but the inquest ruled he'd committed suicide while of sound mind.

Four years earlier, George Melville's body had outraged Melbourne as an oyster shop attraction. Now Captain Melville's cast would be a genteel crowd pleaser as a Sohier lecture showpiece. Yet Le Professeur could only make so much money from people coming to his shows or submitting to his analysis. If only there were a way he could expand the business.

The answer presented itself, courtesy of actress-dancer Madame Lee, who had two months earlier opened Melbourne's first waxworks, on Bourke Street. Her establishment featured more than sixty figures – 'historical, regal, reverend, literary, and otherwise remarkable' – that she'd imported from London. What her waxworks lacked were local villains.

Sohier and his lover Ellen Williams acquiring the business made perfect sense. They could make wax heads from phrenological casts for a Chamber of Horrors, whose population would grow and grow thanks to the city's hangmen.

The city's hangmen, however, were nowhere to be found. Jack Harris had repaid Farie for his kindness by clearing out. The story went that Harris and John Walsh had feared reprisals for hanging Price's killers and, once released from gaol, had taken off with £95 between them in recent earnings. *The Herald* claimed: 'After the executions they started for Sydney, and were never afterwards heard of in Victoria.'

There might have been something to the anticipation of reprisal; Farie's correspondence revealed fears were held for the hulk convict witnesses who'd testified against Price's killers.

Not enough is known of John Walsh to guess at his fate. But a quarter of a century later, in 'The Chronicles of Early Melbourne', Garryowen wrote that Harris had done one last job to fund his escape:

In concert with two or three expert gaol pals he went into an extensive burglary in the city, which was cleverly accomplished, and the robbers wisely shook Melbourne dust off their feet, made a rapid move for Sydney, and got clean off before the Melbourne police had a chance of pouncing on them.

This yarn seems unlikely, given that Harris was sixty-six and a chronic drunk whose previous heists of shoes and carpetbags had seen him collared by civilians. Garryowen's denouement sounded more plausible: 'Harris afterwards relapsed into his bad habits, was convicted of a street robbery in Sydney, and died in bondage there.'

Wherever they went, they weren't coming back. And so Farie faced a problem at the start of September 1857, when Hing Tzan and Chong Sigh, Chinese men convicted of the horrific razor-murder of Sophia Lewis in the heart of Melbourne, were due be executed.

When push came to shove, Sheriff Farie materialised a mystery hangman. *The Age* merely reported that he was a prisoner who'd formerly been a city tradesman. 'It is said that he performed his rightful duty as well and with as much *sang froid* as if this had not been his first attempt,' the paper noted. But however good this fellow had been, he appeared to have no appetite for further engagements. Farie, who'd put the year's hangman fees through as part of incidental expenditure, copped flak from his superiors when he had to admit he didn't know 'what I can procure an Executioner for at all times'. They told him to sort it out.

Fourteen men had been executed in Victoria in the first nine months of 1857 – compared with just two in New South Wales and twelve in the United Kingdom – but Melbourne was again without a hangman. Sheriff Farie had to find a new Jack Ketch.

# CHAPTER ELEVEN

# The Nightman, the New Hangman and Nightmares in Wax

While Sheriff Farie was in the market for a hangman, Elijah Upjohn was starting his career as a nightman in the 'Golden City'.

Ballarat had become famous for the gold nuggets people took from the ground. But as the population soared towards 60,000, the brown ones that residents returned to the earth presented a problem – and an opportunity. 'Nightsoil' was deposited in cesspools under outdoor dunnies. When these water closets were full, they had to be emptied and the waste carted away. Enter the nightman.

The nightman had much in common with the hangman, and suffered from the same double standard. Society needed to get rid of what was disgusting and dangerous, and yet people were repulsed and revolted by the individuals who did this vital work to keep them safe. But there was a difference. The hangman came with a strange fascination that would see people crowd around him if they had the chance. No one clamoured for a glimpse of the nightman and his cart. Just as the hangman was ideally kept out of sight, the cesspool emptier could only legally operate between 11pm and 5am. Hence: nightman.

After Elijah and Ann Upjohn had a second son, Alfred, in 1856, they'd moved to Ballarat. In November the next year, Elijah appeared to be backsliding when he was charged with stealing from a man during a bender at a hotel. The next morning the complainant woke up missing money and papers, and seemed to recall Upjohn pickpocketing him. The problem was that this fellow had come to in the police lock-up, having been detained for being blind drunk. In court, Upjohn was discharged for lack of evidence but his accuser was fined forty shillings for tearing up the hotel.

Elijah and his wife had another boy, Charles, in 1858, so now they had three small mouths to feed. Elijah was going to do it as a nightman. With 'john' already in use as slang for toilet, and the job being to bring muck 'up', it's likely his surname saw him subjected to even more jokes than most men pursuing this profession.

Ballarat was then ruled by two councils – the Western and the Eastern – and these municipal bodies didn't see eye to eye on much. Like many prospective small-business owners contracting to provide a public service, Elijah would have to navigate a system ruled by petty bureaucrats. This would often bring out the disorderly nature that had marked his career as a convict.

Another source of conflict was Elijah's father, who was now living in Ballarat and who would work for him in the nightman business. Henry Upjohn was about seventy-two and still getting into trouble. In June 1857, the old man was charged with stealing four pairs of trousers and, during his court appearance, he offered a 'long rigmarole about the Peninsular war, in which it appeared he had played a most important part'. He then admitted guilt 'but pleaded drunkenness as an excuse' and was sentenced to three months. Elijah and Henry did not have a happy personal or professional relationship – but the son was again to have more in common with his father than he might've liked.

In January 1859, Upjohn went to the Western Council and asked for an exclusive licence to operate as a nightman. The councillors said he couldn't be granted a monopoly but the law would protect him from unticketed competitors. Elijah was granted a £5 annual licence. Then he went to the Eastern Council with the same request and got the same response as well as the advice that 'he could not practise his vocation without a license'. Pushing his point with the Western Council, he presented the town inspector with a list of twenty or thirty people whose water closets needed emptying.

Such neglect was then a major problem. Rather than pay for a nightman's services, penny-pinching householders, business owners, government officials and military authorities often let water closets overflow, or else poured earth into full cesspools, which only forced the shit up and out. Heavy rains caused rivers of stinking filth to run through yards and streets, and it would then collect in stagnant puddles. In Ballarat, as in Melbourne, the stench was pervasive. Hot, wet weather made it unbearable.

Elijah wanted the town inspector to compel the people on his list to empty their cesspools. This official said he'd only do so if their neighbours complained; if he issued summonses, he might be perceived as corruptly boosting Upjohn's business. Ballarat's new nightman wrote a letter to local newspaper *The Star* to force the issue. When that did no good, he wrote to the Western Council to complain that they were doing nothing about countless full cesspools.

Speaking at a council meeting, the town inspector defended his actions and said the nightman had tried to squeeze him for business. The chairman also wanted it known that the uppity Upjohn charged exorbitant prices. By putting these allegations on the record – and thus in the newspapers – they'd put his reputation and livelihood at risk. The council then refused to officially receive Upjohn's correspondence.

Elijah wrote to *The Star* again, saying it was a lie he charged £6 and that he was 'ready to remove all filth at a sum that must be deemed reasonable by every conscientious person'. He also wrote to the council repudiating the accusation and pleading for a personal interview. But because he wasn't present at the next meeting, the councillors said that if he wanted to clear his name, he should advertise his prices in the newspapers.

All in all, it was a messy beginning to a messy business.

Upjohn was on the side of the angels in this dispute. The Eastern Council's health officer said at this time it was 'remarkable' that more people hadn't died or become sick in January, given the 'quantity of offensive and decayed matter, sludge and stagnant water' in his district. An editorial in *The Star* called on the authorities to do more – and to increase their powers to compel people to take action. Under the head-line 'Premature Deaths' a correspondent called 'Health-Desirer' wrote to the paper a few days later:

> The nightman should be constantly at work, removing nuisances of every description, the effect of which would be a great increase of health, and to a very great extent banishment of the sickness which at present carries so many untimely to the grave. Whence the lethargy of the Town Councils in sanitary matters, I cannot imagine.

But the fracas appeared to give Upjohn second thoughts about his new calling. Taking people's crap for a few pounds was one thing; taking the council's crap over taking crap was another. In mid-March 1859, Upjohn advertised the sale of his cart and business. Either there were no takers or he had a change of heart, because by July he'd expanded his operations, as he advertised in *The Star*:

> HEALTH AND COMFORT. Nightman – Elijah Upjohn wishes to inform the public of Ballarat, that he has bought from Mr Wm Gardiner

all his night carts, business, &c., and is prepared to execute all orders in the above line. Closets and cesspools emptied, yards cleaned and rubbish removed on the most reasonable terms. All orders left at Elijah Upjohn's, Lydiard street, near the Gully, Soldier's Hill, will be attended to on the shortest notice, and satisfaction given or no pay.

A month later, Henry Upjohn was convicted of stealing a coat and got fourteen days in prison. This can't have pleased his son, both for the stain on the family name and for strain it placed on the business. Far worse, in mid-October, Elijah and Ann's eldest child, Joseph Elijah, now aged four, fell ill with congestion of the lungs. They took him to the respected Dr Henry Mount but the boy died a week into November.

In June 1860, Upjohn applied again to the Eastern Council for a £5 licence but was refused – as reported in *The Star*. Elijah went rogue and worked the area anyway. The town inspector had him charged, and tried to claim the council had offered him a discounted licence. The magistrate dismissed the case but gave leave for a new complaint to be brought. When that happened in August, Upjohn's lawyer argued that being licensed by the Western Council should be sufficient. But he was fined £5.

Upjohn went on the offensive. The town inspector's claim that he'd been offered a licence was now on the record, so he demanded one and presented the Eastern Council with a list of cesspools that needed emptying. They ignored him. He wrote a letter to *The Star* to claim that Eastern didn't care about public health, and described several locations where closets were overflowing badly. Upjohn said he'd personally waited on the council's chairman and informed him of these and other nuisances, and had again been told they had no power to interfere unless neighbours complained. Elijah wrote that it was 'more than probable that but few of the "neighbours" are aware of this', and that Eastern 'has hardly been mindful of these matters as it ought have been'. As additional proof: 'I may mention that, so long as this has been a municipality, no manure depot has been appointed.' This meant that whoever was emptying cesspools had nowhere to safely deposit the nightsoil, meaning it was probably ending up in creeks or vacant lots. Upjohn appeared to be both a businessman defending his livelihood and a genuinely concerned citizen.

Despite his troubles with the council, Elijah was doing well. Around this time, his good character seemed borne out when he appeared in court as a witness, on one occasion in the case of a woman suing a man to support their illegitimate child, and on another when he had seen a violent assault. In 1861 he and Ann had another son, naming him Joseph Elijah after the eldest brother he'd never know.

But it wasn't all happy families. By July that year, Henry was living as a vagrant. He tried to get into the Ballarat Benevolent Asylum, but was refused because his son was in 'good circumstances'. Whatever had happened between them, Elijah now refused to put a roof over his father's head, or even a few coins in his pocket. Or so the old man claimed in court when he was charged with stealing boots. The police and a character witness told the court that Henry wasn't a bad bloke, and the magistrate seemed to have believed this as he was ordered into custody for only twelve hours.

Elijah can't have liked seeing the headline 'An Undutiful Son' in *The Star*. Henry again applied to the asylum in October, the paper reporting that he had 'been working for his son while able, but eventually becoming incapable of further exertion, had been discarded by the former'. Surely there was more to it than that, given Henry's frequent thieving. But the committee thought it appalling that the well-to-do son had refused to maintain his father; not long after, they found a spot for the old man. Henry died in the asylum three months later.

Elijah had followed in Henry's footsteps when he was transported to Tasmania. But while the father had continued life as a criminal, the son had tried to become a respectable citizen. Now he was rid of Henry for good. Yet Elijah couldn't have imagined that his own future would make his father's final years seem like a comfortable retirement.

~

Sheriff Farie had a new hangman. During the early years of his career, this executioner would remain in the shadows. But when he finally stepped into the limelight, he was enough to make that old sinner Jack Harris look like one of the saints.

William Bamford was born in 1808 in Lancashire. He trained to be a woolcomber but joined the army when he was about thirteen. As a man, he stood five-foot-seven. He had grey eyes set in a long, pale face, with brown hair and thin whiskers. Bamford bore a blue soldier's tattoo on one wrist, and had been branded with a 'D' – for 'Deserter' – on his left side.

Being in a uniform didn't suit him. Later reports depicted him as a troublesome soldier, who on one occasion received 300 lashes. In 1840 he deserted in Ireland but was quickly caught. Bamford was court-martialled in May that year and sentenced to be transported for seven years. He sailed on the *British Sovereign* in December and was noted as being 'well behaved and anxious to be useful' on the voyage.

After reaching Van Diemen's Land in March 1841, Bamford was a reasonably well-conducted convict. By August 1845 he had his ticket of leave, and he was a free man in May 1847. Two months later, in Launceston, Bamford got drunk enough to come under the notice of a constable, who hauled him before the court, where he was fined five shillings. The next day Bamford was back before the bench, for being drunk again and for using improper language, and he was fined the same amount. Bamford's dissolution was minor but rated a passing mention in *The Cornwall Chronicle*. There'd be plenty more such articles in the years ahead.

William Bamford was a free man in 1848 and sailed from Launceston for Melbourne on the barque *Rory Moore* in 1852. What he did with himself then isn't known, but it seems like it wasn't anything good. By June 1853, when Bamford was in the Melbourne court for being drunk and assaulting a constable, his habits were already well known enough for *The Argus* to call him 'a frequent visitor' to the magistrates. He was sent to prison for one month. Bamford was in back in trouble in August – a charge of indecency added to the usual drunkenness. He was to pay a £5 fine or serve a week behind bars.

One night in early September 1857, Bamford lurked in the Old Cemetery, jumped out, seized a man and demanded money. As bad luck would have it, his victim was a police constable, who threw him to the ground. Bamford was in court the next day, with the detective telling His Honour that the accused had, as *The Age* reported, 'long been under the notice of the police for drunkenness, assaults, larcenies, and felonies'. This time it was twelve months in gaol with hard labour.

Shortly afterwards, John Mason, a woodsplitter living in a hut fifty miles north-west of Melbourne, settled a drunken argument with a bullying workmate by putting an axe through his skull. Mason was found guilty, though the jury recommended mercy on account of what other workers said about the victim being such a bastard. There was no commutation.

Cooling his heels in gaol, William Bamford volunteered his services as freelance executioner. On 6 November 1857, he earned his fee and his victim died without a struggle.

John Mason was his first. Bamford would keep count. His tally would mount and mount.

~

By February 1858, Philemon Sohier and Ellen Williams had taken over from Madame Lee. Their new business would operate as Mrs Williams's

Australian Waxworks, while Sohier kept his Phrenological Museum.

The waxworks catalogue – price: sixpence – listed its figures in order of importance. First, of course, was Queen Victoria. Then Prince Albert and other royals. There was also Shakespeare, Voltaire, Sir Walter Scott and the like. But the big attractions were the local villains and some of their victims, Mrs Williams having made heads from Sohier's moulds and outfitted the bodies.

Chong Sigh and Hing Tzan were posed cutting open Sophia Lewis's throat. There was John Price's killer, Thomas Williams, and the bushranger James Condon. John Mason was the most recent addition. But the star of the show was Captain Melville, wearing the man's own clothes and depicted attacking Governor Wintle and the turnkey. How Sohier got these garments wasn't clear. Melville hadn't hanged, so they hadn't passed through the hands of Jack Harris. That the clothes left the gaol would've been up to Farie.

~

Bamford's work on the gallows with John Mason had pleased Farie, who in February 1858 wrote to the chief secretary requesting the governor remit the rest of Bamford's sentence and authorise his release on 1 March, 'on condition of his performing the duties of executioner in the case of the two criminals who I understand are to be hanged on that day, which he is willing to do for £5 and his liberty'. Bamford hanged two racecourse robbers as planned. These executions – and another one a fortnight later – were covered in only spare detail by the newspapers. None of the victims was reported to have suffered unduly. All made their peace with God. The hangman remained in the background, unidenti-fied, unremarkable. As it was supposed to be.

After he was released, Bamford was back in court in April 1858 for drunkenness, but in *The Argus* he was merely listed as one of a dozen pisspots fined ten shillings apiece. He helped maintain his anonymity because he didn't share his predecessor's fondness for screaming about being the hangman or threatening to practise his craft on the magistrate. Even though Bamford lost his left eye in a brawl around this time, he didn't draw attention to how he earned his drinking money.

Yet, as would later be revealed, reporters had known his identity for years. Why had they kept it quiet? It's possible a 'gentlemen's agreement' was in force between Farie and the journalists. Bamford was a boozer but doing his job well and not causing a ruckus, the sheriff might have argued, so why risk scandalising the public unnecessarily while also potentially putting the man in harm's way?

Bamford stayed out of the limelight even when he bungled the October 1858 hanging of Owen McQueeny, convicted of 'The Green Tent Murder' near Meredith. This former convict had shot dead young Elizabeth Lowe while she was nursing her son in the canvas tavern she operated alone after being deserted by her husband. The woman's little boy had nearly suffocated beneath his mother's body. The ruthlessness of the crime, McQueeny's sinister behaviour beforehand and the police's careful investigation all combined to make this a sensational story.

The execution at Geelong was the final act in the drama. After being read his death warrant, McQueeny anticipated a later victim of the gallows, saying, 'Well, I suppose it can't be helped' and objecting to being pinioned with 'Don't let him lay a hand on me more than necessary'. On the platform, he told the hangman the noose was too tight, ordering: 'Don't choke me before my time.' The villain might have wished he'd held his tongue. McQueeny took five minutes to stop twitching entirely and the inquest recorded he'd been 'strangulated'. Then, as *The Star* reported, 'a very singular instance of superstition was manifested' when an 'old crippled woman' asked Sheriff Rede if the dead man's hands could be laid on her to 'remove her infirmity'. It wasn't recorded whether permission was granted.

Despite such detailed press coverage, Bamford wasn't named. Back in Melbourne, he got hammered on his £5 blood money, and though he wound up in court he still wasn't identified as the hangman.

~

McQueeny's cast was added to Sohier's museum. While phrenology was popular, it had its critics. *The Age* would sometimes style it as 'a "science"' when discussing the subject. A Mr Blair had delivered anti-phrenology lectures, in which he criticised the central concept of the brain being the seat of the mind. Melbourne's *Punch* magazine loved poking fun at Sohier with jokes such as: 'Why is Professor Sohier like a new chum passenger by Cobb's coach? Because he is continually feeling bumps!'

Yet Le Professeur was taken seriously enough that he was allowed to give his views to the 'Select Committee of the Legislative Council on the Aborigines'. Based on a number of skulls in his possession, he said, Aboriginal people's inferior temperament, small brains and peculiar combination of underdeveloped mental organs governing firmness, hope, ideality, and so on meant they would be very difficult to improve. Thus, only phrenologists could save Aboriginal people from extinction. Sohier feared that they would meet this fate before sufficient learned men were honest and moral enough to accept the truth of his science.

The committee didn't buy this bunkum outright. The chairman, Thomas McCombie, concluded that the colony's Aboriginal people were even 'perhaps superior to the Negro, and some of the more inferior divisions of the great human family'. He agreed with another expert that their 'perceptive faculties are peculiarly acute, they are apt learners, and possess the most intense desire to imitate their more civilized brethren in almost everything'. But the pseudoscience wasn't entirely dismissed, as his concluding paragraph indicated: '[T]here is considerable deficiency in their reflective faculties, and a certain want of steadiness of purpose in their characters, which appears the great obstacle to be overcome in reclaiming them, and bringing them within the pale of civilization and Christianity.'

Phrenology held that negative traits in the criminal and the savage might be reversed if the right moral education was applied early. Tragically, one piece of Sohier's advice about Indigenous people to the select committee would become government policy long after phrenology had been consigned to the waste bin of history: 'If the young children could be entirely separated from their parents, they might, of course, be more readily and permanently acted upon.'

~

The brutality of the gallows was often masked by blithe descriptions of men going calmly to the drop, and explanations of their long struggles as simple muscular contractions. But in late 1858 a series of hangings was so awful that it was difficult to turn a blind eye.

The first atrocity came during a double execution at Melbourne Gaol on 6 November. Samuel Gibbs, from Santa Domingo, had thrown his wife into a hole sixty feet deep at Ararat. George Thompson, an American from Pennsylvania, had murdered a man at Ballarat. That both were black might help explain why their 'manliness' wasn't protected in the reporting of their deaths, just as Aboriginal men in 1842 and 1847 had been described as being overwhelmed by fear.

Thompson had to be assisted up the ladder because he was so scared. Gibbs too was terrified and had to be pushed up. He struggled and tried to get off the drop, grasping the rail with his pinioned hands and crying: 'Mercy! Mercy! I'm an innocent man; good people, protect me. Oh God! Oh God!'

Gibbs was pushed onto the drop as the bolt was pulled. Thompson fell straight down and died instantly. But Gibbs's forward motion meant his rope hit the lower edge of a scaffold beam and snapped. He hit the ground 'partially executed'. Gibbs was picked up, insensible, and carried back to the platform. There he came to his senses and started screaming. The ends of the rope were quickly knotted, and Bamford and the officers of the law told each other, 'Quick, quick, stand out of the way' as he dropped a second time. Gibbs took two or three minutes to die.

In the inquest on Gibbs, Governor Wintle simply wrote: 'The rope broke in this execution. The rope was of the usual size and character used in executions and was carefully examined before use. I cannot now detect any flaw with it.'

The awful death of Gibbs might have been forgotten if not for what came next. Not wanting to have to deal with another 'partially executed' man, Bamford overcorrected on 24 November, when seeing off Edward Hitchcock, who'd stabbed his wife dead at Strathloddon. But he'd made the rope too short, and hadn't drawn the noose tight enough. Hitchcock struggled for nearly three minutes, 'and not till the executioner brought his own weight to bear, by grasping the feet of the dying man, did the convulsions cease'. Farie's memorandum to the chief secretary just comprised the usual boilerplate: 'Sir, I have the honor to inform you that the extreme sentence of the law was ... this morning carried into effect pursuant to the command and warrant of His Excellency the Governor.'

Less than a week later, Prussian man Christian Von See went to Bamford for murdering a man near the Bendigo goldfields. The hangman drew the bolt. Von See's pinioned hands grasped at nothing. He stepped on air as his feet searched for support. He grabbed his trousers and tried to hold himself up. Then he reached for the rope at his neck. It was four minutes before he died.

Farie picked up his pen and wrote the same words again: 'Sir, I have the honor to inform you that the extreme sentence of the law ...' et cetera. But this horrific hat-trick was too much for Melbourne's newspapers to ignore. For once they didn't simply take aim at the unnamed executioner, but instead focused on Farie's role and the general barbarities of capital punishment.

*The Age* fumed: 'We have said before, and we repeat it, that the employment of a casual hangman is as disgraceful as it is demoralising. If hanging be necessary, let [it] be done in a strictly official manner and by a recognised functionary.'

*The Argus* renewed its call for the abolition of the death penalty, saying the public was brutalised and poisoned by such executions and thus more likely to commit crimes:

Still we hear of men, whose throats have not been properly fitted with the strangling cord, or whose bodies are not sufficiently heavy, requiring the additional jerk and weight of the hangman, who clings to the struggling legs, so that the frightful pair swing together. Still we hear of the rope breaking, and a half-strangled man falling to the earth, and the executioners carefully carrying (oh, miserable tenderness!) the languid, yet too conscious victim, up again to the scaffold, to be once more 'turned off'. Still we hear of – and some of us are eye-witnesses – a man of so powerful a frame, whose tenacity of life is so great, and his imagination so excited with horror, that his struggles continue nearly five mortal minutes (to him how far longer the sense of its duration), while his feet vainly seek to regain the brink of that precipice from which he has been swung over eternity, while his hands try hurriedly to grasp something tangible, and reaching nothing but the air, then seize upon his own body, and strive to lift himself by himself, till they eventually claw up towards the cord, and finding the fingers of Death at his throat, grapple with them to the last. Are such scenes to continue?

*The Argus* suggested a pause in capital punishment: 'It will be easy to revert to barbarism should the amelioration appear to be premature.'

For once, Farie had to go on the defensive – just as he had in 1842, when La Trobe had suggested he and his fellow settlers might have had information about who'd perpetrated the massacre of Aboriginal people. The sheriff's report to the chief secretary, printed in *The Argus*, accused the paper and *The Herald* of false reporting. He admitted Gibbs's rope broke, but this 'most unfortunate and terrible accident' had caused a delay of only two minutes before he 'died without a struggle'. Farie concluded: 'I do not believe he was ever sensible to any suffering.' As for Hitchcock and Von See, neither suffered mentally or physically, and 'I can only say that nothing unusual occurred'.

Farie solicited opinion from Dr William McCrea, Victoria's chief medical officer, and Dr Edward Barker, by now one of Melbourne's most prominent surgeons, who'd both been witnesses to the Hitchcock hanging. Did they believe 'any neglect or blame to be attributed to any of the officers whose unpleasant duty it is to see that capital sentences are properly carried out?' They signed a certificate attesting that the execution had been performed in the 'usual manner' and 'there was no neglect'. While spasmodic convulsions had 'lasted longer than usual', their opinion was that 'the deceased did not suffer pain after the drop fell'.

Farie also solicited Dr James F Rudall to say that within a minute of the airways being obstructed, all consciousness ceased and so a person did not suffer. Muscular spasms extending up to five minutes didn't signify consciousness or life, and only ignorant people saw them as expressive of pain or efforts to escape. Dr Rudall said the recent men had died in the usual time and manner, though he did allow that death on the gallows was only instantaneous when the neck was broken by the drop.

In response to these medical defences, *The Argus* argued that the science of hanging men wasn't conclusive, and so the onus was on civilised society to err on the side of the humane. The paper witheringly noted that Farie had seen 'nothing unusual' at executions where the hangman had swung from one victim's legs and another strangling man had clearly been trying to free his neck from the noose. The sheriff 'cannot bear to think that his duties involve the infliction of agony upon any of his fellow creatures'.

By February 1859, *The Argus* had refined its argument. While it hoped capital punishment would someday be abolished, in the meantime civilised society should not make men suffer unduly because 'some unhanged rascal, who had volunteered his services, did not understand the business! ... It should by no means and on no account depend upon the skill or bungling, the strength or weakness of nerve, of a low ruffian, whose very nickname is a reproach to civilised society.'

So it was back to blaming the lowly functionary rather than his establishment boss.

# CHAPTER TWELVE

# Out of the Shadows

William Bamford's anonymity meant the spectacle of a sloshed Jack Ketch didn't give more ammunition to the anti–capital punishment critics. Nearly five months without a brutal hanging also took much fire from their argument. When he performed three executions in mid-1859, the malefactors were reported as having died without fuss. Things settled down again.

Bamford – his count now at thirteen – was next to hang another rebellious prisoner. Richard Rowley – like Captain Melville – had been convicted of three counts of robbery and Justice Redmond Barry had given him three sentences totalling thirty years that were to be served consecutively. Hearing this, Rowley had said: 'Sentence me, Your Honour, to be hanged, for you have done as bad.'

Like Melville, Rowley claimed he'd been brutalised. In June 1859, in Pentridge, he attacked and seriously injured overseer Denis Kilmartin – a convict who'd been John Price's crack enforcer – along with another warder. Rowley's spree was only stopped by the intervention of a prisoner named Michael Gately.

Hearing this might have made Bamford smile, because Gately had been transported with him on the *British Sovereign*. Back then, it had been hard to miss the tiny lad with the red hair and freckled face. Since then, Gately had grown into a flame-haired man mountain and habitual crook. For his bravery in saving the guards, though, he was going to be rewarded with early release.

When Rowley came to the scaffold in July, *The Argus* was paying close attention with its timepiece: 'A slight convulsive shudder ran through his frame, and in a few moments he ceased to live, death taking place in 42 seconds from the time of his fall.' In November, the paper saw child rapist William Siddons hang 'without struggle'. Soon afterwards, former American slave Henry Brown – who'd been convicted of murder – strangled for three minutes and twenty seconds because Bamford hadn't adjusted the rope properly.

But this time there was no impassioned *Argus* commentary, perhaps because the paper had new conservative editors who would set the tone for its next century. In July 1860, when the double murderer George Waines endured a 'few muscular spasms', the paper's reporter said 'there was no sign of suffering; in fact, a more merciful execution, if any can be merciful, could not have taken place'. Nor was *The Argus* to note anything more than a maladjustment with the rope when wife-murderer John McDonald took nearly three minutes to die in September.

~

Sometimes it wasn't suffering that made the death penalty unpopular. Sometimes it was a man cheating the noose that led to cries for its abolition. Such was the case in early 1861.

On New Year's Day at Geelong, a young man named Laurence Shanklin fought with another fellow about a girl and came off second best. A few hours later he stabbed his sleeping adversary to death in front of a witness. An insanity defence was rejected by the jury and Shanklin was sentenced to hang. But a petition arguing that he hadn't been of sound mind – signed by prominent clergymen and others – was accepted by the government as justification for commuting his sentence to twenty years. Controversy erupted when newspapers alleged that the real reason for mercy was that Shanklin had family connections to a cabinet member – and that this man had swayed the Executive Council and perhaps the governor.

Shanklin's reprieve stoked anti–capital punishment sentiment. A massive 'indignation meeting' at Geelong heard that sparing him meant every previous execution had been a foul judicial murder. In parliament, the chief secretary was asked if the government now intended to abolish the death penalty. Surely it couldn't justify hanging anyone ever again after sparing Shanklin.

But it could. There was no reprieve for William Smith, who'd drowned his wife in a waterhole near Wangaratta, with Bamford hanging him in April 1861 at Melbourne Gaol, *The Argus* now admiringly noting that 'the executioner did his office with promptitude and precision'.

That sort of reliable efficiency was the dream of Dr Edward Barker. This surgeon, who had defended Farie, was an aficionado of executions and had a theory: the knot should go at the back of the neck instead of beneath the left ear, as was by then customary. Martin Rice, who'd murdered a popular racing identity, was to be a test case in Melbourne Gaol at the end of September.

*The Herald* painted another unseemly scene allowed by Farie. As soon as the gates opened, there was a rush and 'many who ought not to have been admitted succeeded in gaining entrance'. These people – some of whom were said to know Rice – pressed forward to see him. The Melbourne newspapers recorded Rice dying quickly. But *The Geelong Advertiser* claimed Dr Barker's knot hadn't done the trick. Instead, 'death was attended, apparently, with so much suffering as to cause the hangman to strive to press upon the body to put the wretch out of his misery; but Dr Barker would not admit of it.'

A similar scene played out a month later. Farie again allowed a rabble to attend the hanging of rapist Thomas Sanders. Some pushed to get to the gallows first; others followed the condemned man as he made his last walk. Sanders, *The Argus* said, 'behaved, under the circumstances, much better than the spectators'. Dr Barker supervised. *The Age* reported: 'Death was not so instantaneous as in some cases, through it is said, a slipping of the knot; but it certainly took place within three minutes.'

~

As Bamford worked in the shadows, and as Sheriff Farie and Dr Barker oversaw these spectacles, Professor Sohier and Ellen Williams went from strength to strength phrenologically and personally.

In January 1859 they'd taken the 'Australian department' of their waxworks and phrenological museum to Castlemaine and then Bendigo. 'For One Week Only', customers in each town could marvel at murderers, including recent additions Von See, Thompson and Gibbs. Country folk could also consult Le Professeur, now modestly rewriting history to tout himself as 'the Phrenological lion, who introduced, in 1853, Phrenology into Australia'.

As Mrs Williams's husband was now dead, the lion and his lioness married in Melbourne in April 1859. Their certificate listed his occupation as 'phrenologist'. Hers was left blank, even though she was a talented figure-maker and enterprising businesswoman. Perhaps it was enough that their establishment would from then on be known as 'Madame Sohier's Waxworks Exhibition'. Within a few years her name was also over the door of a Sydney branch.

By 1861, Melbourne had more phrenologists. Bourke Street barber James Doubleday had expanded his business to include bumpology, which made a kind of sense as he already spent his days working on men's heads. In October he cast the noggin of Thomas Sanders, displaying the result in his shop window. The death mask was advertised as a 'bushranger' – presumably because 'rapist' was deemed less likely to bring the customers in for a shave and trim. Across the road, Sohier added Sanders to the waxworks, spruiking his realistic creation as 'all but breathing'.

Melbourne also had a new wax wizard in Maximilian Kreitmeyer. Originally from Munich, this anatomical sculptor had spent a small fortune to make 200 models of every part of the human body for his 'Grand Anatomical Museum'. One of his close associates was Dr Louis L Smith, who'd use an 'anatomical Venus' to illuminate his presentation of 'Life, Health, and Disease'.

But Dr Smith – who was soon to open his own anatomical museum with a focus on venereal diseases – was more than just a progressive lecturer who might titillate by talking about sexuality. He was also a populist politician and the colony's new crusader against capital punishment.

~

Dr LL Smith specialised in 'Nervous Affections, Loss of Power and the Diseases of Married Life'. He also sold 'Vegetable Pills', the 'best domestic medicine in the colony', which he marketed with big newspaper advertisements, making enemies of some in the medical establishment, who believed he should be prosecuted as a qualified surgeon peddling quack cures. Like Sohier, Dr Smith wasn't apologetic for being a relentless self-promoter, and viewed himself as fighting the good fight against ignorant vested interests.

Dr Smith really was a man of the people, offering free consultations several times a week, which was a boon to the poor. So too was his annual *Almanac*, which contained 'useful family, medical and other information', such as taking opium for insomnia, amyl nitrate for nervous headache and enemas of liquor bismuth for anal prolapse. Dr Smith's popularity saw him elected to the Legislative Assembly in 1859. From irrigation to aquaculture, he had a lot of big ideas. One was that hanging was immoral and ineffective.

In January 1861, amid the debate in Victoria over the fate of Laurence Shanklin, Henry Parkes brought a bill to abolish capital punishment in New South Wales, the first such move in Australian history. Though Parkes was defeated by twenty-five votes to sixteen, Dr Smith resolved to make a similar attempt in Victoria. In November, he sought to bring an abolition bill but was opposed by the chief secretary, and he backed down for the time being.

Dr Smith put his case before the parliament in mid-January 1862, explaining that he was merely presenting the arguments used by abolitionists in England. Dr Smith said he didn't mind being ridiculed as a 'wild enthusiast' because, in addition to following his conscience, the reality was that, in practice, 'an eye for an eye' justice didn't work. Juries and judges were more hesitant to convict and condemn because they didn't want to risk 'being the instruments of the strangulation of an innocent man'. If Victoria abolished the death penalty, then this anxiety would be removed; if new evidence came to light, it wouldn't be too late to save the man.

Dr Smith also spoke about the uncertainty surrounding who was hanged and who was spared, making reference to the cases of Shanklin and others who'd been reprieved. What's more, he argued, many rapists were never even charged, because delicate-minded victims shrank from the responsibility of taking a man's life. Given his very prominent and specialised practice, it's likely he encountered more women and girls who suffered as a result of rape – including pregnancy and venereal disease – than anyone else in the colony.

Attorney-General Richard Ireland opposed Smith's motion. The colony of Victoria was very different to England, he said, having many remote settlements that were preyed upon by that uniquely local criminal genus known as the bushranger. Abolishing capital punishment would 'imperil the well-being of society', because it would remove the reason many bushrangers stopped short of actual violence.

Not many people realised it, Ireland said, but highway robbery was not a capital offence unless accompanied by wounding or attempted wounding. In anticipation of this debate, which had been on the cards for months, he'd requested Farie prepare a return of bushranging convictions to show how many were committed with violence and how many without. Regrettably, Mr Ireland had to tell parliament, Farie had not yet provided this document. But if it *had* been furnished, he said, it would show that most bushrangers refrained from hurting people because they feared the noose. Ergo: deterrence.

Graham Berry, the former Eureka juryman turned radical who'd recently been elected to the parliament as an 'extreme liberal', spoke in support of Dr Smith. When campaigning six months earlier, he'd been reported by *The Herald* as telling Collingwood voters: 'Our criminal jurisprudence required revision and amendment, even perhaps to the abolition of capital punishment.' Now in parliament, Berry claimed that civilised societies tended to abolition. Public executions had once been thought a deterrent, but the accepted truth now was that they simply brutalised the populace. Berry therefore supported a reading of the bill and a full parliamentary discussion, saying he preferred a system in which capital punishment was reserved for first-degree murder.

Chief secretary and Premier John O'Shanassy praised Berry's passion and said he'd made a better case than Dr Smith, who should have sought a royal commission or select committee inquiry rather than demanding abolition. Seeming to argue against himself, O'Shanassy said that in Ireland the previous year there had been just one execution, from a population of six million. The point he was trying to make was that it hadn't been deemed necessary to abolish capital punishment there.

As for uncertainty, O'Shanassy said Victoria's court system – inquest, trial, appeals – gave criminals every chance to 'escape'. When it came to the Executive Council reprieving some and condemning others, it only looked like uncertainty to outsiders because the cabinet was a secret tribunal, and 'therefore, neither the public nor the press could know what transpired in it'. Sometimes, he said, 'most important evidence was received at the last moment'.

Citing a parliamentary return that *had* been produced by Attorney-General Ireland, the premier said there wasn't wholesale hanging in the colony, nor was there undue leniency. Between 1855 and 1861, eighty-five people had been sentenced to death, and another fifteen had sentences of death recorded (which was when a judge wanted to acknowledge a capital crime but knew the Executive Council would reprieve). Of these 100 cases, fifty-four related to murder, two to attempted murder, five to shooting with intent to kill, fifteen to rape, two to rape and carnal abuse of children, five each to sodomy and bestiality, two to arson and ten to robbery or burglary with violence. Of the 100 offenders, the premier said, forty-three had gone to the gallows and fifty-seven had seen their sentences commuted to long prison terms with hard labour.

As for Dr Smith's contention about rape, the premier believed this crime's frequency was *because* not all cases were punishable by death. His return cited seventeen men with rape convictions, yet only Siddons and Sanders had swung for their offences. Without saying it in so many words, the premier had, during a debate about the abolition of capital punishment, expressed his belief that another fifteen men should have been *added* to Sohier's Chamber of Horrors.

The motion was put and negatived without a division. *The Argus* – until recently the champion of abolition – approved wholeheartedly:

We are glad to find that there is no disposition in the Legislative Assembly to entertain the propositions to abolish the punishment of death ... If death be, as we contend, the most effectual warning, we should not relinquish it ... Victoria is one of the last places in which the dangerous experiment should be tried of abolishing capital punishment.

Dr Smith vowed to try again, confident of success, not realising he'd been born a century too early. Graham Berry, meanwhile, would later face a far more intense debate about hanging men – or at least one man – as premier of Victoria in November 1880.

~

In November 1862 – five years after he'd hanged his first man – 'John' Bamford was named in *The Herald* as 'The Colonial "Jack Ketch"'. *The Argus*'s phrasing – 'an individual who has been for many years employed in the capacity of hangman' – indicated that its newsmen had long known his identity. The occasion for the unmasking was Bamford's appearance in Emerald Hill court on a drunkenness charge. Having now offended many times – including just a few days earlier – he was given the severe sentence of three months in gaol.

Why he was abruptly exposed isn't known. Perhaps he'd just got into strife one too many times. But the revelation wasn't accompanied by any editorial handwringing. Capital punishment was off the agenda: there hadn't been a hanging for nearly a year. Besides, the Bamford issue was dealt with for the next few months.

By mid-March 1863 Bamford was out and again playing up in Emerald Hill – later renamed South Melbourne. The hangman now seemed happy to channel Jack Harris, being, as *The Herald* described, 'in a state of brutal intoxication, and behaving in the most shameful way to passers-by'. *The Argus* called him an 'incorrigible drunkard who spent three-fourths of his time in gaol'. *The Age* was more cynical, detecting some method in the man's madness: '[T]he prisoner is somewhat proud of his public calling, and is apprehensive lest another should usurp his office; for no sooner does he complete one sentence than another charge is preferred against him, which provides him with food and clothing at the country's expense.'

This commentary presumed that Bamford didn't mind being in gaol because he'd be looked after and wouldn't be overlooked when Farie needed a hangman. If that was the case, he was rolling the dice when it came to magistrates, who had a lot of latitude in the punishments they handed out. In this instance, Bamford was sentenced to twelve months. But even with good behaviour, Bamford would be out of sight and out of mind – as well as out of the taverns and out of trouble – for the rest of the year. Again, the hangman question was forgotten for the time being.

On 6 November 1863, Bamford got the shock of his life when he arrived in Geelong to hang the constable murderer James Murphy. The doomed man was *the* James Murphy he'd been mates with back in their Tasmanian convict days. Just as his Sydney predecessor Thomas Hughes had cried when forced to hang an old drinking buddy, so Bamford now burst into tears, having to suffer the turnkeys chiding him for his weakness. The hangman sobbed: 'I can't help it; he was a pal o'mine t'other side.' Composing himself, he wiped away his tears and pinioned Murphy. *The Geelong Advertiser* reported that it was a 'rather affecting scene', but the hangman 'got through the remainder of his thankless office creditably'.

Five days later, on 11 November, Bamford faced a first for the colony when he had to hang a woman. This was the task that had greatly disturbed Australia's first hangman, and that would later be the death of one of Bamford's successors.

At the age of thirteen, Elizabeth Scott had been made to marry an older alcoholic man. They'd operated a refreshments tent near Mansfield for a decade and she bore him five children, though only two survived infancy. Elizabeth became friendly with local David Gedge and with her Macau-born cook and servant Julian Cross. In October 1863, the Crown contended, she'd induced Gedge to cast a bullet and load a gun.

Elizabeth then plied Cross with brandy so he'd shoot her husband as he lay in bed suffering delirium tremens.

The public interest in her hanging was intense, with a large crowd assembling outside. To avoid a scene, Farie secretly brought forward the execution to 9.30am. Several reporters would arrive only to find they'd missed it. But not *The Herald*, which observed that 'Jack Bamford' awaited the condemned trio with 'some of the implements of his loathsome calling'. Cross held up when he was pinioned, while Gedge broke down in a flood of tears. Elizabeth Scott emerged last. She was dressed in black, her hair neatly arranged, and was holding a white handkerchief. *The Herald* reported:

> There was no trembling of the limbs, no paleness of cheek or lip, no quiver of the eye, and indeed no indication that she was filled with dread of the hangman's touch as any woman not altogether of adamantine heart might be expected to be. She seemed entirely unsexd; and in point of nerve far excelled her fellows.

Those still arriving rushed through a narrow door, creating, as *Bell's Life in Victoria and Sporting Chronicle* reported, 'a very unseemly crushing and scrambling' as they strove not to miss the big moment. From beneath her white cap on the scaffold, Scott said one last time that she was innocent. A second later, Bamford drew the bolt. All three died quickly.

Elizabeth Scott still held the handkerchief when Bamford lowered the bodies so they could be laid on trestle tables, the ropes coiled beneath their heads. When the caps were lifted, she'd been all but decapitated, her head and face swollen and purple.

Even though Scott had denied Philemon Sohier permission to cast her features, as did one of her accomplices, the professor was able to buy their clothes from Bamford. Within a week, the trio were on show.

Though the femme fatale's face had not been made from life, the phrenologist told *The Herald* that some of her relatives had been given a preview and pronounced it 'an excellent representation of the wretched woman'.

Farie allowed another rowdy gallows scene a few weeks later when James Barrett was hanged for the tomahawk murder of a woman at Woodstock. Forty people, 'behaving most indecently', according to *Bell's Life*, jostled for position through the narrow gate. The condemned was a few minutes in dying. The public could soon see him at Sohier's, holding the murder weapon, whose provenance was unexplained, and wearing the clothes in which he died, the sale of which no doubt added to Bamford's purse.

Two weeks after that, Sohier might've hoped to have a unique cast and clothes when John Wilson was convicted of 'The Fitzroy Unnatural Crime'. The court heard that Wilson was in the practice of wearing women's clothes and 'decoying' men to his Fitzroy house. Chief Justice William Stawell noted that no one had been executed in the colony for sodomy, but he was going to do his best to set a precedent. The judge passed the death sentence, rather than just 'recording death', as was usual for this offence. His Honour said, 'if ever there was a case in which that sentence should be carried into effect, yours is that one'.

Wilson's punishment was commuted by Executive Council – to life with hard labour, the first three years to be spent in irons. Sohier didn't get his cast but Wilson's figure went into the waxworks anyway, billed as 'an extraordinary scoundrel'. In any case, the real John Wilson suffered what amounted to a death penalty, dying six years later of illness in the Pentridge hospital.

~

At this time, a new criminal problem was emerging north of Melbourne, near Beveridge. James Kelly, Red's brother, had in 1862 been twice charged with cattle stealing in the Kilmore court, but each time the case was dismissed. In April 1863 he was on trial again for thieving thirteen cattle from a Beveridge blacksmith.

Despite the ill-omened number, James was likely hoping it would be third time lucky. After all, he had a couple of defenders who could alibi him. His sister-in-law Ellen spoke in his defence, as did one of his little nephews. But it did no good, and James and an accomplice were sentenced to three years with hard labour.

At the age of eight, Ned Kelly had got a taste of how justice and injustice worked. Given that his uncle had been convicted despite his testimony, the boy had, by implication, been branded a liar.

~

Around the time that little Ned Kelly was seeing his uncle convicted in court, William Bamford was emerging from the shadows and Philemon Sohier was making bigger bank from his growing body count, Elijah Upjohn was beginning his long slide from respectability to roguehood.

In March 1862, Ballarat's most ornery nightman was in court under fairly shitty circumstances. Before 11 o'clock one night, a citizen had spied his minions taking nightsoil along the main road to the manure depot the Eastern Council had finally established. This snitch summoned the police. Upjohn was in trouble for working before the permitted time and because he didn't have a licence for that part of Ballarat.

Elijah's counsel argued that his client had been unaware he needed a licence. The police pointed out, quite reasonably, that the accused had already been found guilty of a similar offence. He had to cough up a fine of forty shillings.

Upjohn's woes mounted. In July 1862, he was fined twenty shillings when he was taken to court 'for allowing a dog to worry a flock of sheep'. In August the next year he was slugged five shillings for drunkenness.

A few days later it was £1 for emptying nightsoil into a creek. This put him at a disadvantage the following month, when he sought to renew his licence in the Western district. The council refused, then made him jump through hoops before giving him his ticket, warning that it would be revoked if he transgressed again.

In 1863 Elijah and Ann had another son, whom they named Ernest. The nightman's seesaw with the law continued. On a particularly bad day in October 1864 he was fined £1 for being drunk and disorderly, and then faced a further charge of dumping nightsoil in a street. Upjohn was fined £3, in default of which he had to spend six days in gaol. Even so, his licence was renewed the following year, though he had to pay a bond in addition to the standard fee.

That meant Upjohn was back on the street early one morning in May 1866. Spying two boys walking with a bag, he approached; they dropped it and fled. A couple of chooks popped from the sack. Upjohn chased the lads, crying out, 'Stop, thief!' A third boy broke cover and started running. The nightman couldn't catch the little thieves – aged eight, ten and twelve – but a constable soon rounded them up. Upjohn gave evidence and these boys were each sent to a reformatory for three years. Given that he'd been gaoled and flogged for a similar offence at their age, he perhaps thought they got off lightly. Little did he know *The Star* headline 'Fowl Stealing' would also describe the beginning of his end.

Two months later, Elijah's son Joseph, named for his dead brother, himself died of measles and pneumonia at the age of five. In February 1867, Upjohn was charged with breaking into a shop and smashing up toys. Whether this was drunken anguish for his lost sons wasn't revealed. The shop owner didn't turn up to give evidence, and the case was dropped.

Upjohn's unravelling continued. A week later he was in trouble for using abusive language against the widowed landlady of the Golden Fleece Hotel and then following her daughters and hurling insults at them. In court, Upjohn did himself no favours by making 'unwarrantable' assertions against all three women. He was fined twenty shillings, in default of which he could do a day in gaol. Upjohn took the latter option.

The next time he was brought to court, the magistrate warned, Upjohn would get a month behind bars. It wouldn't be long before that came to pass.

## CHAPTER THIRTEEN

# The Best Job in the Country

In August 1864, William Bamford had a £15 payday with a triple hanging at Melbourne Gaol. William Carver and Samuel Woods were guilty of shooting and wounding a bank manager in Fitzroy. There was a petition to spare these men because they weren't murderers, but they were victims of bad timing. As *The Herald* noted:

[I]t may be that, but for the outrages in New South Wales, their sentences would have been commuted. But it appears to us that, in carrying out the capital sentence, the Executive have decided wisely. Who can tell how many young men there are amongst us who are even now burning to emulate the deeds of Gardiner and Ben Hall, Vane and Morgan. Into the minds of all such the terrible end of Woods and Carver will strike terror.

So these two men were to die not for their own sins, but for the sins of more notorious bushrangers – and to prevent youngsters like Ned Kelly from sinning in the same fashion.

The third man on the scaffold, Christopher Harrison, who'd murdered a business partner over a business dispute, had as his champion Dr George Halford, Professor of Anatomy at Melbourne University, who argued that the condemned should be spared because he was morally insane. Harrison's wife, adult son and friends said he'd acted in madness. Numerous medical men – including Dr LL Smith – gave sworn statements saying he was insane. Government surgeons said the opposite. Harrison wasn't reprieved either.

About fifty people – ordered by Farie to behave – were present to hear the trio's final words and see them hang. From the scaffold, Carver said he'd changed his mind about having himself displayed at Sohier's, and hoped his image and biography would serve as a warning to others. Woods let fly with 'ruffianly ravings, ribald jests and braggadocio songs', his various outbursts including swearing at Bamford to rope him properly because he didn't want to strangle like a dog. Harrison's last words were to request his brain be given to Dr Halford, who might yet prove that he was innocent because he was insane. Farie wouldn't honour this request, because a condemned man could make no disposition of property – and that included the contents of his own skull.

Besides, Farie had already allocated who was getting what. In protecting himself and the establishment, it didn't make sense to give Dr Halford the brains that might prove the defence had been right. Once the trio was cut down and the inquest was over, Dr Barker and two colleagues each took a body to anatomise, while the brains were set aside for another surgeon, and only the stomachs were designated to go to Dr Halford. But that wasn't what Harrison had wanted.

So Dr Halford just stole the brains. He made his getaway and was using this purloined grey matter to deliver a lecture to his peers at Melbourne University when Farie and Dr Barker arrived.

'How is this, Dr Halford?' the sheriff asked.

Dr Halford replied: 'The brains are mine, Sir.'

'No,' Farie said, 'they are the government's brains.'

Graciously, the sheriff and Dr Barker allowed him to finish the lecture. Then Farie took the brains into custody. The story went that he wrapped them in a newspaper page, popped them in his pocket and was then stalked by the city's stray dogs all the way back to the government offices.

~

William Carver got his wish and was added to Sohier's waxworks. One hundred thousand people were now visiting the exhibition each year; it was *the* essential attraction for any visitor to Melbourne. One wide-eye was eighteen-year-old English lad Marcus Clarke. In a January 1865 letter, he described the phrenologist 'Mohier', white hair streaming in the wind, spruiking his museum as 'de greadest vonder in Melbourne'. Inside the chamber, by then bulging with four dozen or so horrors, Clarke thrilled to the past decade's worth of murderous Melbourne and vicious Victoria.

By this time Sohier was cashing in on the public fascination with the boldest of the new breed of bushranger. Working from photographs, he'd added Frank Gardiner and Ben Hall, who'd pulled off the Eugowra gold escort robbery, worth £14,000. The former had been caught in Queensland in July 1864 and got thirty-two years, but the latter continued his prolific robberies in New South Wales.

In mid-September that year Sohier added Mad Dan Morgan, who'd just fatally shot his second policeman. Sohier advertised in *The Argus*: 'This portrait-model was obtained in New South Wales at great expense and trouble, and competent judges have pronounced its fac-simile [*sic*], in our Sydney exhibition, an excellent and characteristic likeness of this Bloodthirsty Outlaw.' He didn't know how right he was.

Yet it seemed likely Sohier would soon update these displays to show these bushrangers in death. That was because they'd inspired New South Wales to introduce *The Felons Apprehension Act*. This was a darker variation of 1830's *Bushranger Act*. It stipulated: 'the outlaw may at any time – either by a constable or a private individual, and either with or without demand to surrender – provided he be armed or reasonably suspected of being armed, be shot dead'.

We don't know whether young Ned Kelly visited Sohier's. But he is believed to have followed the exploits of Ben Hall and Mad Dan, so their waxworks would likely have been high on his list of things to see. But if Ned couldn't get to Melbourne, there was some bushranger excitement closer to home.

Allen Lowry was a handsome chap of twenty-three years of age who'd already done three years in gaol for larceny and horse stealing, and had recently become a highwayman around Benalla. In a November 1864 shootout with constables, this outlaw was lucky to turn his head in the nick of time so that a bullet grazed his lip rather than blew his brains out. Arrested and awaiting trial in Kilmore Gaol, Lowry escaped over the wall just before Christmas and went back to bushranging. All this had to be thrilling for Ned, particularly as he was said to have met Lowry, who was known to his family.

Young Ned Kelly might also have been excited in January 1865, when the colony got a surprise visit from some world-famous outlaws. The Confederate American cruiser *Shenandoah* spent almost a month in Melbourne as it underwent repairs, its presence dividing the colony into a civil war of words. Whichever side you were on, these American 'pirates' were fascinating. But the most fawning was the Melbourne Club, which put on a lavish dinner for these defenders of slavery. Young rebel sailor John Mason recorded in his diary that he'd been seated next to Dr Edward Barker, whom he called the 'hanging doctor' because his table conversation was all about the art and science of executions:

> He contended that instead of placing the knot behind the ear as is usually the custom, it should be just behind the neck immediately upon the neck-bone where the fall would snap the neck off and produce instantaneous death, whereas with the old custom of placing the knot behind the ear always five or sometimes ten minutes was required to produce death.

In April 1865, Bamford got to use Melbourne Gaol's brand-new gallows on child killer John Stacey. *The Age* thought it a 'great improvement on the old arrangement'. Reporters previously hadn't been able to witness the entire process, with prisoners pinioned in a corridor some fifty yards away and then marched to the gallows. Now everything happened above the spectators on the first floor.

Well before the appointed time, *The Age* explained, the condemned man was moved to the 'press cell', while the hangman would wait in the cell opposite. The two cubicles were connected by the balcony that ran around the building. The drop was built into this platform. Above the trapdoor was a thick beam, to which the fatal rope was affixed. No longer would shaky-legged condemned men have to ascend stairs to their gallows.

Farie presented Stacey's death warrant to Governor Wintle and demanded the body of the condemned man. Bamford got to work pinioning, noosing, capping, dropping. *The Age* enthused that 'the melancholy office is performed with an expedition and decorum which could not be attained while the old machinery for carrying out the last sentence of the law was in use'. Stacey's execution took five minutes, including the couple it took him to stop twitching.

There was another innovation. *The Herald* reported that his body was the first to be dealt with under the recent statute that ordered all murderers interred within the gaol in a cheap coffin. 'The remains are placed in a shell, and after being covered with quick-lime, are buried beneath the ground in one of the yards, and nothing is left to mark the spot.'

The day before Stacey was hanged, Dan Morgan, who'd robbed his way south towards the Murray River and then crossed the border, stuck up a station at Little River in Victoria, twenty-five miles north-east from Yackandandah. On the day Melbourne's new gallows was used for the first time, he was robbing another station, twenty-five miles south of

Wangaratta. As Morgan rode on, raiding a hotel and bailing up team-sters, he'd proudly announce just who the hell he was. But many needed no introductions, because they'd visited Sohier's.

A publican's daughter, on seeing him pass by, said: 'Why this man is very like Morgan; he just resembles the man in the Waxworks.' The north-eastern paper *The Ovens and Murray Advertiser* reported another waxworks-fan and bail-up victim 'knew him to be Morgan before he mentioned his name'. Morgan was cognisant of his celebrity and commercial appeal. When exchanging boots with a drayman, he said: 'I hear they have got my phiz in the Waxworks; these are a policeman's boots, if you sell them you may get something for them!' For Sohier, this was promotional gold. But the best was yet to come.

On 8 April 1865, Morgan bailed up Peechelba Station and held the householders and their servants hostage. The erratic bushranger made the mistake of letting a nurse out of his sight to care for a sick child. She alerted the station's co-owner, who summoned the police, and in the early hours they surrounded the place, helped by armed citizens. Like Jepps & Co., Morgan had stuck around for breakfast – and to do his hair and beard. When he stepped out, he was stalked and shot in the back by one of the vigilantes.

Morgan took hours to die. Then souvenir hunters swooped to cut off locks of his hair. His corpse was put on public display and photographed holding a revolver. A Benalla doctor flensed his beard so it could be souve-nired, and then Morgan's head was cut off and a cast made. What was left of his much-abused head was sent to Melbourne University. There, poor Dr Halford, unable to catch a break when it came to murderers' brains, proclaimed it too decomposed for study.

Mad Dan's posthumous degradation led to some newspaper revul-sion, and to minor reprimands for the district coroner and the Benalla police superintendent. But mostly the bushranger's demise was the subject of fascination. Despite how brutal he'd been, some still regarded him as a hero, and all were curious to see his updated waxwork. Sohier obtained the bushranger's aforementioned footwear and his recently removed hair. He advertised: 'MORGAN IS CAUGHT! – Looks, Locks, Boots, Barb, and all.'

Less than a month later, Ben Hall met his end. Shot and wounded in a police ambush, he said, 'I am wounded, shoot me dead.' The constables obliged and riddled him with thirty pieces of lead. Ben was the antithesis of Mad Dan: a 'gentleman bushranger', he hadn't murdered anyone. His death was tragic, perhaps even noble, and Sohier played to this with a revised waxwork: 'Ben Hall – Falling mortally wounded – A splendid figure.'

~

With the brisk hanging of Stacey, and his remains bound for a quick-lime grave, execution inside Melbourne Gaol had reached a new peak of efficiency. Bushrangers – whether they acted gallantly, wounded civilians or murdered policemen – could now expect to excite a new level of press interest on their way to dying in the gallows or in a shootout. Death held the prospect of hideous posthumous photographs and post-mortem brutality, but also of public lionisation and waxworks immortality. Many of the elements that would attend the end of Ned Kelly were now in place.

In 1865, Red Kelly was on a downward slide and had moved the family to Avenel. Ned was about ten years old and getting some schooling in arithmetic, reading and writing. During this time, he proved a hero by rescuing a younger boy named Dick Shelton from drowning in a nearby creek, the lad's thankful parents giving their son's saviour a long green sash, which he'd treasure for the rest of his life. Unfortunately, it seems Ned's heroic deed wasn't covered by the newspapers. Clippings might have afforded easier proof of his good character than having to explain the provenance of a sash.

In May 1865, in the immediate wake of the demises of Dan Morgan and Ben Hall, Ned temporarily lost another of his heroes when Red stole a heifer to feed the family and was arrested by Constable John Doxey. It was said that this Irish policeman had been a gold escort, and by the side of commissioner Robert Rede at Eureka. Further, when Mad Dan had threatened to murder Judge Redmond Barry, Doxey was reported to have been his bodyguard.

Thanks to Doxey's policing, Red was found guilty of illegally possessing a cowhide and sentenced to six months with hard labour. Remissions would bring that down, but for the time being, young Ned was without his father.

~

In August 1865, having now used the new drop on two more murderers, William Bamford went up to Castlemaine to attend to David Young, sentenced to die for cutting a woman's throat. There was widespread doubt about his conviction on circumstantial evidence. In its long considerations, the Executive Council had 'retried' the case under the guidance of Barry, before deciding the law would take its course. As *The Herald* reported, '[T]here has never been an execution in Victoria about the justice of which the public mind has been so much divided.'

Hopes for a last-minute respite were dashed. Bamford got his £5 fee. Young was added to Sohier's, with the Professor offering *The Herald* his final phrenological verdict: 'No benevolence, large destructiveness, very large secretiveness, no sympathy, no soul, thoroughly selfish, a brute!'

Red Kelly was released in October. In Melbourne at the end of that month, Bamford was convicted of stealing a hand truck in Fitzroy and sent to gaol for two months with hard labour. The timing was handy. Beechworth hadn't been able to find its own Jack Ketch and there was a murderer there who needed hanging. Bamford was taken in handcuffs aboard the gold escort, which, given that hangman transportations tended to excite the locals, probably caused a stir as it passed through Avenel. Young Ned Kelly may even have heard about the policeman who'd caught the killer and been clobbered for his trouble, Senior Constable Arthur Steele.

Patrick Sheehan had stabbed a hotel landlord during a drunken brawl in the appropriately named hamlet of Rowdy Flat, near Yackandandah. His arrest was more notable because one of the witnesses, a big, boozed-up bruiser named Frank Neville, had hit and kicked the uniformed constable Steele when he had the killer in custody.

Upon Bamford's arrival at Beechworth, *The Ovens and Murray Advertiser* reported: 'The executioner is by no means an amiable-looking specimen of humanity, such as the celebrated Calcraft is described.' William Calcraft, elected to the job in London nearly forty years earlier, was still held up as the epitome of the gentleman hangman.

Sheehan was lucky that John Castieau was Beechworth Gaol's governor. He'd been promoted to the position in 1856, shortly after he married English immigrant Mary 'Polly' Moore and they were now raising their growing brood of children within the penitentiary's walls. If nothing else, it tugged on Castieau's heartstrings that Sheehan was a father of five.

This condemned man also had an innovative final request: that his photograph be taken as a keepsake for his family. Castieau granted permission, and a man from the telegraph office undertook this 'melancholy duty'. As the execution neared, Castieau witnessed Sheehan's final confession, and on the gallows the condemned man would give his best thanks to the governor.

Bamford pinioned Sheehan and walked him to the drop. Now he followed what had become his custom. As *The Argus* later recounted: 'One sickening attempt to show good feeling to those he executed he never omitted. After he had pinioned his man and so rendered him helpless, he used always to shake him by the hand, and murmur a "God bless you" before he pulled the fatal bolt.' Having given Sheehan this send-off, Bamford adjusted the rope and dropped the cap.

'Raise it for a minute,' Sheehan said.

Bamford did him the courtesy.

'God bless you all, and God forgive me,' the doomed man said. 'That will do.'

The bolt was drawn and he died quickly.

Castieau had to be relieved. Hangings burdened his soul. He'd later write in his diary 'as usual before an execution I feel nervous for fear any bungling may occur'.

Frank Neville's penal journey would last far longer. He got two months for attacking Senior Constable Steele. Later in the year, while being taken to the Yackandandah lock-up for being drunk and disorderly, Neville attacked this same officer again. In the police version, Neville grabbed Steele by the throat and threw him down. Two other constables hauled Neville off. Then the prisoner attacked Steele again.

Steele testified at the trial: 'Then in self defence I used my staff freely.' That he said it took him and his men an hour to fully subdue the man made it sound like police brutality. But Steele's account was corroborated by another constable, and by a civilian.

Yet Neville had his own witness. James Gould – aka 'Tom the Devil' – had been in custody at the same time and could testify to what *really* happened. But when Neville questioned him in court, Tom spilled the beans:

When you were brought to the lock-up by the police, they did not ill use you. What hurts you got, you did yourself by your own violence. You gave yourself a great swing round, and the police who had hold of you left go to avoid falling; you then fell with your heads against the handle of the pail. You swore that as soon as you were out again, you would murder the policeman Steele.

Who needed enemies with friends like Tom the Devil? Neville was sentenced to three months. It didn't make him any better disposed to his fellow man. Sometime later, Neville was again in the Yackandandah lock-up, when who should be tossed into the cell with him? As *The Ovens and Murray Advertiser* reported:

> Tom's cries for mercy – for although a hardened and brutal villain he was like a child in the hands of the giant Neville – brought the police to his assistance; and after a great deal of trouble the men were torn away from each other, and locked up in separate cells.

Neville reportedly went down on his knees, pleading with Steele for ten more minutes with Tom. But the police – who'd surely known what would happen if they put the men together – were done with their fun for the day.

Steele would again tangle with Neville – and Tom the Devil would get his turn at the gallows – after which the senior constable became a sergeant, on the way to facing his greatest adversary, who was then just a young boy proud of saving a littler chap from drowning. A few years hence, Arthur Steele and Ned Kelly would hate each other. As the lawman's obituary would claim: 'Steele knew the family, and Ned Kelly always vowed that he carried about a grudge against the police officer from the days of his youth.'

In October 1865, Bamford went to Geelong to hang the murderer Thomas Menard – aka 'Yankee Tom' – under the supervision of Deputy Sheriff Robert Rede. The condemned man was reported to have verbally admitted six other murders. But when this confession was printed in the papers, Menard merely hinted at such atrocities: 'I do not wish to say any more – the secrets of my heart go to the grave with me.'

Was Bamford hoping for a gallows confession? Such a scenario had to occur to every hangman. But Yankee Tom kept his lips buttoned.

Geelong Gaol had a new gallows like the one in Melbourne, so the man only had to take a few steps from his cell. But it was a long journey to death. While he barely moved after the six-foot drop – apart from his right hand clutching convulsively at the prayer sheet it held – Menard's heart didn't stop beating for ten minutes, according to *The Geelong Advertiser*, with *The Herald* reckoning it took seventeen. The post-mortem showed that the doomed man's vertebrae hadn't been injured in the slightest, though the sternomastoid muscle in the neck had been almost ripped in two.

~

Red Kelly was arrested by Constable Doxey in mid-December 1865 for drunkenness, and forfeited five shillings for his troubles. Then, on Christmas Day at Avenel, the same intrepid policeman arrested the escaped bushranger Allen Lowry. This time he'd be sentenced to four years.

The following year, Ned was progressively robbed of Red as he became ever more mired in drink. By November 1866 he had 'dropsy', now known as oedema, which results in painful swelling caused by fluid retention. It must have been hideous for the boy to see his father like this at Christmas. Two days later, Red was dead at the age of forty-six.

~

Though more than a decade older than Red, and far more dissolute, Bamford kept on keeping on. But his survival seemed to have some-thing to do with the enforced periods of sobriety that resulted from the arrangement *The Age* had hinted at a few years earlier.

Such suspicions were strengthened by striking coincidences. On 22 February 1866, William Bamford got three months for trespassing, just as country courts were about to sit and hear a number of capital cases. Sure enough in the next week, at Maryborough Circuit Court, a Chinese man named Long Poy was found guilty of murder – on what was popularly believed to be perjured evidence – and sentenced to death. At the Ballarat Circuit Court, James Jones was found guilty of murder and ordered to endure the same dread punishment. The timing was excellent. Bamford was already incarcerated and getting sober, and as he was a prisoner of the Crown the government would foot the bill for his transportation to conduct these executions.

Shortly afterwards, on 10 March, Bamford saw to Long Poy. *The Mount Alexander Mail* gave the impression that the hangman did the job right, having 'made his arrangements previously as to the rope, length of fall, etc.' Bamford, it said, 'performed the operation of pinioning with his accustomed sang froid and skill'. On the scaffold, Long Poy, who barely spoke English, had little understanding of what was about to happen; *The Castlemaine Daily News* reported that the 'doomed Chinaman was certainly not cognizant of the English mode of execution'. So much so that Long Poy indicated the rope around his neck was too loose, and asked the hangman to tighten and raise it so as to 'not let me fall down'.

*The Mount Alexander Mail* – which was of the opinion that Long Poy had been unjustly convicted – reported that what followed was 'to most spectators a very painful scene'. Long Poy's every muscle convulsed – so much so that one of his boots shook off. When the spasms subsided, he was observed to be breathing heavily – 'the action of his lungs could be seen distinctly even at a distance'. That lasted five minutes. It wasn't until eight minutes after the fall that his pulse ceased. The *Mail* called it 'butchery', but simultaneously believed that because the post-mortem showed a dislocated vertebra, 'it is clear that the poor creature did not suffer pain after the drop'. Was that true? No one really knew for sure. But the 'harrowing scene' was enough, the paper said, that it felt 'quite sure that the faith of many as to the expediency of capital punishment was much shaken by their experience'.

Next Bamford was off to Ballarat to see to James Jones. Fifteen hundred people applied to watch him hang. As many as 150 were admitted to see the man's last moments and this rowdy crowd had to be brought under control. Perhaps playing to his audience, the hangman went to work, with, as *The Geelong Advertiser* reported, the 'celerity and method which has gained him a notoriety'. Jones died with a 'dislocated spine' so *The Age* may have been right when it said 'there can be no doubt that all sensibility ceased immediately after the drop'. Even so Jones's heart took ten minutes to stop beating.

Such scenes didn't cause outrage as they once had. This was just the way it was. The vagabond hangman would get it right as often as get it wrong. Sheriffs made a mockery of the private execution law. Some culprits appeared to take a long time to die, but medical men always said they didn't feel a thing, so newspaper reporters could describe the ghoulish spectacle while reassuring readers that no one was suffering. Sohier was fed a steady supply of new monsters for the public to savour. Brutality was normalised, legalised, commercialised, *civilised*.

If Sohier – who by now had announced his retirement as a practising phrenologist – had been able to make money displaying the corpses of these hanged criminals, he would have had them in tanks of formaldehyde in no time. In August 1866, he had the next best thing in the form of the 'Queensland mummy'. This was an Aboriginal man who'd been chased up a tree, shot dead in the back by a settler and left for years to desiccate in the sun. The body was displayed in a glass case.

*The Herald* fired the public's prurient imagination by reporting that 'many portions which might be expected to have disappeared are still remaining', and offered educational justification to the morbidly curious by saying that Sohier's exhibit would be of interest to 'those who wish to make themselves acquainted with the feuds which have sometimes broken out on the borders of Australian white and black territory'.

This real-life murder victim would be toured for years.

~

Back in England, there were some who tried to make hanging more humane. In July 1866, the polymath doctor, reverend and mathematician Samuel Haughton wrote that the present short-drop method was 'extremely clumsy and also painful to the criminal'. His studies led him to believe that people died in one of three ways: apoplexy, caused by constricted jugular veins; asphyxiation, the result of strangulation; or shock to the lower part of the brain, from a broken neck.

In his article 'On Hanging, Considered from a Mechanical and Physiological Point of View', published in *Philosophical Magazine*, he wrote: 'In the first two cases death is preceded by convulsions, lasting from five to forty-five minutes, which are caused by the cessation of the supply of arterial blood to the muscles. In the third case death is instantaneous and painless, and is unaccompanied by any convulsive movement whatever.' Haughton set out calculations, based on the victim's weight, to ensure the drop was sufficient for the third result.

*Philosophical Magazine* had some subscribers in Melbourne, although Bamford probably wasn't leafing through its pages in his gaol cells or seedy haunts. But it seems unlikely that it had no readers among the politicians, gaolers, sheriffs and doctors who haunted the Melbourne Club and the medical rooms of the city.

What Haughton's article made clear was that some hangings in Victoria – as elsewhere – were adding prolonged torture to the judicial death sentence. Even when this view did become broadly accepted, and when a method for more merciful hangings was ordered by London, things would be very slow to change in Melbourne.

~

Melbourne wasn't simply unconcerned by legal brutality – it was actually clamouring for more. In early 1867, there was increasing concern about crime in Victoria and the cat-o'-nine-tails was proposed as a cure-all. Twenty years earlier, when Jack Harris had arrived in the city, newspapers had called for the dismissal of magistrates who ordered that prisoners be flogged. Now there was a groundswell of support for whipping men who indecently assaulted women and girls.

But Redmond Barry went further to prove how firmly he believed in the maxim 'spare the lash and spoil the child'. In March 1867, William Parsons, just fifteen years old, bought a pistol in Bourke Street and headed out to Nunawading. The lad held up a convoy of wagons and demanded, 'Your money or your life.' He scored just £1 from his first victim. The second wagon driver said he had no money. The third wasn't going to be robbed, and he grappled with the young desperado. The gun went off, the ball passing through the bushranger's chin.

At Parsons' trial, Justice Barry said: 'It is almost impossible to believe that you, with arms in your hand, actually stopped three men to rob them. I think you have had a lesson about the danger of practicing [sic] bushranging, for you gave yourself a severe wound, and nearly blew your own brains out.'

Parsons – a 'fine-looking lad, with an intelligent face' – no doubt breathed a sigh of relief.

Barry continued: 'Were it not for the seriousness of the offence the affair would be almost laughable. I think I know a proper way of dealing with you.' The judge then read aloud excerpts from the Act that allowed him to direct offenders under sixteen to be flogged in addition to their sentences. Barry, always fond of pontificating self-importantly, said he was reluctant to inflict this 'most degrading punishment' but, alas, if Parsons had been whipped when he was young, he wouldn't be in court now. His Honour sentenced him to five years in gaol, and to receive twenty-five lashes on 1 April and twenty-five more on 1 September. He told the trembling youth: 'I trust, young gentleman, this sentence will prevent lads at your time of life attempting to make distinguished heroes of romance of themselves.'

If Parsons had to be whipped, that meant Bamford had to be found. Through the latter part of 1866 and into the present year, he'd been in and out of gaol for crimes that included drunkenly assaulting a constable and smashing up a fence in the Botanic Gardens. This time he was found in the latter place doing nothing apart from keeping company with a 'miserable-looking lot of creatures ... in a state of squalid misery'. All of them got a month for vagrancy.

*The Bendigo Advertiser* would later hit the nail on the head, noting the 'singular coincidence' that Bamford was 'generally cooped up some little time before his professional services are required'. *The Kyneton Observer* would also be fine with this, approving the 'enormous elasticity' of the vagrancy act, 'this excellent statute' that could ensure Bamford was 'all there' when called upon to ply his 'ghastly trade'.

So Bamford was in Melbourne Gaol, close to forty-eight hours sober, when April Fool's Day dawned and young Parsons was strapped to the triangle. Bamford laid into him. *The Mount Alexander Mail* recorded that the boy 'yelled so lustily before half the work was done that his screams of pain and fear, it is said, could be heard beyond the outer walls of the building'.

Parsons was reportedly the first person flogged in Victoria for about fifteen years. There was little backlash. But neither was flagellation reinstated. At least for now.

~

Six weeks or so after the kid was flogged, Ned Kelly, now twelve, was accused of horse stealing. No charges were laid. But that didn't stop him from making his debut in the *Police Gazette* in June 1867. This publication of record mistakenly reported him as being 'Charged with Horse Stealing', and described him as two or three years older than he was, standing five-foot-four or five-foot-five, stoutly built with light-grey eyes in a smooth face beneath brown hair.

Was Ned pleased at the flash of notoriety or angry at the incorrect report? It may have been both. He might also at this time have dreamed of being a better bushranger than that idiot William Parsons. For that matter, young Ned might have fantasised about being a better bushranger than the *other* Edward Kelly.

*That* Ned was part of the Blue Cap Gang – 'a band who openly declared war against society' – then operating in the Riverina region of New South Wales, led by Robert Cotterell, who was light-sensitive and wore a blue visor. From July 1867 they raided a few stations and bailed up Chinese quarters. Leaving a hotel they'd stuck up at Stony Creek, the gang was fired on by police but got away in the darkness. In the months following, various members were caught, other men joined and one unlucky fellow drowned with his horse while trying to cross a swollen creek. By mid-October there was excitement in Gundagai when the gang turned up to buy some supplies and have their steeds shod. A couple of weeks later, Cotterell was caught at Humbug Creek when he was riding a clapped-out nag on a road and couldn't escape constables coming the other way. Two of his mates were arrested at the end of November. That left just gang members John Payne and Edward Kelly.

In early December, Payne held up a Whealbah pub and told the proprietor he was riding out to a station but would return soon. When a constable coincidentally called in at the hotel, he learned that if he stuck

Jack Ketch's botched execution of the Duke of Monmouth ensured his name became the nickname for hangmen ever after. (Etching by Jan Luyken, 1698, Rijksmuseum, Amsterdam)

Executed in 1842, Maulboyheenner (left) and Tunnerminnerwait (right) were the first people hanged in Melbourne. (Paintings by Thomas Bock)

CLAUD FARIE.—FROM A PHOTOGRAPH BY BATCHELDER AND CO.

Claud Farie, Melbourne's sheriff from 1852 to 1870, who presided during the busiest period for Victoria's hangmen. (State Library of Victoria)

Justice Sir Redmond Barry, Ned Kelly's eventual nemesis, had a cruel record as a hanging and flogging judge. (State Library of Victoria)

Melbourne Gaol governor John Buckley Castieau worked in Victoria's penal system from 1852 to 1884, showing compassion to doomed prisoners.
(State Library of Victoria)

Dr Edward Barker, 'the Hanging Doctor', had plenty of bad ideas about where the hangman should place the knot. (Photograph by John William Lindt, State Library of Victoria)

Melbourne Gaol *c.*1861. (Photograph by Jean-Baptiste Charlier, State Library of Victoria)

Inside Old Melbourne Gaol.
(Author's photo)

'The fatal beam', rope and drop at Old
Melbourne Gaol. (Author's photo)

Explorers Robert O'Hara Burke and William John Wills with expedition survivor John King, as portrayed in wax at Professor Sohier's, 1862. (Photograph by Samuel Clifford, State Library of Victoria)

Professor Sohier as satirised in *Melbourne Punch*, 25 June 1867. Note the death masks watching on. (National Library of Australia)

PHRENOLOGY.

*Prof. Sohi—r (loq.)—*"VERY EXTRAORDINARY DEVELOPMENTS! I CERTAINLY SHOULDN'T HAVE THOUGHT IT." CONSCIENTIOUSNESS LARGELY DEVELOPED! TRUTHFUL, TO A FAULT!!—*(Walker!—M.P.)*

HEADS OF BURGESS

HEADS OF KELLY

HEADS OF LEVY

Sohier's rival bumpologist Archibald Hamilton stole death masks to produce the 1866 booklet *Practical phrenology: a lecture on the heads, casts of the heads, and characters of the Maungatapu murderers, Levy, Kelly, Sullivan, and Burgess.* Fourteen years later, Hamilton got his hands on Ned Kelly's head.
(State Library of Victoria)

Marcus Clarke, aged twenty. He wrote a brilliant series about Melbourne's underworld, which culminated in his portrait of hangman William Bamford. (State Library of Victoria)

Young Ned Kelly. Believed taken around 1873–74, by which time he had already been dubbed a 'candidate for the gallows'. (State Library of Victoria)

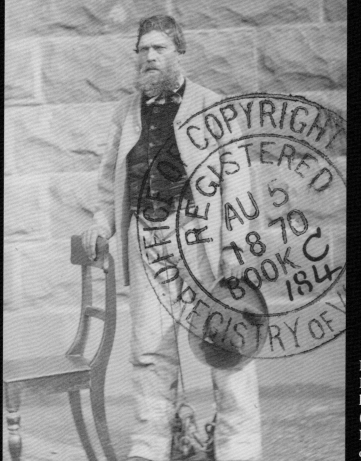

Ned Kelly's mentor Harry Power after his 1870 capture. (Photograph by Charles Nettleton, State Library of Victoria)

Michael Gately in the 1860s, during his 'John Andrews' days. In his prison file, he claimed previous experience as an executioner. (Public Records Office of Victoria)

Michael Gately, c.1873, when he succeeded William Bamford as hangman and flagellator.
(Public Records Office of Victoria)

Michael Gately, mid-1870s. With wild red hair and beard, the hulking hangman was a terror on Melbourne's streets.
(Public Records Office of Victoria)

TREVARROW, AFTER HIS SECOND FLOGGING, ON PENTRIDGE GREEN.

*Police News*, forerunner to modern tabloids, made a horrifying hero out of Gately, depicted flogging a paedophile in the 21 August 1876 issue. (State Library of Victoria)

Edward Feeney (left) and Charles Marks (right) rehearse their murder-suicide, on the day the latter died and the former was charged with his murder. One of the letters that Marks wrote to Feeney reads in part: 'I do not attempt to deny but am proud to say I love you as a brother and perhaps more, and I know you are fond of me or I at least hope you are … I want us not ever to part.' (Photograph by Davies & Co., State Library of Victoria)

Death mask of An Gaa. There were grave doubts about his sanity and thus the fairness of his conviction. (Old Melbourne Gaol, author's photo)

Death mask of Basilio Bondietti. There were serious concerns about the evidence used to convict him, but a reprieve campaign failed. (Old Melbourne Gaol, author's photo)

John Weachurch. Before Ned Kelly, he was arguably Victoria's most infamous criminal and a 'martyr' of the penal system. He plead his case to the Governor of Victoria on 22 November 1875 as follows: 'I am now under the sentance of death and wateing your decision under the most unjust elegal and disgracefull circumstances …' He was hanged two weeks later. (Public Records Office of Victoria)

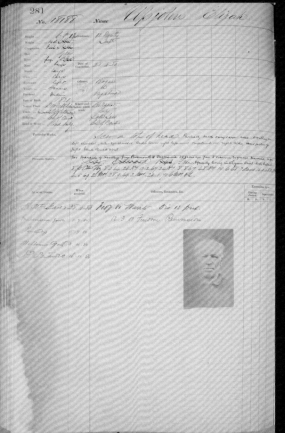

After a long period of freedom, Elijah Upjohn was back in gaol in April 1880 as a 'rogue and vagabond'. He volunteered as the hangman soon afterwards. (Public Records Office of Victoria)

The front page of *Australasian Sketcher* on 3 July 1880 took readers to Kelly's last stand. (National Library of Australia)

Sergeant Steele on 3 July 1880. The fowling piece he holds is presumably the one used to shoo Kelly. (Photograph by William Edward Barnes, State Library of Victoria)

Like 'Mad Dan', Joe Byrne was propped up for 'action' in what's considered Australia's first news photograph. (Photograph by John William Lindt, State Library of Victoria)

Ned Kelly, in irons, the day before he hanged. (Photograph by Charles Nettleton, State Library of Victoria)

Ned Kelly, from the same photoshoot the day
before his death. (Photograph by Charles Nettleton,
State Library of Victoria)

One of hundreds of Kelly petition pages. Note phrenologist AS Hamilton fifth from top on the left. (Public Records Office of Victoria, author's photo)

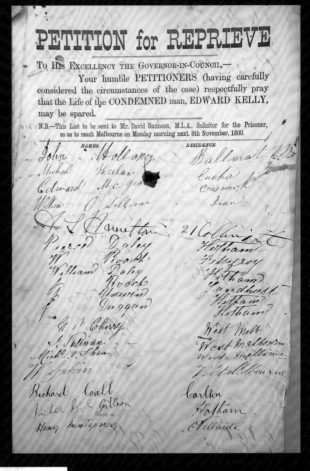

## PETITION for REPRIEVE

To His Excellency the Governor-in-Council,—

Your humble PETITIONERS (having carefully considered the circumstances of the case) respectfully pray that the Life of the CONDEMNED man, EDWARD KELLY, may be spared.

N.B.—This List to be sent to Mr. David Gaunson, M.L.A., Solicitor for the Prisoner, so as to reach Melbourne on Monday morning next. 8th November, 1880.

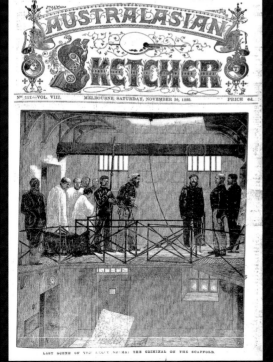

*Australasian Sketcher*'s front page put readers inside Melbourne Gaol in Ned Kelly's last moments, as he stood face to face with his hangman, Elijah Upjohn. (National Library of Australia)

SOONER OR LATER.
THE UNERRING ARM OF JUSTICE.

*Melbourne Punch*, 18 November 1880, saw Ned Kelly's hanging as the long arm and rope of the law extending a long way back; given Victoria was a British colony, this presumably meant all the way to London. (National Library of Australia)

Death mask of Ned Kelly. (Old Melbourne Gaol, author's photo)

around, he'd be served an outlaw to go with his beer. After the policeman arrested Payne, the chastened outlaw said Kelly was in the bush and not in a good way because he'd shot himself in the foot. On the promise of a lesser sentence, he directed the constable to his mate. When the law came for this Ned Kelly, he simply said, 'All right.' Kelly got thirty years, Payne twenty and 'Blue Cap' Cotterell ten years.

Such was justice. Though soon forgotten, the Blue Cap Gang 'outbreak' was then in all the colonial papers, and it's reasonable to assume young Ned knew of his namesake.

~

In April 1867, Bamford turned off the murderer Denis Murphy at Ballarat. *The Star*'s graphic report – which was widely reprinted – said he dropped eight feet, heaved convulsively, blood staining his cap and trickling onto his clothes, 'and although the executioner endeavoured to accelerate the work of death, the pulse continued quite distinct for about 10 minutes'. This wasn't a case where different journalists saw different things. *The Argus*'s man said 'the culprit's death appears to have resulted from asphyxia or strangulation'.

William Bamford wouldn't perform the next execution, but not because of what happened to Murphy – no one seemed to care about that. The reason was that it was to take place at Beechworth, and there was a transport problem. Initially it was reported that the government wanted to save money by using a local. Later it'd be said there was no gold escort going up from Melbourne on which he could hitch a ride, and Cobb & Co. had refused to take the hangman. Either way, Bamford would miss out on this £5 fee.

The man to be hanged was John Kelly, convicted of raping an infant; Justice Barry said it was the most abominable crime he'd encountered. Beechworth Gaol's governor, John Castieau, posted notices offering any prisoner who volunteered for the role £5 and the dead man's clothes. No one put his hand up. It began to look like the duty might fall to Deputy Sheriff William Gore Brett.

Then a prisoner stepped up: Tom the Devil. He'd recently been sentenced to three years for robbery with violence. Interviewed by Castieau, Tom claimed he'd turned off one or two men in Tasmania. In a strange coincidence, he said, over there he'd been pals with the very John Kelly who was now sentenced to hang.

Tom got the job. Castieau hosted a reunion of the two old mates. At first Tom didn't tell Kelly why they were meeting. Then he broke it gently: 'You know it's to be done, Jack, old pal – more's the worse; but you wouldn't mind an old friend getting what he can out of it, would you? I'll turn you off, old pal, as well as any of 'em. I will, s'help me.'

Fifty to sixty people saw Tom the Devil see his old mate out of the world. He made good on his promise to do a good job, *The Ovens and Murray Advertiser* reporting he 'acquitted himself as if he had been born to it'.

Bamford, back in prison for six months, got a change of scenery when he went up to Castlemaine at the end of July to put the murderer William Terry to death. The hangman was reported as shaking more than usual. One hundred people watched his victim struggle for eleven minutes. Bamford – who likely hadn't soaped or stretched the too-short rope – had to employ a new approach to finishing off his victim. A journalist for *The Star* later recalled that he 'drew the dangling mass towards him, and placing a foot first upon one shoulder and then upon the other of the dying man, pressed upon the body with his whole weight until the last spark of existence was crushed out of him'. Contemporary reports said the same thing, albeit in less graphic language. There was no controversy.

Eight days later, Bamford was back at Ballarat to hang murderers George Searle and Joseph Ballan. On the scaffold, the two men at first didn't acknowledge each other – there being no forgiveness for the bad blood of their trial. Bamford roped Searle and dropped the cap. For all his *sangfroid*, he hadn't pinioned the man so tightly that he couldn't push up his cap and loosen the rope. 'Don't choke me, don't choke me just yet, for I want to speak,' Searle said. As Bamford attended to Ballan, who gazed coolly at the hangman and fifty spectators, Searle claimed innocence, adding: 'I hope and trust that this gentleman alongside of me will confess the truth too.' But Ballan merely continued his prayers.

Bamford readjusted Searle's noose and dropped the cap. As he reached for the bolt, Searle wanted one last connection with Ballan, asking, 'Will ye shake hands with me now, Joe? Let's shake hands.' The sightless men turned to each other, pinioned hands groping as the reverend stepped closer to help their rapprochement.

Bamford drew the bolt and the drop opened with a thud. Ballan pulled up with his toes half an inch from the ground. Searle fell to within a foot and half of the floor. Ballan seemed to die in an instant, but Searle did not. *The Ballarat Star* said he 'struggled a good deal and the executioner had to pull down by his own weight the body'. But Ballan hadn't expired either. It was fifteen minutes before the men's hearts were still. The post-mortems found that both men had died of asphyxia.

This time, Bamford actually had some explaining to do. He said he hadn't noticed the men's last gesture. As to why Ballan almost hit the ground – which would've required him to be hanged again – Bamford said the rope must have stretched somehow since the day before. *The Star* called this absurd, as both lengths had been cut from the same piece of rope. 'But in the interests of decency and mercy, it seems that greater care should have been taken by the executioner.' That was as far as the admonishments went.

Far more column space was given to Mr T Wright, a Ballarat phrenologist, who took their casts and did a quick analysis with a 'phreno-physiometer'. This gizmo measured the angle formed by the ear and eyebrow. In normal people it was 25 degrees. But Professor Bridges of Liverpool had discovered that all murderers had angles between 35 and 45 degrees. Bingo! Wright wrote: 'I found they possessed the murderer's type of brain, for the angle was 38 degrees.'

Of course, this wasn't news to anyone who'd seen Searle and Ballan in the waxworks, Sohier having made them an attraction even before their trial, with no consideration as to how this might have affected potential jurors.

Over the next year, Bamford would hang two other murderers in Melbourne Gaol. But he'd miss out on his £5 when John Hogan went to the gallows in Castlemaine in August 1868. This time a man named George Aldridge – serving twelve months for stealing a side of bacon – performed his duty well and the murderer died fast with a dislocated spine. *The Ovens and Murray Advertiser* noted the sheriff had received a large number of applications from people wanting to see the execution, including 'one from the respectable head of a respectable family, asking for a ticket for himself, his wife, and three children'.

~

An execution was no place for a child. Neither was a courtroom, especially if you were watching a relative stand trial on a capital charge.

It's believed that Ned Kelly got his first look at Redmond Barry in April 1868. As the 'man' of the house, he would have been expected to be present in the Wangaratta Court to support his mother in a case that pitted Kelly against Kelly.

In January 1868, Jim Kelly, Red's drunkard cattle-thieving brother, came to the former hotel in Greta where Ellen was stopping with her two sisters and the thirteen children they had between them. Jim made an advance on his dead brother's widow, and for his shameful behaviour got a gin bottle cracked over his head, before Ellen chased him off with a stick. He took his revenge by setting fire to the building. Thanks to a neighbour who came to their aid with water, the women got all the children clear before the building burned to the ground. If not for their quick action, it could have been a massacre of innocents.

Jim went to trial at Wangaratta before Judge Barry. Having heard from Ellen and her sisters, along with other witnesses, the jury found him guilty. The judge pronounced sentence. For a moment, young Ned might have thought his uncle was going to hang. But Redmond Barry was merely recording death. People didn't swing for arson, and amid some critical newspaper commentary, the Executive Council commuted Jim's sentence to ten years on the roads.

So William Bamford wouldn't add this Kelly to his tally. But how he kept score became part of his lore. As *The Argus* would later report, around this time he'd said, after hanging a victim, 'The best job in the country – that makes 47.'

# CHAPTER FOURTEEN

# For the Term of His Unnatural Life

William Bamford was a far more brutal bungler than Jack Harris, and had a far higher body count. But what was such a creature like up close? Marcus Clarke, now twenty-five and working under the pen name 'Peripatetic Philosopher', wanted to know. From mid-June 1869, he began publishing his six-part series 'Lower Bohemia' in *The Australasian* – and it seemed the young writer structured his long investigation so it would culminate in introducing the reader to the lowest of the low in the personage of the hangman Bamford.

'Lower Bohemia' was a deep dive into the underworld that was out of sight and out of mind for most Melburnians. Clarke said the demimonde's denizens comprised three overlapping classes: criminals, the poor, and the sick and diseased. Some would work, some would steal and some could not or would not do either. Some took their dinner at sixpenny-a-plate eating houses and some slept in sixpenny-a-night lodging houses. The worst of the down-and-outs lived on wharves, in pipes, behind sheds, in parks and around swamps.

Clarke started at the Immigrants' Home, the city's largest charitable institution, observing it was over capacity by 'sixty human creatures, in every possible stage of dirt, raggedness and poverty'. One such wretch was a mate of Bamford's. Clarke used this as a hook, saying he already knew the hangman rarely stepped inside this place, preferring to live amid the stones and swamps. But the writer was also savvy: Bamford wouldn't be found there then because he was in gaol, 'at which fact criminal Bohemia smacks its lips, and scents a hanging'. Clarke teased readers: 'I have had several interviews with him, which I will relate to you in due course. Here I will premise only that he is an old man, with white hair, and has the cheeriest laugh of anybody that I know.' It was a tantalising juxtaposition, making the hangman sound like a jocular grandfather.

But Clarke's readers would have wait for future instalments. In the meantime, a special reporter for *The Age* wrote 'The Drinking Dens of Melbourne', a panoramic phantasmagoria depicting the Gomorrah created by recently changed licensing laws that had soaked the city in cheap booze and seen filthy gin palaces spring up like poisonous mushrooms. The writer counted at least eight such establishments on Bourke Street, the 'great main sewer of iniquity in Melbourne', which were open day and night, even on Sundays and holidays, and packed with criminals and disreputable characters. One place boasted 'The Playground', a big, dark room packed with miscreants visible only by the flames of a flickering fire that rendered the scene 'perfectly demonical'.

The police and judiciary did nothing – indeed, they were corrupt and complicit, even though bargain booze was making whores of women, who'd guzzle gin all day and then sell sex to buy more. One of the places they prostituted themselves was the wastelands beyond the Prince's Bridge. This was Bamford's domain. *The Age* writer too had missed him – because he was in gaol – but offered a scandalous portrait of the government contractor cum underworld king:

Here it is that Bamford, the public hangman, lords it over his crew when he is emancipated for a time from gaol. At present he sojourns in durance vile, but just before his removal thither, a few weeks ago, he was living in a gully about half way between the Immigrants' Home and the Botanical Gardens, and there he kept a party of half a dozen women, some of them mere girls, acting as a procurer for the group, and guiding soldiers and others to their retreat.

Marcus Clarke's 'Lower Bohemia' series concluded here in *The Australasian* on 21 August. The final instalment, 'In Outer Darkness', saw him among the city's true wastrels, in the presence of an unnamed guide. Wet, filthy and infamous, Melbourne's most wretched lay under bushes, lurked in hollows and peered from behind boulders, wearing their rags, tattered blankets and coats of advertising posters. 'Here are the dwellers in the wilderness, huddled together indiscrim-inately – men, women, children,' Clarke wrote. Stepping over a drunk man on a narrow pathway, they reached a tiny hovel built around a hole in the ground:

> This is where the hangman lives. We knock upon the stones and shout. A stone withdraws itself noiselessly, a tarpaulin which it fastened down uplifts itself, and forth into a momentary gust of ghastly moonlight rises the head of an old man with flowing white hair. Sitting up thus, with head protruded from his lair, he looks like some wild animal. 'There is a hanging on, Jack,' says a companion. Jack laughs, with his body still in the hole, and asks who it is. A name is mentioned, at which he laughs again more heartily. 'I knowed him,' he says, and then ruefully, 'You're gammoning a cove,' and breaks out into savage blasphemy.

Clarke wrote that Bamford was old but muscular, and not poor in the strict sense because he was paid £5 per hanging. '[H]e told me that he had only hung some dozen people in all his life; but I believe that he makes money in other ways,' Clarke noted. Surely he didn't believe the former claim – by now Bamford had presided over dozens of executions – though the latter suggestion chimed with *The Age*'s suggestion that he was a procurer.

If Clarke asked Bamford why he did this work, and what he felt when he hanged a man, he didn't include the answers in his article. For these insights, Melbourne would have to wait for a later interview with a future hangman. What struck Clarke – and what would prove an increasing problem and shape how Bamford's successors lived and died – was that this man was forced to live in the stone heaps, because 'if criminal Bohemia knew that he had a settled abode, they would annoy and maltreat him'.

Clarke reflected on this far more deeply than previous colonial journalists who'd considered the lot of the hangman. He saw him as a victim of – and monster created by – a system that had gone unchecked and become entrenched:

It struck me as a curious comment upon capital punishment, that the executor of justice should be forced to live like a dog by reason of his office. The man who pulls the bolt does not more than the judge who sentences, or the jury who decide upon guilt or innocence. Yet the spectacle of the old man with laughing mouth, eager eyes, and white locks streaming, half buried in that dismal pit, in such a wild bleak night, made me shudder. I was in the midst of the Crusoe's desert island of modern civilisation, and I had suddenly come upon that Footprint – instinct with a terrible significance – which was alone wanting to make the parallel complete.

In William Bamford, Marcus Clarke had the ending to what would become regarded as his best piece of journalism.

~

During the publication of Clarke's series, Bamford had been in gaol. But he hadn't been idle. In July 1869, the Crown unearthed the 295th section of the Criminal Law and Practice Statute to allow 27-year-old Joseph Harris to be sentenced to five years and fifty lashes – delivered in two instalments of twenty-five – for using a garrotte during a robbery in Carlton.

Bamford would be paid £1 for this flogging. As his victim went to the triangle for his first dose, prison officials and reporters took a step back in apprehension of the brutality they were about to witness. But they were bitterly disappointed. *The Argus* reported that 'the first stroke was sufficient to show that Harris was to be let off lightly. The hangman made a show of coming down heavily on the man's back, and that was all. There was no severity in his style'.

Farie warned Bamford that if he didn't put his back into it, he'd be the next to feel the cat-o'-nine-tails. That made no difference and 'the work was completed without Harris being called on to suffer more pain than many a boy has received at school'.

*The Star* reckoned the 'affair was something very much like a farce'. Editorial writers complained that Harris had been 'tickled' because the hangman was on the side of the criminals. Marcus Clarke put up a droll defence:

> Not that I blame poor old Bamford; I feel a positive affection for that dear old man (he has rid me of so many of my fellow creatures), he did his best, I have no doubt. Besides, 'flogging' is not in his bond; 'hanging' is all he is engaged for.

A couple of months later, Bamford was released from gaol and within hours of regaining his freedom was arrested in a 'beastly state of intoxication'. *The Age* was moved to note that there was a 'serious defect' in a system whose intended 'moral effect' was neutralised to a large degree by using 'so degraded an agency'.

Sprung from the watch house the next morning, Bamford took himself to the Eastern Market, where *The Mount Alexander Mail* observed him gobbling a pie and boasting he hadn't yet guzzled all his drink money. Even when he had, no matter, because he looked forward to another 'job' soon. The paper rated his glib, gobsmacking presence 'one of the most revolting sights that has been seen in Melbourne for some time'. It asked whether he could be kept in prison permanently so he didn't 'set common decency at defiance'.

*The Telegraph, St Kilda, Prahran and South Yarra Guardian's* columnist 'Figaro' was similarly appalled: 'This is the man whom the law employs to preach a great moral lesson!' Figaro believed Farie should do the floggings; Bamford was the strongest argument against capital punishment that its opponents could want: 'I say it is a disgrace to the law to be obliged to make use of such a debased man as this.' *The Age* agreed about Farie taking over: 'But fancy such a liability being brought home to him!'

Given Bamford had been behaving this way for a dozen years, and that his latest antics were no worse than previous shenanigans, the timing of this chorus was curious. The likely explanation was that they'd all been reading 'Lower Bohemia' and 'The Drinking Dens of Melbourne', and that Bamford was in their thoughts. Even more so for making such a farce of the cherished return of corporal punishment.

In mid-September, Bamford was presented with the backs of a couple of street thugs who'd robbed and half-choked a sailor. Farie, Castieau, a magistrate, the colony's chief medical officer Dr William McCrea and a gaggle of reporters were watching. The pressure was on. If he 'tickled' these men, he might really lose his job. But Bamford put in a pleasing performance, breaking the skin and making the prisoners cry out in agony. The doctor expressed no disapproval when the lash a few times twisted around one man's loins, which was against the regulations. Neither did *The Herald*:

At the last flogging in the gaol it was felt that well-nigh a farce had been played. Not so now, and if criminals know what they have to expect, and the lash is held *in terrorem* over them, garrotting and midnight assaults will soon disappear from our list of offences.

Melbourne had rekindled a love of the lash, and what had been considered a barbaric punishment would now be increasingly inflicted for crimes of decreasing severity.

Bamford's duties had been expanded, and this would transform the lives of future hangmen. Executed felons didn't come back for revenge. Flogged men were often serving short sentences and *would* soon be back on the streets, where they might run into their torturers.

Bamford had proved himself at the triangle but he can't have been pleased at the prospect of missing out on £10 from a double hanging scheduled for Beechworth on 11 November 1869. Wild drunken giant Frank Neville had finally beaten a man to death at Rowdy Flat and had been nabbed by his nemesis, Senior Constable Arthur Steele. Neville was sentenced to hang. Wife-killer Peter Higgins – alias James Smith – was also set for the Beechworth scaffold.

Tom the Devil was still in gaol and was up for this payday. The chance to string up Neville must have seemed a godsend. Yet he wasn't to have his revenge. In one of its inscrutable decisions, the Executive Council commuted Neville's sentence and packed him off to Pentridge for twenty-one years. But Tom did good work on Higgins, as *The Ovens and Murray Advertiser* reported: 'Death was instantaneous; not a movement was observable after the body fell.'

That was two for two for Tom. If Bamford's critics were paying attention, they might've suggested Tom was the man to regularly earn the £5 with far less trouble. Except Tom was cut from the same cloth as Bamford. Perhaps even worse. When he finished his sentence on 22 November, he got drunk and disorderly, and punched and bit a constable, who said he was 'more like a cannibal than a human being'. Tom went back inside for three months. Melbourne would get by with Bamford. Perhaps better to stick with the devil they knew than dice with Tom the Devil.

~

Early in this same year of 1869, Melbourne witnessed departures and arrivals that would have future significance.

Harry Power escaped his work detail at Pentridge and was off to Victoria's north-east, where he'd make his name as a gentleman outlaw, and as early as May start teaching young Ned Kelly the ways of the bushranger.

John Castieau farewelled Beechworth Gaol to take over as governor of Melbourne Gaol, where just over a decade later he'd oversee Kelly's final days on earth.

Philemon and Ellen Sohier said goodbye to the city and sold their waxworks to Max Kreitmayer, who would eventually ensure the most famous hanged outlaw forever had a physical presence in Melbourne.

Understandably, none of these came under Marcus Clarke's notice. But he'd soon have something to say about another Melbourne arrival.

The larrikins were here.

# CHAPTER FIFTEEN

# Young Ned Kelly: Juvenile Bushranger and Promising Scoundrel

'I wonder if any "person present" has heard a song called Sam Hall.' So asked Marcus Clarke in his column on 19 March 1870. For those not in the know, he explained, the ballad was a bawdy celebration of an English villain who was fond of saying, 'Damn your eyes,' and whose exploits ended when he 'jump[ed] boldly into the Great Unseen with the assistance of a leg up from the hangman'. Clarke was asking because it seemed to him Sam Hall was:

> the unconscious exponent of the larrikin section of our community. The larrikin lives, he has an entity of his own, and he doesn't care a fig for you or anybody else. Why should he? 'His name is Sam Hall, —— your eyes!' He has a vote, a pipe of tobacco, and a threepenny drink – for the rest the world may go hang ... The larrikin has been a little noisy lately. The daily press records his doings with unction.

That was damn true. In the past month, these Sam Hall types had exploded seemingly out of nowhere to cause chaos and generate newspaper hysteria. But 'larrikin' was merely a new label for an established problem that had already caused plenty of angst.

Since at least 1864, any youthful miscreant had been dubbed the 'boy nuisance' or the 'big boy nuisance'. *The Argus* in November 1868 had warned:

The Australian stripling of a particular and uncompromising type becomes more numerous. His characteristics are not pleasing. He wants the diffidence and the reverence which are natural to youth. He is bumptious. Notoriety is his ruling passion ... But he is often worse than noisy, demonstrative, and troublesome, in all places of public resort, for he too frequently clutches with energy the gravest vices of mature life. This sort of flash and fast youth is a plentiful crop in New South Wales, and it also begins to abound in the rising generation here.

That was who they were. The question was: what to do about them?

In October 1869, when an 'atrocious young ruffian' abused a Melbourne woman with obscene language, the magistrate expressed regret he couldn't order him flogged for the offence. The newspapers echoed the sentiment, and soon politicians were talking about a new criminal amendment bill to allow the whipping of such boy nuisances. Spare the lash and you might end up with another young highwayman. Like that little bastard up in the north-east that *The Ovens and Murray Advertiser* called 'A Juvenile Bushranger'.

By now, young Ned Kelly had fallen in with Harry Power, become his apprentice and helped out in bailing up victims. The verbally diarrhetic 'Old Fox' would've filled the ears of his 'Cub' with his stories – from what it was like on the hulks and in Pentridge to the time he'd been framed for shooting at a constable, and the other time he'd stood trial for the murder of Owen Owens and felt Jack Ketch's breath on his neck.

Kelly wouldn't have learned only about bushranging from Power – he would've received an education in the history of the colony's crime and punishment from an old lag who'd lived it. But after the kid froze when they came under fire in late May 1869, Power sent him packing for the time being.

While they were on the outs, in October 1869, Ned Kelly allegedly robbed a Chinese hawker, Ah Fook, on the road between Winton and Greta. 'I'm a bushranger, give me your money,' this colonial youth had said, 'If not I will beat you to death.' Kelly denied the charge but spent weeks on remand. If he was found guilty, there was a chance the magistrate would order him flogged, like the boy bushranger Parsons. But at Kelly's trial in Benalla, three witnesses – including his sister Annie and future Greta mob member William Skillion/Skilling – corroborated his claim that Ah Fook had been the aggressor. The magistrate dismissed the charges and, as *The Ovens and Murray Advertiser* reported, 'The young lad then left the dock inwardly rejoicing.'

~

An old lag like Harry Power seems to have been the first person to use the word 'larrikin' in print in Australia. Up in Sydney, where they'd had their own 'boy nuisance', *Empire* newspaper in October 1867 published 'The Autobiography of a Convict', recalling the writer's long penal experience, including the time many years earlier that an overseer had labelled him a 'little bit of a larrikin'. Whether the term was used that early – perhaps the writer had heard it recently and included it so his article had more currency – 'larrikin' soon became a label for younger troublemakers.

The earliest Melbourne press manifestation appeared to be on 3 February 1870, when *The Herald* headline 'Emerald Hill Larrikins' appeared over an article depicting these offenders as a scourge: 'Now that the Emerald Hill Council have offered a handsome reward for the detection of roughs infesting the sea-bathing places, it is to be hoped that the parties frequenting those places will help the local authorities in bringing the offenders to justice.'

The next day, *The South Bourke Standard* reported that three 'larri-kins' were in city court for assaulting police; each was fined £20, in default of which he'd do three months. Setting the tone, the *Standard* suggested: 'It would have been a saving to the State if they were made to "kiss the gunner's daughter" instead.' 'Kiss the gunner's daughter' was Royal Navy slang for when a man was laid across a cannon so he could be flogged. From then on, Melbourne's newspapers seethed with larrikins, who inspired louder and louder arguments about whether they should be lashed.

Debate also raged about where the word 'larrikin' had come from. It was said an Irish constable with a thick accent had told a court a youth had been 'larking' and it had caught on. But a *Herald* correspondent had this to say:

> I think it is of much older date, and comes from the slang word 'leary' or a 'wide-awake' or 'knowing' one. We used to say 'he's a leary card,' meaning he was extra sharp. The 'kin' is used as a diminutive, the same as it is in the word mannikin, a little man, and a pannikin, a little pan. I should give its meaning thus: Larrikin, leary-kin, a knowing youngster.

Whatever its origin, Thomas Tracey, member of a Bourke Street gang, was a prime example of the genus. Since 1866, when he'd been in his mid- to late teens, Tracey had been charged with being drunk, street fighting and obstructing a constable. His punishments had ranged from cautions to small fines. Then he'd graduated to clobbering coppers, for which he was fined £10 in default of three months with hard labour.

But Tracey wasn't intimidated. In March 1870, he and two other gang members beat and robbed a man at one of those gin palaces *The Age* had warned about. When the victim had them charged, Tracey said he wished he'd smashed in the man's skull. The judge was appalled at how many like him – 'the worst grade of the class now designated "Larrikins"' – were coming before the bench. His Honour resolved to strike terror into their cocky hearts, and sentenced Tracey and his mates each to one year and twenty-five lashes.

'Dying game' wasn't much good to the man on the gallows, because he didn't get to enjoy his fame. Standing up to a lashing with a laugh could make you a hero to your mates while you were still alive. But just as private hangings stayed that way without reporters, so too prison floggings could only be revealed to most people via the newspapers. When Thomas Tracey went to the triangle in April, journalists could scarcely have done more to make him a hero.

*The Age* said he 'walked up the corridor with a jaunty, careless demeanour. On stripping, he was seen to be tatooed [*sic*] on the arms, in sailor fashion; he laid himself out on the triangle, bending his back slightly, and throwing up the muscles of his body in hard ridges.'

Bamford began his most severe flogging yet. Twice the doctor told him to strike lower. But the larrikin didn't seem to feel it. On the fifteenth lash, *The Argus* said Tracey called out: 'Lay it on Bill; what you're giving me wouldn't kill a mosquito.' In *The Age*'s version, it was on the twentieth and he'd said, 'Lay it on, Jack, don't be afraid.' *The Bendigo Advertiser*'s correspondent put it at the eleventh or twelfth stroke, as: 'Play up, Jack, old fellow, you've not got the dummy to practise on now.'

When it was over, *The Bendigo Advertiser* said Tracey's back 'showed signs of severe punishment, being puffed and surcharged with blood, looking like dry liver'. But he wasn't fazed. According to *The Argus*, 'On being released, the hardened young ruffian coolly put on his shirt and swaggered off as if nothing had happened.' No doubt larrikins all over the colony were breathless with admiration.

Tracey's fellow larrikins also bore up well that day, though they weren't as mouthy as their mate. Despite the evidence that Bamford had delivered severe floggings, *The Herald* regarded his effort as a farce because it'd been treated as a joke by the ruffians: 'A boatswain from Sandridge would punish far better than the decrepit hangman.'

That night Bamford got drunk in the city and was gaoled for a month. Columnist Figaro launched another attack: 'What would we think of a judge, or a jailor, or a turnkey who was ever and again being sent to gaol for drunkenness?' Figaro argued that if he wasn't dismissed, then hanging should be abolished. But the writer didn't really want that: he wanted Bamford gone. The man was old, dissolute and likely to die soon. Then he'd have to be replaced. 'Why not, then, anticipate that event,' Figaro asked, 'and get somebody to fill his offices who will at least refrain from such offensive obtrusions of himself on the notice of the public?'

Why not indeed?

~

Harry Power was still on the loose and making fools of police sent up from Melbourne to capture him. Although the Old Fox and Cub had reunited for a time, the bushranger had got sick of his apprentice and sent him home to his mum. There, at Greta, ragged and ill from his time away, at daybreak on 4 May 1870 Ned Kelly was arrested for his highway robberies. Two days later, he was before the Benalla Police Court, to face the first of several charges. He was remanded for seven days at the request of Superintendent Charles Nicolson.

When Kelly next appeared before the bench, the court was crowded with people eager to see the young highwayman. *The Benalla Ensign and Farmer's and Squatter's Journal* reported that his appearance had improved thanks to the prison diet and since his incarceration 'has become quite "flash". We are told that his language is hideous, and if he recover[s] his liberty at Kyneton and again join[s] Power – as no doubt he soon would – we are inclined to think he would be far more dangerous than heretofore.'

But Ned Kelly wasn't going to gaol. All the charges would be dismissed – either because witnesses could not identify him or witnesses couldn't be found. And the *Ensign*'s fears that he'd team up with Power again proved unfounded. The two men were now opposed, with no chance of rapprochement. Kelly was believed to have given information to the police that would help them catch his mentor – which they did on 5 June 1870, though actually through the treachery of Ned's uncle Jack Lloyd.

Though Kelly seemingly hadn't provided information of much use, he was troubled by the rumours that he was an informer. When he wrote to a friendly sergeant on 28 July to ask for help, he complained that 'everyone looks on me like a black snake'.

~

On 4 August 1870, William Bamford hanged wife-killer Patrick Smith in Melbourne Gaol. Most papers didn't report that he'd been placed too far back on the drop, so his body hit its edge as he fell, resulting in two or three minutes of spasm because his neck hadn't been broken by a stiff noose. Even *The Kyneton Observer*, which provided these details, was sure that 'death had been caused at once by the hanging'. What was more of a novelty that morning at Castieau's chateau was the arrival of Harry Power, temporarily lodged in the gaol before being sent back to Pentridge.

Harry's defeat gave *The Argus* cause to reflect on society's curious relationship with such outlaws: 'Since the time of Robin Hood, bushranging is a crime which has somehow or other been surrounded with a fictitious halo of interest that in the eyes of a certain section of society has half absolved the criminal.' The likes of Power clothed themselves in an air of romance and could rely on a certain amount of sympathy and admiration. As such, 'in the minds of the rising generation the bushranger is an interesting being ... who rides splendidly, robs the rich for the sake of the poor, and can obtain no higher fate than the one in store for him, namely, to be put in the waxworks and labelled'. But Power's long sentence had robbed him of romance, because 'to die game is the felon's *cordon bleu*'. Nevertheless, *The Argus* warned against giving 'any motive to the criminal classes to cultivate a spirit of egotism and self-admiration, or ... to raise up any splendid association in favour of being hanged'.

Two weeks later, after hanging the murderer Andrew Vair at Ararat, Bamford went on his usual bender in Melbourne and was fined. *The Advocate* reiterated the revolting cycle: the hangman did his job, collected his pay, shouted drinks in vile dens for hangers-on, and kept the debauch going until the money ran out and he was gaoled for another job so it could start all over again. So far, so familiar. But this new Catholic newspaper made a new penetrating point. The government knew the cycle better than anyone, but still they gave him the £5 that paid for this pandemonium and degradation. 'It is impossible not to regard those who gave it to him as accessories before the fact.'

*The Advocate* said a long-sentence prisoner should take over the role. Such a policy would keep Jack Ketch where he belonged – in seclusion – and save the city from 'that most disgusting sight – the debauch of a common hangman with the funds he had earned by the performance of his odious office'.

*Punch* mocked the booze-to-bust cycle: the Victorian government was like the cruel father who gave his only son a penny each night, stole it while the boy slept and the next morning punished him for losing it. 'We consider the conduct of the Government equally mean towards its only executioner. It professes to pay him for his services, and then, when he gets into a state of obliviousness, fines the money out of him again.' When it penalised Bamford ten shillings, it meant: 'Forty pints of colonial snatched away from his very lips, and swallowed by the greedy Government'.

*Punch* asked: 'Should Bamford strike?'

He didn't.

~

Sheriff Claud Farie's long reign was over when he died on 22 August 1870 after a short illness. Castieau was saddened by the loss of the man he said was his best friend. There was speculation as to who'd take Farie's place. For the time being, deputy Louis Ellis became acting sheriff. Ellis had been in the job since 1854 and was a gallows aficionado. Back in 1844 in Sydney, as a thirteen-year-old lad, he'd played truant from school so he could be part of the 10,000-strong crowd that had watched Alexander Green hang the aristocratic murderer John Knatchbull outside Darlinghurst Gaol. That lark had got young Louis in trouble. Now he liked to remark that the law *ensured* he attended every execution!

Ellis was nothing if not a man with long experience. A week into his stint as acting sheriff, he supervised as Bamford despatched the wife-murderer James Cusack. Though his neck was supposedly broken, he spent three minutes struggling at the end of his rope. As *The Argus* recorded: 'So apparent did it seem that the prisoner was not dead, that twice while he was hanging the chaplain recommended reading prayers for him.'

Castieau noted in his diary:

When the body was cut down I examined the neck as I could not under-stand why there was so much muscular movement & I found that part of Cusick's [sic] flannel shirt had been between the rope & the neck. This I imagine must have prevented the rope from getting quite close to the other portion of the neck & perhaps delayed immediate strangulation.

Bamford collected his £5 and caroused in a way that seemed calculated to stick it to his critics. The hangman held what *The Argus* dubbed a 'lawn party' and 'noisy orgie' for 'fellow outcasts' behind the Immigrants' Home. If Bamford was sending a message, so was the magistrate who fined him £5 – which he couldn't pay, so back to gaol he went for two months. The mean father giveth, the mean father taken away, but Melbourne was really the one being made to pay.

But one letter writer had the solution – himself! He'd witnessed what he called the 'disgraceful exhibition' of Andrew Vair's hanging at Ararat, and wrote to the deputy sheriff of the western bailiwick to say Bamford was too long in the tooth for such work. 'Should you require any one in the future,' he stated, 'I should be most happy to offer my services.' The aspirant added a postscript: 'I am prepared to do it for 10s. per head, but will expect their clothes. I undertake to do the work in a workmanlike manner.'

*The Ararat and Pleasant Creek Advertiser* printed his letter. The man was miffed that he was ignored by the deputy sheriff, and the newspaper published his follow-up: 'I feel rather surprised that you have not answered my letter; you will not get such an offer again.' Now he made his offer direct to Acting Sheriff Ellis, promising to work with 'utmost despatch and promptitude'. The correspondent said that just because he was applying didn't make him unfit for the role. He merely considered it'd be a welcome supplement to his other incomes.

Both letters were reprinted with amusement in city and country papers. Yet why not entertain this man's offer? He couldn't be worse than the incumbent. Both Tom the Devil and George Aldridge had done well on their first attempts. At the very least, the man might save the cost-conscious government a considerable amount of money.

But even if Louis Ellis wanted to replace Bamford, something his boss hadn't felt the need to do, he likely wouldn't have felt empowered to do so, because he was merely keeping the seat warm for an incoming gentleman: William Wright, Esquire. Claud Farie, who'd protested that he knew nothing of Aboriginal massacres in Victoria, was to be replaced by a man who'd ordered one in New South Wales.

In the years since Wright had tried to prevent Robert Rede from ordering the slaughter at Eureka, he'd had a trajectory befitting one born to a 'good English family': he'd become a member of the Legislative Council, president of the Melbourne Club, secretary of the railways. Now he wanted to be sheriff, and would take over in April 1871.

~

Larrikins and garrotters weren't the only offenders sent to Bamford's triangle. Rather than 'recording death' and letting homosexuals rot in prison for life, judges could now give them the maximum number of lashes and lengthy gaol sentences.

John Robert Morrison was such a victim. He was convicted of sodomy at Beechworth, sentenced to ten years and 150 lashes, to be administered in three instalments during the first six months. On 7 November 1870 he went to Bamford, who reportedly had 'trained' for a week. *The Argus* reported the punishment lovingly: 'The first stroke slightly raised the skin. At the second the prisoner winced. At the third he commenced to roar.'

During the next dozen strokes Morrison screamed, 'Oh, my God', and, 'Oh, I'm killed.' He begged Dr McCrea to stop the punishment several times. Bamford looked at the medical man, who bid him to continue. From the eighteenth stroke, Morrison went quiet, characterised by *The Argus* as resigning himself to his fate. Bamford took a breather after the twenty-fifth lash. Morrison's back was now black and the skin cut. When the hangman resumed, it was with less vigour, but harsh enough for the prisoner to scream for the last fifteen strokes. *The Weekly Times* provided a blow-by-blow for readers that concluded: 'This was the greatest number of lashes inflicted at one time in the colony since the convict days of yore.' Despite furnishing similar gory details, *The Argus* thought Bamford not up to the task and the punishment not brutal enough.

Such bloodlust became increasingly common. In late November, a quartet from the larrikin tribe was lashed by Bamford. What disgusted Castieau was the crowd – reporters, 'quasi gentlemen' and sundry others – who'd been admitted by Acting Sheriff Ellis, and for whom the hangman's heavy efforts weren't nearly enough:

The crowd's anxiety seemed to be that [the larrikins] should get it hot & not a sign of compassion or disgust was shown by any of the lookers on. We read with horror of the brutal exhibitions of the Romans with their Gladiators pitted against one another or opposed to wild beasts & wonder how the populace could delight in such cruel amusement. I do not however think the men of the modern age are much different & I feel confident if a scene of the kind was to take place in Melbourne to-morrow there would be any number of applications for admission & some very severe criticism on the deportment of the Gladiators when dying or the want of pluck shewn by the hyenas in not taking their gruel quietly.

*The Ovens and Murray Advertiser* felt the bloodlust. Reporting Morrison's first flogging made the paper wish a judge had been able to serve up similar to a lad they called 'A Promising Scoundrel':

The young man Kelly, who for a time acted as mate and bush telegraph of Power the bushranger, was brought up at the Wangaratta Police Court on Thursday, for a serious assault on a hawker named McCormick, and grossly indecent conduct towards McCormick's wife. It seems a pity that the lower courts have not the power to award similar punishment to that inflicted on Morrison in the beginning of the week. Twenty-five or fifty lashes would more efficacious in deterring such as Kelly from crime than a sentence of two or even four years' imprisonment.

The lad's crimes – fighting the man and pranking the woman with a gift of bull's testicles – were classic larrikinism. Instead of being lashed, he got six months, which commenced in Beechworth Gaol on 11 November 1870.

Ned Kelly had ten years to the day until he would meet Elijah Upjohn.

# CHAPTER SIXTEEN

# Young Ned Kelly: A Candidate for the Gallows

Elijah Upjohn seemed to be looking for a new start, a way to be rid of the stains attached to his name. The past few years hadn't been easy, and he hadn't behaved as well as he might have. Perhaps now he could clean up his act.

Upjohn had kept fighting the Ballarat authorities and kept running afoul of the law. In November 1867 – having a month earlier been again fined for illegally dumping nightsoil – he complained to *The Star* about the council's 'inspector of nuisances'. Elijah said servants were emptying the cesspools of their masters in broad daylight, and dumping the waste into piles of cow manure in fields. When farmers found these festering heaps, they left them where they were. The inspector had done nothing about this. But he punished Upjohn if – in trying to get to his first job on time – he was on the streets with his perfectly clean and empty cart before 11pm!

Upjohn's prison record shows he did seven days in gaol in June 1868, though it doesn't specify the offence. There came more fines for working without a licence, and more court actions against customers who didn't pay. In February 1869, Upjohn was a witness for the Crown in a false pretences case: the defence accused him of perjury, citing his 'prison experiences'. The jury didn't think it mattered and the man was found guilty. Nevertheless, it can't have been pleasant for Upjohn to have this appear in the newspapers. Two months later, he was again found guilty of dumping nightsoil – this time in an old quarry in a swamp – and said he'd rather do the month in gaol than pay the £5 fine.

Trouble kept finding Elijah – and he kept finding trouble.

In mid-October 1869, Ballarat's cesspools – and everything else – were overflowing when heavy rains caused a disastrous flood. Upjohn's house and stables were near a creek, and were soon under two or three feet of water. No sooner had the waters receded than he was back in court for dumping nightsoil. He was fined £10 – and, unwilling or unable to pay, this time served two months.

In May 1870, Elijah's son Alfred was in all the papers. On a Saturday night, a Ballarat ironmonger went to the tinsmith's shop where the boy worked. The man asked Alfred whether the owner's wife was in. This woman came out to see her visitor and young Upjohn stepped outside. That left a shopgirl to see what happened next: the ironmonger drank poison, grabbed a shotgun and blasted the tinsmith's wife, before shooting himself. Alfred was called to testify at the murder-suicide inquest, the crime electrifying Ballarat for its gory details, and because it appeared to be the killer's horrific response to a souring adulterous affair.

It wasn't long before Elijah Upjohn was up on an unlovely charge that had tongues wagging and heads shaking. On a July night he was found trespassing on Charles Chamberlain's property, lurking near the stables with a ball of dough he'd been about to pop into a horse's open mouth. Upjohn apparently scrammed but was silly enough to leave the morsel behind. When Chamberlain had it tested by a chemist, the dough was found to be laced with poison.

Why should Upjohn want to do such a thing? Or why would Chamberlain manufacture such a charge? The newspaper reports didn't offer a clue. But Chamberlain was also a nightman. Had Upjohn been trying to ruin his business by killing the horse that pulled his cart? Or was Chamberlain trying to frame Upjohn to get rid of a competitor?

Under the headline 'A Rascally Affair', Ballarat paper *The Courier* reported that in court the Chamberlains withdrew the attempted poisoning charge, while Upjohn was dismissed on the trespassing citation because he convinced the magistrate he'd been on the premises in search of work. Upjohn walked free, but it was bizarre and likely hard to live down.

In late October 1870, history repeated as rains hammered down and created an even worse flood than the year before. Elijah and Ann got their three sons to safety, but stayed to try to protect their house. By 3am the next morning, the waters of the nearby creek were up to their waists. As *The Star* reported: 'Mr Upjohn got on the roof and gave the alarm, and Trooper Laverton was soon on the spot with a lantern and ropes but alone he could do no good.'

With the help of other men, and a lucky break when a floating roof wedged against the house to provide a rescue raft, the Upjohns were tied to ropes and pulled free. *The Age*, *The Argus* and other papers reported their close call as part of their disaster coverage. But the Upjohns weren't made into heroes, *The Star* calling them foolish and saved only 'at the peril of their rescuers'.

Then, just as in the previous flood year, Upjohn was charged with dumping nightsoil. When the matter came to court in late November 1870, he was fined 20 shillings, in default of which he'd serve six months. Back to gaol he went from early January. It seems he somehow added to his time rather than earned a remission, because he wasn't released until August.

Elijah Upjohn had now been in Ballarat for about fifteen years. He'd come to the Golden City trying to do work that was honest if disgusting. At first he'd been be frustrated in his business by bureaucrats with little regard for public health or common sense. But his subsequent actions had stained his record and character. Including offences proven against him, charges he'd beaten and circumstances he'd put himself in, Upjohn had been labelled in the papers as a drunk, a perjurer and a pickpocket, a toy shop smasher, a worrier of sheep and would-be horse assassin, a fool of the flood and a serial dumper of shit.

But Elijah was also a husband, a father of three surviving children and a hard worker. The court had relied on his good character as a witness, and when chickens were stolen by little larrikins, he'd been the one giving chase. For well over a decade he'd performed an essential service for Ballarat.

Now, released from gaol, Upjohn appeared ready to change for the better. For years his penal record would show no further convictions, and his only newspaper mentions came when he sued for monies owed him and when he applied to the council for employment.

In 1871, Ballarat's sanitation laws were amended to compel residents to have a licensed nightman empty any full water closets. This was what Elijah had wanted when he first clashed with the councils. If they'd listened to him them then, how different things might've been. Ballarat's new cesspool rules should have been a boost to his business, but Upjohn was done with toiling in the darkness and filth.

At some point in the early to mid-1870s, Elijah and Ann began taking in washing. It was lowly work, hot and hard, the sort of thing Chinese migrants did. Nevertheless, you could do it by day, and what was produced was welcomed by customers as fresh and clean. Elijah would regularly be seen at his trade by a *Ballarat Evening Post* reporter, who described how, when on a break from wheeling his barrow, the laundryman would sit on its handles in the shade and smoke his pipe with a 'complacent and contemplative air'.

We don't know what Elijah Upjohn was thinking about during these smokos. But there's a good chance his thoughts strayed to the many mistakes he'd made, and how he could make a better life for himself, his wife and his boys.

~

William Bamford started the year of 1871 doing twelve months for vagrancy. He had work inside to keep him busy, starting with John Morrison's second instalment of fifty lashes, delivered despite the man suffering heart trouble since his first torture. The doctor pronounced him fit to flog. Bamford went to work. 'He frequently begged for mercy, and called upon the doctor for God's sake to stop the flogging, as they were cutting his back off,' *The Ballarat Courier* reported. 'When taken down, the criminal's shoulders and back down to the waist presented the appearance of so much raw beef.'

*Punch* drolly described Bamford's 'artistic finish' and the 'force and colouring' of his floggings. But it was more serious when echoing a familiar refrain: 'If the Government would only consent to furnish Mr Bamford with a larger supply of subjects, in the shape of an assortment of larrikins, woman-beaters, and general ruffians, we have no doubt that he would in time become an ornament to his profession.'

Not everyone was so enthusiastic. Marcus Clarke attended the flogging of a garrotter in mid-February, and met John Castieau for what seemed to be the first time. In his diary, Melbourne Gaol's governor noted that this was the most severe flogging he'd seen. Of Clarke, he recorded: 'I was glad to see he did not believe much in its efficacy as a rule though he believed flogging could occasionally be resorted to with advantage.'

Flogging wasn't only about prevention and punishment. It was about sadistic pleasure. Castieau a few months hence recorded a double flagellation attended by 'the usual little knot of connoisseurs gathered to see the sport'. Morrison provided sport for the third and final time in April. Then this scourged man had to endure the rest of his sentence – which he did, outliving most of the people in this book, only dying in 1914 at the age of seventy-nine, by then an 'old colonist' of Yackandandah.

A few weeks after Morrison's last whipping, a man convicted of bestiality was sent down from Ballarat for the first instalment of his 150 lashes. He claimed heart disease and, unlike Morrison, got a reprieve. Bamford still got paid that day because he had three other customers. They included a sixteen-year-old and a lad two years older convicted of stealing just eighteen pence from a boy in the street. The *Weekly Times* columnist 'Hylax' heartily approved:

> I would stand by willingly and see the back of such ruffians cut to pieces. I should not certainly like to shake hands with Mr Bamford, but when I read of his improvement in the art of laying it on to these ruffians, I feel what may well be called a distant admiration for him. May his arm never wither.

But reports occasionally hinted that Bamford wasn't all monstrous. Once his flogging work was done, he sometimes handed water to bleeding prisoners and helped others away from the triangle. Once he was heard to console a victim by saying of the pain: 'Not to mind it; it would soon be off.' Perhaps these qualities – as much as his cheery laugh and grandfatherly appearance – were what Marcus Clarke had responded to, and what led Castieau to refer to him as 'Old Jack'.

~

Ned Kelly was beyond the whip now. Six months earlier, *The Ovens and Murray Advertiser* had been baying for the blood from his back; now, its headline 'A Candidate for the Gallows' envisaged the day Kelly would meet Jack Ketch.

The lad had been committed to stand trial for stealing the Mansfield postmaster's horse. *The Ovens and Murray Advertiser* admiringly reported that clever senior constable Edward Hall had given him a good revolver-whipping around the skull during the arrest. The paper predicted deadlier legal violence lay in the larrikin's future: 'From the number of times that Kelly has already appeared before the public, in the position of a criminal, it is quite evident that, like Rogue Riderhood, he has little to fear on the score of danger from drowning.'

This seemed harsh, given Kelly's youth, the fact that horse theft wasn't a capital crime, and the reality that he hadn't even been convicted of it yet. When he was found guilty – after more than three months of time on remand, and on very shaky evidence – Kelly got three years. Now he'd see the places Harry Power had been, Pentridge and the prison hulks, but first he was going to Beechworth Gaol.

~

Ballarat Gaol had been Bamford's destination in mid-May 1871, while Kelly was still on remand. He was going up to Upjohn's neck of the woods on the night train to flog a man. Such was Bamford's celebrity that when the train stopped at Geelong, there was a commotion as people gathered to see him, noting he carried a small bundle, wrapped in scarlet cloth, from which protruded what looked like the handle of a whip.

Going to see the hangman of your own volition was one thing, but having him thrust upon you was in very poor taste. Six months later, Bamford was sent to Beechworth on the mail coach. *The Ovens and Murray Advertiser* was appalled that he'd been transported in this fashion – and that prisoner Richard Chute had a few days later taken the same conveyance: 'We look upon this as a great outrage on the public, which ought to be done away with.' The paper said additional expense should be incurred to send the two men by separate vehicles, as it affronted 'every sense of decency that ladies and children should be compelled to be shut up for hours with a murderer or worse'. 'Worse' put Bamford below Chute, an insane wife-slayer who'd end up locked away in Ararat asylum.

Bamford was in Beechworth to hang the murderer James Quinn. But even *The Ovens and Murray Advertiser*'s reporter had to admit the executioner wasn't quite the monstrous apparition he had expected.

Bamford was 'an elderly looking man, rather bent in figure, and with little to distinguish himself from an ordinary swagman, except perhaps a somewhat peculiar look of the eyes'.

Bamford might have seemed benign at a glance – apart from that missing eye – but watching him hang Quinn in Beechworth Gaol was to see something dark in the man's soul. 'Bamford performed his duties with apparent relish, and quietly proceeded with them while Quinn was speaking,' the reporter wrote.

Knowing that a hanging was being carried out within its walls cast a pall over any prison.

Somewhere inside Beechworth Gaol that morning – 10 November 1871 – Ned Kelly was marking the first anniversary of the conviction that had put him inside. One year down, two to go. Less if he kept up his good behaviour.

~

Bamford was back at Ballarat just before Christmas, to whip homosexual man Ah Chow before a large and appreciative crowd. *The Ballarat Evening Mail* reported: 'Bamford, with arms bared, seemed to take a fiendish delight in his beastly work.' Victoria had sent a clear and terrifying message to homosexual men. If caught, they'd be shamed, flogged, and thrown in gaol for a decade or more.

In this atmosphere, on an afternoon in March 1872, two well-dressed, youngish men, Edward Feeney and Charles Marks, walked into a Melbourne photographic studio to have their pictures taken. In one image they posed facing each other and holding hands. In the next they stood every bit as amiably, though they held pistols at each other's breast. These men, who had worked together at Melbourne Hospital as wardsmen, were all but inseparable. They were also desperately melancholy, and both had reportedly previously attempted suicide.

Leaving the studio, they went to a wine bar, wrote letters to their families, bade the proprietors a farewell and went to the Treasury Gardens. A single gunshot rang out. Witnesses found Marks breathing his last, shot in the chest, his clothes bloody and torn and smouldering. Feeney lay a few feet away, smoking a cigar. Placed under arrest, he said: 'We were to have died together, and he tried to shoot me, but could not.'

*The Herald* called it a case of 'extraordinary insanity and suicidal mania on the part of both men. They are described as inoffensive, well-conducted, and intelligent men.' Castieau wrote that they'd had 'an almost or quite a romantic affection for each other & feeling disappointed with the world made up their minds to leave it altogether'. The guns were to be used 'not out of animosity but in brotherly love, trusting their shades would fly to the same sphere & there be united'.

They were reunited – as figures in Max Kreitmeyer's waxworks – even before Feeney went to trial. The Crown contended the men hadn't meant to commit suicide. Rather, they'd planned 'cross-murder'. In sentencing Feeney to death, Judge Williams added a personal touch of hatred when he said the condemned man should that day in the park have taken the pistol that'd remained and 'blown his own brains out'. Castieau wrote: 'I hardly think it was quite the sentiment to proceed from the Bench.' He also noted: 'Here is material for a Sensational Novel who dare use it.'

That 'sensation' was more of a worry for Feeney than his imminent death. *The Herald* reported: 'During the last few days of his life he has been most anxious to leave the impression that he is entirely innocent of the charges made against him in connection with his unfortunate victim.' Feeney went to so far as to solemnly deny to Castieau that he'd been intimate with Marks, and asked him to relate this to the press. The governor honoured his request. The next morning, 14 May 1870, Feeney went to the gallows.

A hungover Castieau wearily recorded the execution. 'Old Bamford' pinioned the man 'a little more clumsily than usual', he wrote, and had difficulty getting the cap over the man's hair. 'At such a time a second seems like a minute & a minute almost an hour.' In his diary, Castieau offered a rare insight into how what he saw from the platform differed from what others witnessed down below – and why other executions might come to be described in different ways by different reporters: 'He was evidently in a great state of fear & shook a good deal. This I could see being close to him. The bystanders some little distance off thought he showed little signs of concern.'

Predictably, the hangman bungled:

Bamford did the pulling tight of the rope a little too hard & when the bolt was drawn the body scarcely fell fairly, the rump catching the side of the scaffold & thus breaking the fall. Feeney seemed to struggle much longer than men who are hanged usually do. Dr Barker however styled the horrible spasmodic movement as simply 'reflex' & of no consequence.

Unlike reporters who constantly parroted the 'hanging doctor' and his ilk, Castieau even after two decades of watching men strangle wouldn't accept this blithe reassurance: 'He could not however answer my question as to why some when executed were troubled with reflex movements & others were not.'

Feeney's indignity wasn't over. Castieau wrote that, away from the prying eyes of the press, Dr Barker and his medical students 'revelled in the luxury of a fresh & healthy corpse'. There was a special reason for their enthusiasm: this was their chance to settle the stories.

Barker exposed Feeney's rectum & both he & Dr Youl said it told of a vicious indulgence. I was asked my opinion, or rather to coincide in theirs, but I declined as I had no experience of what a healthy rectum would represent. Doubleday took a cast of Feeney's head.

The head-reading hairdresser did more than that. Six days later, *The Age* reported: 'The cast of Feeney's head, exhibited in the window of the Waxworks Exhibition, has attracted a large number of gazers. It is stated that the proprietor had obtained the actual hair and beard of Feeney to place on his wax model.'

~

Supreme Court judge Redmond Barry had now been handing down severe punishments for twenty years. But his wisdom was called into question in mid-August 1872, when he sentenced Angus Adams to serve thirteen years and receive seventy-five lashes for bestiality. This eighteen-year-old lad – who looked fifteen – was an intellectually disabled orphan who'd been dumped in an Industrial School. It was at this institution that he'd committed his offence. Adams told the arresting policeman that he'd only been copying other boys in how they behaved with goats.

Castieau was deeply disturbed at a sentence he believed would bring 'tribulation' for Barry. With Adams under his care in Melbourne Gaol, he tried to find out more about the lad but to no avail: 'He walks about without taking notice of any one or anything & is more like an animal than a human being.' Even the often vicious *Ovens and Murray Advertiser* suggested Barry might've enquired further into the boy's background, and dared to question His Honour's judgement: 'It is doubtful, however, whether the administration of floggings was called for.'

Despite widespread unease, the Crown refused to remit the corporal sentence. When Adams was due to be flogged on 2 September, it was one of those rare occasions when Bamford couldn't be found. Castieau wrote: 'Old Jack had'ent put in an appearance & Rowley did'ent know where to find him.' Then Bamford sent word he was on the way.

But to Castieau's relief, he wouldn't be needed. Dr McCrea certified Adams unfit to be flogged, and the Governor remitted this part of the sentence. The youth was soon admitted to Yarra Bend Asylum and he remained institutionalised until his death in 1908.

~

All bad things must come to an end, and in 1873 Bamford was like an old clock winding down.

The year got off to its usual start with the hangman creating a comic ruckus. Out of gaol for longer than usual, Bamford was squatting, in every sense of the word, on a patch of vacant land by the old railway station on the corner of Flinders Street. A respectable man and his family lived in the building and were dismayed to see Jack Ketch making his toilet in broad daylight. Passers-by were similarly disgusted at the hangman letting it all hang out.

Bamford was hauled into court.

The mayor asked him: 'Have you no visible or lawful means of support?'

Bamford: 'None.'

The mayor: 'A good job too!'

Everyone erupted in laughter – Bamford included – because everyone was in on the joke. Melbourne needed him, and he needed food, shelter and money for drink. The *Vagrancy Act* served them all. The mayor sentenced him to two months. As *The Herald* reported: 'Bamford made a *salaam*, and trotted out nimbly, overjoyed to get home again.'

The killjoy 'Figaro' wasn't laughing, using his soapbox to argue that it'd be better to abolish capital punishment than have 'the law's last dread and solemn office' carried out by 'such a disgraceful old loafer'. It had now been a quarter of a century since Jack Harris had provoked the same commentary. Melbourne had plenty of other longstanding and more serious problems, such as the appalling lack of sanitation, which caused deaths from dysentery and other diseases, and which could only be solved with enormous political will and government expense. But the ongoing Jack Ketch dilemma wasn't like that. Bamford served at the pleasure of Sheriff Wright. He could've consulted his bosses – the chief secretary and the inspector-general of penal establishments, George Duncan – and replaced the hangman at a pen-stroke. Figaro, echoing critics of the past twenty-five years, asked: 'Have the authorities, I wonder, ever made a serious attempt to secure the services of some less objectionable person that Bamford?'

The answer was no. But it hadn't needed to be like this. William Calcraft was now approaching his forty-fifth year as London's hangman. Up in Sydney, Robert 'Nosey Bob' Howard was about to start a nearly thirty-year career as an inoffensive 'gentleman hangman'.

~

Ned Kelly was on the move in mid-February 1873, transferred from Beechworth to Pentridge. His initiation was as a solitary A Division prisoner, made to wear a hood as he walked to and from the yard for his one hour of exercise a day. After six weeks, he began regular prison life in B Division.

Ned was a good inmate. His only infraction was handing tobacco to another convict, which merited a seven-day extension. If Kelly kept this up, he'd be out early with remissions and ready to start over.

~

Bamford had been whipping larrikins, garrotters, flashers, sodomites and men who lay with animals. But wife-beaters evaded such a penalty. Indeed, they often evaded any punishment. As the law stood, a man would likely hang for murdering a woman. But a husband could beat his wife almost to death, and receive a lesser penalty than the hangman got for hosting a drunken 'lawn party'.

*The Weekly Times* set out six cases that had come before the courts in a recent week: 'The man who beat his wife till she became insensible, and then attempted to burn her alive, was sent to gaol for two months, and the other old reprobate who, "for a long series of years," had used his victim "very brutally" was sentenced to a fortnight's imprisonment.'

The *Times* recorded that one man who hammered his wife, already suffering a broken arm, was simply bound over to keep the peace. Another offender received a ten-shilling fine. The other two were discharged. 'When Parliament meets, it will be a discredit to hon. Members if they do not alter the law so that Bamford and wife-beaters can become legally acquainted,' the *Times* concluded.

They would not. Women continued to suffer horrifically while the law shielded their husbands from serious punishment. Years later, in an unintended consequence, this legal double standard would help kill a hangman – and see a cloak of invisibility fall over future Jack Ketches.

~

In May 1873, Bamford was off to Beechworth to execute Thomas Brady and James Smith for a murder at Wooragee. He again travelled by public coach, and *The Ovens and Murray Advertiser* was again apoplectic. It was even more outraged because Bamford was out of gaol and thus a private citizen, yet the government had paid his fare and facilitated this 'gross outrage against decency and social law'.

The paper was less concerned that Bamford, 'more nervous than usual and in a hurry to despatch the men', seemed to bungle one of the hangings pretty badly: 'Smith, or Smith's body, we hardly know which, struggled and writhed for, what seems to the spectators, five minutes, but was probably less than one. It was, at any rate, a most painful spectacle.'

Later that month Bamford was in Castlemaine, making a mess of Pierre Borhuu, who'd shot a woman while in one of his 'mad paroxysms of drink'. As *The Mount Alexander Mail* observed, Old Jack 'bungled the matter considerably by running the hitch so tight as to half strangle his victim before he fell, and thus prevent the knot slipping into its proper place on the fall of the body'.

After fifteen years in this job, and having now hanged sixty men, Bamford still only got it right half the time – if that.

~

At least Ned Kelly didn't look like he'd be fulfilling *The Ovens and Murray Advertiser*'s prediction that he was 'a candidate for the gallows'. After four months in Pentridge, he was in June 1873 transferred to the hulk *Sacramento*, and was soon put to work as a stonemason building sea walls at Williamstown. Back when Harry Power had been on the hulks, such labour had been a punishment. Now honest toil and a shilling a day – which he'd soon receive as a 'first-class prisoner' sent to live ashore – were the rewards for good behaviour.

Ned Kelly was making a go of things.

~

When Bamford wasn't up to whipping three prisoners in July 1873, *The Ovens and Murray Advertiser* presumed he was indisposed because he had 'in an evil hour neglected business for pleasure'. The paper was tickled to imagine his superiors in a panic:

What was to be done in such an awful extremity? The Inspector Duncan could not do it, and Mr Sheriff Wright is too respectable; he would have resigned first. Mr Ellis, the under sheriff, would be too small for the office ... Consternation reigned within the prison, when, lo! A happy thought struck some one, that within the walls dwelt one Fagan, a Tasmanian, now under the special care of the Victorian Government.

'Fagan' was Michael Gately. Just over thirty years earlier, he'd been that little urchin on the *British Sovereign* when it had transported Bamford to Van Diemen's Land. Fifteen years earlier Gately had saved the Pentridge warders and got early release. Now he was about to embark on a new career with the cat-o'-nine-tails.

William Reynolds was one of the prisoners on Gately's triangle. He was fifteen or sixteen and sentenced to one month in solitary and twenty-four lashes for attempting sodomy with another boy, who'd been let off entirely because he was drunk at the time. Reynolds was so slight – just five-foot-two and nine stone – that Gately used a junior version of the cat – called 'the kitten' – to deliver his first instalment of a dozen lashes. Reassuring readers that the flagellator wasn't Fagin from *Oliver Twist*, *The Ovens and Murray Advertiser* offered a glowing review and predicted he'd soon be the colony's hangman:

> The masterly and energetic way in which he handled the cat lifted him at once into high favour ... it is more than hinted that Fagan may yet supplant Jack altogether even in the higher grades of office. At all events, it must have the effect of making Jack more attentive in future.

Bamford wasn't being inattentive. His health was failing. But he still felt equal to heading up to Ballarat to hang an African American man named Oscar Wallace, who'd been convicted of raping a white woman. The racial angle of the case was pervasive. *The Courier* observed, 'As a coloured man, he was passably good-looking when a smile lit up his features, but wore the mischievous scowl of a demon when he frowned.'

Wallace had plenty to frown about, claiming he should have had a mixed-race jury – and that he should have discharged his own counsel, because he would have cross-examined witnesses better himself. Saying there was a white conspiracy against him, in gaol he had 'chafed like a wild beast in his cage' and said he would '"die game" because he would rather be off this earth than upon it'.

On 11 August 1873, some thirty spectators rushed into Ballarat Gaol, given access by Robert Rede, now deputy sheriff of the southern bailiwick. The scene reminded *The Star*'s reporter of 'the crowding to a ticket-office after the opening of the pit door of a theatre'. Three extra guards were positioned on the scaffold, which added to the audience's excitement.

Wallace maintained his defiance. When Bamford put the noose around his neck, the doomed man growled at him: 'Take off the rope, take off the rope.'

The hangman shook his head.

Wallace asked: 'Ain't I allowed to speak?'

Rede told him to say his piece, but the noose was staying in place.

'Well,' Wallace said, 'I've a good deal to say; how long shall I be allowed to speak?'

Rede: 'Go on.'

'Well, I want to have a say about how I've been treated since I came to the colony ...'

Rede gave Bamford a look. They weren't going to listen to this.

Bamford said roughly, 'That'll do,' and dropped the white cap over Wallace's head. The condemned man struggled for a moment. Then he relented and said: 'Well, I may as well get to hell at once.'

It wasn't quite 'at once', as *The Herald* made clear in one of its multi-deck headlines that gave all the highlights at a glance:

The
Execution of Wallace
Obdurate to the End
Maintains his Bravado to the End
Tries to Dodge the Hangman
Does Not Succeed
Please Take the Rope Off My Neck
I may as well go to Hell at once
Is Launched into Eternity, but Takes Five Minutes to Die

Bamford's escort had a hard time getting him back to Melbourne on the train because the hangman was weakening. That he'd made it to sixty-five was something of a miracle. By using him so cynically, incarcerating him so frequently, the government had preserved him by enforcing stints of sobriety. But his hard life had still taken its toll. Suffering dropsy and heart disease, Bamford was admitted to Melbourne Hospital. He sent for a reverend. What Bamford confessed can only be guessed. The hangman followed his victims into eternity on 9 September 1873.

Unlike Sydney's early executioners, and his Melbourne predecessors, Bamford's lengthy unbroken reign and the level of celebrity it saw him attain meant he merited numerous obituaries. While acknowledging he'd been a drunken pest, the major newspapers offered portraits that bordered on affectionate. Further rewriting history, his superiors were depicted as having treated him with compassion and brought order to his chaotic existence.

*The Herald* reflected on how this 'necessary evil' had been 'shunned and abhorred even by the most degraded criminal'. For years he'd been unable to get a roof over his head, 'except that prison home provided for him by a beneficent Government'. The hangman hadn't been a creature of the wasteland but an almost romantic vagabond: 'When not enjoying royal hospitality, Bamford lived a nomadic life, passing his days in haunts of crime and low dissipation, and his nights beneath the canopy of heaven.'

While acknowledging he'd often been hauled in as a vagrant, *The Argus* otherwise depicted a dutiful public servant operating in his own eccentric but efficient manner:

> To send notice to 'Jack' that he was required to come into the gaol was sufficient. This would be given him two or three days beforehand, and then he would at once voluntarily imprison himself, sleep off his drunkenness, make himself clean, and be ready to hang or flog, as his 'job' might be.

As for the sadistic relish and frequent bungling that had led the newspapers to frequently call for his removal from office? None of it was mentioned. 'Bamford, as a rule, performed the terrible work allotted to him quietly and efficiently.'

Wistfully, *The Age* recalled how he'd wept before hanging his old mate in Geelong, while *The Herald* said it had many funny tales but space for only one anecdote – about the time in court he cheekily won over the mayor by wearing the man's old election propaganda.

Bamford might not even 'be going to hell at once' like his last victim. *The Herald* believed even he might be saved: 'Let us hope that at the eleventh hour this unfortunate creature became in some degree sensible of his dignity and responsibility as an immortal creature.'

*The Ovens and Murray Advertiser* was unsentimental, and its obituary more accurately reflected how newspapers had reported Bamford when he was still alive: 'He was a horrible fellow; his heart seemed to be in his ghastly work.' A reporter for *The Star* placed the hangman in the context of the system when he professed himself 'unequal to the task of doing justice to the wretched creature, whom society found it convenient to brutalise in order that he might obey its behest'. According to this writer, two first-hand experiences 'suffice to show how utterly callous he was' – one was Bamford stepping onto Terry's shoulders to finish him off; the other was Bamford gazing on the body of another victim and proudly saying: 'The fifty-eighth; the best job I have done yet.'

Bamford's passing caused some reflection on the death penalty. *The Star*'s man hoped he wouldn't have many successors – or at least that his brand of barbarity would soon pass. 'I think the time is not far distant when capital punishment will cease, or cease, at all events, in the offensive form that it has been carried out in my day and generation.'

*The Ovens and Murray Advertiser* considered the question also: 'There is such a feeling of horror and disgust almost universally felt towards the man who carries out the last sentence of the law, that it is impossible to avoid asking ourselves whether there must not also be something vile and unnatural in the sentence itself.' But, of course, that was throwing out the baby with the bathwater, and 'we do not see that instinctive horror of the hangman affects the righteousness of the sentence which he executes. The opponents of capital punishment are numerous and able, but the day of their triumph is still afar off.'

A century, in fact.

Bamford's death meant that Sheriff Wright had to find a new hangman. This offered a chance for reform. But now one might be given to ask whether there had really been a hangman problem. After all, the obituaries in *The Age* and *The Herald* might lead you to believe Bamford wasn't so bad, and the system actually worked pretty well. If it wasn't broken, why fix it?

*The Ovens and Murray Advertiser* learned that twenty men had applied to fill the vacancy. Surely some were solid, sober, sane. But this paper had two months earlier correctly predicted who'd get the job: Michael Gately. Out of the frying pan and into the fires of hell.

Jack Ketch was dead. Long live Jack Ketch.

# CHAPTER SEVENTEEN

# A Great Brute Who Would Boil Babies

Michael Gately was Melbourne's new hangman. Given what the city had endured over the past thirty-five years as Harris and then Bamford had careened through the streets, the lack of journalistic curiosity about this new Jack Ketch was unfathomable. Gately's prison records had previously been in the press. Anyone perusing them would have to ask: why him?

Born around 1824 in Mullingar, Ireland, Gately's criminal career began when he was a child. Caught stealing apples and potatoes, he served three months. Next it was clothes, earning him another three months. Then he graduated to burglary – he'd claim he stole £24 from a post office – which in July 1840 got him ten years on the other side of the world.

It was a big sentence for a small lad. Gately then stood just four-foot-ten and gave his trade as 'sweep'. The boy had blue eyes and a fresh complexion, a broad nose and a small mouth, all set in a freckled face with a high forehead framed by red hair. Perhaps to remind himself of his real name – for there were a lot of aliases ahead – he'd tattooed 'M.G.' on the inside of his left arm. Young Gately cooled his heels in

Kilmainham Gaol until December 1840, when he was transported on the *British Sovereign*, arriving in Van Diemen's Land in March the next year.

As Gately grew into an imposing figure of five-foot-nine, he racked up the usual minor misconduct punishments – though not on par with the far more disorderly Elijah Upjohn. Gately wandered off without permission, absented himself with frivolous pleas of sickness, neglected his duty and disobeyed work orders. But one offence anticipated what Victoria could look forward to in the future. While in the lobby of a police office, Gately let fly with obscene language and profane swearing that got him fourteen days in solitary.

Gately had his certificate of freedom in July 1850 and set his sights on the other side of Bass Strait. But while Upjohn had tried to reform himself, Gately brought his old ways to his new home.

In February 1853 Gately stood before Redmond Barry at Geelong's Circuit Court charged with horse stealing. By now he was going by a couple of aliases, had added a 'DOG' tattoo to his lower right arm and acquired a scar over his left eye. More intriguingly, his new Victorian prison file noted he was 'formerly an Executioner'.

However, a man named Solomon Blay had been Hobart's executioner since 1840 and had worked all over Van Diemen's Land. Gately possibly assisted him, or took his place on occasion. But convicts also often lied about jobs they'd done in the hope of landing easier or better work. Why would Gately have done this in February 1853? Perhaps because Jack Harris had just been sentenced to four years on the roads, and he believed the hangman's office was vacant.

If that was Gately's hope, it wasn't to be. Barry sentenced him to eight years and he was off to Pentridge. Not long after admission, Gately was declared to be 'shamming mad'. His prescription was a six-month stint on the dreaded hulk *President*. Then he was transferred to the *Success*, before being bounced back to Pentridge in June 1854. In addition to the occasional reprimand for insolence and misconduct, Gately on one occasion got twenty days in solitary for 'disgusting conduct in his ward'.

In August 1857, Gately was discharged on a ticket of leave. He'd only been out a few weeks when he stole a coat and cheques at Ararat. Back to Pentridge he went on a three-year sentence, and soon bounced to the hulk *Success* for six months as punishment for his 'violent and dangerous conduct'.

Then, in June 1859, back at Pentridge, Gately became a bona fide hero. Convict Richard Rowley – under sentence of thirty-two years – hit brutal overseer Denis Kilmartin on the head with a stone and pushed him into a quarry. Next the berserker rushed warder Mathews, throwing the stone at him. As *The Age* reported: 'Rowley then rushed towards an axe that was lying near, evidently with the intention of committing farther violence. He was at this moment seized by one of the prisoners who stood near him.'

Gately went to Kilmartin's aid. The man had head injuries, broken ribs and a busted arm and leg. Mathews suffered a fractured skull. But – thanks to Gately, reported to have suffered a minor wound in the affray – at least Rowley hadn't killed them or anyone else with the axe.

At the trial, Gately's evidence helped convict Rowley and the culprit soon died in Bamford's noose. For his bravery, Gately was released early. But a month later he was sentenced to twelve months in Ararat Gaol for vagrancy. No sooner was he out than he was back inside for another year, for illegally working cattle at Kilmore.

Gately was in court in June 1862 at Sandhurst for horse stealing and burglary. He made such obscene threats to the magistrate, Mr McLachlan, that he reportedly had to be gagged. Gately was sentenced to five years. Under the new remissions system, he might've been out much sooner. Instead, he committed so many offences in gaol that he served almost the full stretch.

The next time Gately was in court, at Heathcote in April 1867, getting six months for petty larceny, *The McIvor Times* reported: 'The vagabond appears to have lived almost exclusively in gaol or under the surveillance of the police since his arrival in Van Diemen's Land.' Just as his criminal record kept growing, so did his bewildering list of aliases, which included 'John Kelly', 'John Andrews', 'John Gatehouse', 'Fagan' and the strange and sinister-sounding 'Ballaran' or 'Ballyram'.

In August 1868, having just been released after another six-month stint for pinching a ring worth £1, Gately used a jemmy to break into a hut at Wild Duck Creek so he could steal clothes worth forty shillings. In court, Magistrate McLachlan recognised his old acquaintance and said: 'Ballaran, are you here once more?'

Gately shot back: 'Yes, —— you; the next place we meet will be in hell.'

The '——' might've been 'damn' but was likely far cruder. As *The Bendigo Advertiser* reported, the prisoner 'used the most disgusting language towards Mr McLachlan, and hoped he would soon be in his grave'. Melbourne's *Herald* called his outburst a 'comical incident' and it was reported elsewhere. If the young larrikin Ned Kelly heard this story, it might have given him some ideas on sentiments you could express to a judge. After a week on remand, Gately was sentenced to a hefty six years.

The man of many names and many crimes remained a gaol gadfly. He racked up another couple of dozen minor infractions in Pentridge, including insolence, disobedience, defiance, having contraband, refusing to work, refusing to shave, and making false and malicious accusations. For these he usually received minor sentence extensions, sometimes in solitary or under hard labour.

By July 1873 he'd calmed down a little and been trouble-free for just over a year. Likely this recent good behaviour – along with his willingness, his claimed hangman experience, his link to Bamford and what he'd done to save the warder Denis Kilmartin – is the reason he got the chance that month to take Bamford's place at the triangle.

But elevation to hangman? Gately's record should have given the authorities pause. He'd been in gaol for almost all of the past thirty years. When in custody he'd been in continuous strife, been violent and disgraceful, and demonstrated obscene contempt for authority. Perhaps Gately might be controlled if he had years to serve. But he was due for release in just a few months.

Castieau noted that Gately was still going by the name Andrews when he became a regular at Melbourne Gaol to flog men, reporters approvingly noting the severe punishments the new man delivered unto the assortment of miscreants.

Gately was released in November 1873 and followed in his predecessor's sodden footprints by camping out in the city's public parks with a tribe of fallen women. In mid-January 1874 he was in Flagstaff Hill Gardens, enjoying an 'al fresco repose', when he was approached by a couple of Crown Lands bailiffs, who ordered him off. He threatened to stab these officers of the law.

Gately was arrested and found with a jemmy. In court he claimed it was a tool for legitimate work. See, he'd been trying to make a living hawking fish and fruit, and his little crowbar was for opening oysters. In fact, his industrious efforts to make an honest living had been thwarted by bailiffs scaring off customers with their blather about him being a flogger and hangman. While Jack Harris and William Bamford had been able to spin the odd 'plausible lying yarn' to secure their freedom, they'd never been in the habit of threatening to kill bailiffs. While the charge of having housebreaking tools couldn't be proved, Gately was sentenced to six months for these menaces and for trespassing.

Handwringing began at this happening all over again. In Ballarat, *The Star* opined:

Gately the hangman seemed to be as abandoned a wretch as his predecessor Bamford ... It is to be regretted if capital punishment must be inflicted that we cannot devise some other plan of disposing of criminals than by employing wretches of the Bamford and Gately type to strangle them.

Yet it shouldn't have been a surprise, given the record of the man the government had chosen. To paraphrase a later aphorism, the authorities were making the same insane choice over and over and expecting different results.

Before Melbourne was marvellous, this was its madness.

~

Gately returned to gaol with a case of gonorrhoea. Dr McCrea ordered him kept in his cell on a low diet, and the prisoner grumbled sorely at this prescription. But what really alleviated the patient's pain was inflicting pain. Castieau noted that 'when he was told of the "job" for this afternoon, he brightened at once & professed himself as ready. His sickness & his want of food did'ent save the man he operated on from getting a severe hiding.' Gately, as *The Bendigo Advertiser* reported, took a 'savage delight in what he calls "a givin of 'em it hot and strong".'

Even though Castieau once suspected him of taking a bribe to go easier on a prisoner, Gately most often far outdid his predecessor at the triangle. In June 1874, a journalist for *The Ballarat Evening Post* gave readers a lengthy and graphic account of what the doctor declared the most severe scourging he'd witnessed at Melbourne Gaol. The reporter concluded: 'Jack Ketch did his bloody work well, and looked every inch of him – a fellow well suited to his ghastly employment.'

But Gately was more than that. He was a savage animal, at least according to a later report in *The Age*:

One of his favourite pastimes was to place a number of live rats in a circumscribed place, and, getting in among them, catch them in his teeth like a terrier dog and shake them to death. Afterwards he would put them on a 'spit', roast them, and eat them with every expression of relish.

Such a story – hangman as rodent muncher – might beggar belief, if not for the fact that long before his worst verified excesses, Castieau viewed Gately as strange and sinister, 'a great brute who would boil babies if ordered to do so'.

# CHAPTER EIGHTEEN

# Who Shall Hang the Hangman?

Around the time Castieau was making his bestial observations about Gately, a phrenologist was supposedly coming to similar conclusions about Ned Kelly. This 'Professor Nimshi' – who had been lecturing for the past few years – reckoned:

The head of this man is non-intellectual. The base of the skull with the whole basilar section of the brain is a massive development of the lower animal proclivities, and which being vastly in excess of the moral sectional measurement, inclines him to the perpetration of sensual animal vices, and which, with an adverse facial angle, prompts him to the commission of vicious brutal acts of outrage and aggressiveness. He has large organs of self esteem and love of approbation, which give self conceit and vanity. If the one be wounded, or the other mortified, his animal nature would know no bounds. He would be likely, under sudden surprise, to commit the grossest outrages, and being uncontrolled by any moral sentiment, stamps his character as wolfish and ravenous, his notions of moral right giving him a dangerous range of action.

Nimshi reputedly published his findings in *The Wangaratta Star* in 1874. The first reprint was dated four years later, though, by which time Kelly was infamous and such opinions were a penny a pound. But if Nimshi did make such an analysis, then it was startlingly prescient. Not least because Ned had remained close to a model prisoner, and had walked free from Pentridge on 2 February 1874.

Kelly left prison with £2 10s in wages. Since he'd gone inside, things had changed in Melbourne. The train now went all the way to Glenrowan. But catching it meant going into the city, bustling with a population of more than 200,000, going hither and thither by foot and on horse, by coach, omnibus and even velocipede.

There was much to see. Redmond Barry might have been a hanging judge, but the city had a magnificent library due to his efforts. Collins Street was lined with ornate bank offices and topped by the imposing Treasury Building. The slope from the parliament down Bourke Street was a cascade of lively attractions, from shops in the Royal Arcade to the raucous rifle galleries, bowling alleys and billiard halls.

Of course, Kreitmeyer's Waxworks remained a top attraction. If Ned Kelly did visit – seeing Mad Dan and Ben Hall and so many others – he might have thought: *There but for the grace of God* ... When Kelly got back to Greta and the bosom of his beloved family, he appeared determined to make an honest living, and never to stand in wax at Kreitmeyer's or have his death mask gazed upon by visitors.

~

Michael Gately was also supposedly going straight.

In June 1874, he was selling fruit from a basket on his head in Brunswick. He was also drunk. When Gately fell down in a street, he didn't blame the grog but accused a boy of pushing him and went after the kid with his knife. Local women stepping in to protect the lad received a filthy tongue-lashing from the flagellator. Gately got two days in gaol, got out and got drunk, and got abusive when, as *The Herald* reported, a cab stand worker 'pointed him out as the public hangman ... to which Mr Scraggem objected'. Perhaps injury was added to the old insult for him because he still hadn't necked anyone. Gately got two further days in gaol, got out and got after the Brunswick boy in court. He sued for £2 for his damaged basket but had to pay nearly that much in costs when witnesses said he'd fallen down drunk and the case was thrown out.

Gately's dealings with the city's youth took a darker turn. He was said to have been consorting with a thirteen-year-old runaway in what the *Mount Alexander Mail* called a 'shocking case of depravity'. The hangman wasn't charged but the girl was sentenced to two years in the Industrial Schools. Soon after, Gately was staggering through Coburg and scaring children, who fled into the house of a Pentridge warder. Gately grabbed this man – whom he surely knew from prison – and threatened him with a bottle. For this the hangman got three months.

In his first year on the job, Gately had racked up sentences of nine months. As long-critical Figaro lamented in *The Telegraph*: 'Bamford was bad, but his successor seems to out-Bamford him.'

~

Gately was a threat to the young but it also worked the other way. In Carlton Gardens in December 1874, he had a run-in with a wild colonial boy who was far from your run-of-the-mill larrikin. James 'Tippo' Hayes was, according to *The Herald*, 'bullet-headed, square-jawed, ruffianly-looking' and so fond of clobbering cops that if the police heard he was on Bourke Street, they'd patrol in pairs for their own protection. Tippo stole Gately's £2 watch. The hangman might have let this go rather than risk making an enemy of the 'noble commander of the West Melbourne larrikin forces'. But he had Tippo charged and hauled into court. The larrikin was remanded for eight days – over Christmas. It can't have made him happy.

The case was dismissed. Gately couldn't testify that day as he was in court himself, accused of assault. The hangman got three months and the larrikin walked free. Returned to Melbourne Gaol, Gately was forced to have his wild red mane and beard cut and shaved, leaving Castieau bemused that this would-be baby-boiling brute took it so badly: 'He fairly blubbered this morning about the loss of his hair & told a terrible tale of his troubles.' Gately made his complaint to the visiting magistrate. The governor noted: 'Mr Sturt is however at times a very unsympathetic man & showed himself to be so on this occasion for he sent the gentle flagellator howling away without any consideration for his grievances.'

Gately would meet Mr Sturt again, and the magistrate's lack of sympathy would have people laughing all over Australia. It would also be a link in the chain of circumstances that would decide the last face on earth seen by Ned Kelly.

~

Gately had yet to hang anyone, but Castieau dreaded the inevitable. In 1874 he'd written in his diary, 'for hours the ugly rope and its dreadful load kept dangling before my eyes whenever I chose to doze.' Castieau recorded that, as much as he dreaded hangings, Gately was itching to prove himself, and was to write that the flogger was 'impressed with the belief that he would shine as a Hangman and has been, for a long time, anxiously abiding his time for an opportunity of distinguishing himself as "Jack Ketch"'.

In November 1874, Gately surely thought he'd have his first customer in John Weachurch – aka John Taylor, aka John Hallam – who, before Ned Kelly rose to infamy, was the most notorious criminal in the colony. A minor crook with a string of convictions, Weachurch was given six years for burglary in 1866. During his stretch in Pentridge, he was a very badly behaved prisoner, receiving numerous punishments decided by the 'star chamber' of visiting magistrates. When Weachurch had served his entire sentence, he was kept detained in the brutal A Division on a special magistrate's warrant. Told he had to serve out his various time extensions, which amounted to more years, he declared he was being held illegally and warned he'd wage war on the warders. In a bid to commit a crime that would get himself into open court, where he could air his grievances, Weachurch burned down the prison's shoemaker shop. But he wasn't put on trial – just given more custodial time.

In August 1872, Weachurch stabbed Pentridge's boss and the inspector-general of penal establishments, George Duncan, in the abdomen. This time he went to trial and was charged with attempted murder. His defence was that he hadn't meant to kill the man, only to get his claims of abuse and unlawful incarceration heard. Weachurch said his bit, was found guilty and sentenced to death. But the Executive commuted this to life in prison. Back to Pentridge he went and, by February 1873, with Ned Kelly now a fellow prisoner, Weachurch continued his one-man war. In November 1874, he split a prison warder's face open with a hoe, was again charged with attempted murder, and again said he'd only wanted his grievances heard in court. Surely he now had to swing as Gately's first victim.

Though Weachurch was damned in the press as a 'human tiger' whose 'rabid thirst for human blood' called to mind the 'ghouls in Eastern tales, or the stories of *loup garous* in France, and *wehrwolves* in Germany', he was acquitted by a jury who believed his claim that he hadn't meant to murder. Back to Pentridge he went, to continue his life sentence.

As this drama had been playing out, Gately was suddenly in the Melbourne Gaol orbit of another celebrity monster: Joseph Sullivan, who everyone agreed should have already died in the noose. In Maungatapu,

New Zealand, during June 1866, Sullivan and three accomplices had, over a couple of days, robbed five unresisting gentlemen of their gold, and then proceeded to strangle, shoot and stab these victims. Sullivan's atrocities were bad enough, but he was considered even more of a fiend when he testified against his fellow killers. The trio swung and he got a life sentence. After only seven years, Sullivan was released from gaol with a free pardon on the proviso he leave New Zealand and not go to the Australian colonies. He had been reported bound for California or England. Instead, in December 1874, Sullivan was caught near Wedderburn, 130 miles north-west of Melbourne, having come back to see his wife and children. He was charged with being illegally at large in Victoria. Of course, Gately couldn't earn £5 by hanging this villain, who'd already 'paid' for his Maungatapu mass murder. To much outrage, his lawyer would successfully argue Sullivan had been illegally detained and this five-time killer was to walk free. After being hounded from Wedderburn and other towns, Sullivan was to disappear from view, his whereabouts a mystery discussed by many Victorians – including Ned Kelly.

Around the time Sullivan was wriggling free of custody, Gately had another good bet for his debut in Richmond wife-killer Joseph Husler. But the hangman wasn't to collect £5 for him, either, because in February 1875 the jury believed he'd been insane with delirium tremens at the time of the crime.

Upon his release a month later, Gately was soon in a similar state, drunk in the street and trying to take a bite out of a constable's leg. His delirium tremens in the watch house was so severe that 'his howls of murder and shrieks for mercy reached the interior of the police court, where they caused mild excitement for the time'. To the magistrate, the arresting constable said Gately had been 'more like a wild beast than a man'. He went back inside for twelve months.

The *Weekly Times* columnist who'd adopted the Dickensian alias of

'John Peerybingle' said Melbourne might soon be rid of the hangman, as his habits meant he was not 'likely to cumber this vile earth much longer'. Peerybingle wasn't so sage about the fate of 'Fagan'. Bamford had shown that being a frequent guest in Castieau's sure-fire dry-cure hotel could lengthen the life of a dissipated Jack Ketch. The government was similarly punishing and preserving his repulsive replacement.

Gately's gallows moment finally came in August 1875. It had been nearly two years since there was a hanging in Victoria, and the prospect of this one pricked the colony's conscience and again seriously called into question the judgement of Redmond Barry and the Executive Council.

Chinese man Ah Cat had been living in an adulterous relationship with a married woman at Dunolly. Caught out, she'd hit her husband with a poker; Ah Cat had taken the weapon and laid into the man, and then his friend had stomped whatever life was left out of the hubby. All three went to trial for murder.

The Crown's principal witness was the accused woman's seven-year-old daughter with the deceased; indeed, this child's testimony was so vital that Barry said he'd have to dismiss the charges without it. Based on what they heard, the jury convicted Ah Cat but acquitted the wife and the friend. Yet even this confused jury recommended mercy, as they believed Ah Cat had acted in self-defence and without premeditation. But Barry sentenced him to death, and the Executive Council let the law take its course.

*The Dunolly Express* was amazed at the 'deplorable failure of justice on the one hand, and an unheard of severity on the other'. Despite the controversy, and the novelty of the first execution in a long time, city reporters didn't go to Castlemaine to see Ah Cat hang. Their editors instead relied on a brief article from *The Castlemaine Representative*, which used Confucian stereotypes and said the usual things: 'Like most fatalists, he appeared resigned to his fate. The drop fell, and a few convulsive struggles terminated his existence.'

But *The Mount Alexander Mail* had sent a reporter and its readers got a different view. Ah Cat had been pale and trembling, and repeated his claim of innocence:

> The executioner, a horrid specimen of humanity, seemed rather hasty in performing his last duties, and scarcely allowed Ah Cat time to speak before he pulled the cap over his face, and kicked the spring. The body dropped and through some horrible bungling in fixing the knot life was not extinguished for some seconds, the hands forcing themselves up to the face in a nervous twitching. However, in a few minutes all was over, and Ah Cat was no more.

*The Maryborough Advertiser* thought the matter funny, and enjoyed a joke made by the lawman in charge:

> It is said that a cat has nine lives. Whether this be the fact or no, it is certain that Ah Cat was the ninth man hung at the Castlemaine Gaol. It is equally true, as Deputy Sheriff Richard Colles remarked, that Ah Cat, on being hung, died as hard as a cat, and stood a great deal of hanging before he died.

Three weeks later, back at Melbourne Gaol, Gately hanged another Chinese man, An Gaa, who'd been found guilty of murdering his miner mate at Vaughan. This case was also troublesome, coming so soon after white wife-slayer Joseph Husler's successful insanity defence. When the police came to arrest An Gaa, he'd been calmly eating dinner in the presence of his still palpitating and bloody victim. After he was convicted and sentenced to death by Justice Barry, the killer's behaviour was so eccentric that he was transferred to Melbourne Gaol for Dr McCrea and other medicos to observe. They declared him fit to hang.

An Gaa's execution was taking place in the city, so there were more reporters present. *The Herald* introduced the new Jack Ketch, who'd found a way to express his hirsuteness: 'The person who officiates as hangman at present is a big red-haired fellow named Michael Gately, standing as nearly as possible six feet high. This morning his shirt was thrown open displaying a chest covered with tawny hair some three or four inches long.'

After pinioning An Gaa, Gately led him to the drop, where 'the detestable finisher of the law adjusted the noose, grasped the dying man's hand with one hand, whilst with the other he reached over, and almost before he had left the drop the body of his victim fell with a thud'. An Gaa reportedly died without a twitch.

Gately's third victim went to the gallows in October. Frankston hotel keeper Henry Howard had murdered his mistress and a barman who'd come to her aid. Gately appeared nervous, which might have explained why the noose was loose and the knot slipped under the man's chin when he hit the end of the rope. Howard convulsed so violently that it seemed clear to *The Age* he was 'expiating his crime by a slow process of suffocation'.

Gately had botched two out of his first three. He really was out-Bamfording Bamford.

~

Yet if any columnists were moved to begin anti–capital punishment screeds, they might have binned them when that hellbent rebel Weachurch stabbed a warder at Pentridge a few days later.

After he'd been returned to the prison, Inspector-General Duncan gave Weachurch special treatment 'outside the regulations'. He was kept caged in chains while being half-starved and repeatedly punished. Somehow he sharpened a tub handle, stabbed a guard and got himself back in court, charged yet again with attempted murder. Duncan testified under oath that Weachurch had been treated well. The jury convicted and the judge sentenced him to hang. This time he was going to die.

Even though *The Herald* thought this just, it wrote that 'there is something radically wrong in that system of prison discipline which, inflicting petty annoyances on prisoners, renders life an intolerable burden, and death, even at the hands of the hangman, a happy escape'. This minor criminal had been goaded into a 'state of ferocity bordering on madness' as the 'butt of any petty official, who chose to vent his temper on the prisoner, or to make experiments as to how far human endurance could go'. It argued the government must 'Abolish the star chamber of enquiry, so hateful to English men, adopted by Visiting Justices. Let these gentlemen hold open court to which both press and public are admitted.'

*The Herald* accused its rivals of publishing sanitised views of the penal system in their reporting of Weachurch. But it was worse than that. They wanted Weachurch to die for reasons beyond 'justice'. *The Leader* argued that killing him would save the cost of keeping a 'useless and life-sentenced prisoner'. *The Age* said he'd had a bad effect on other prisoners, and an example had to be made. Weachurch said that such press demonisation had made him a 'by word for mothers and nurse-maids to frighten children with'.

But one boy wasn't afraid of this bogeyman. Castieau's little son Jack, aged six, had lived his whole life in family residences inside the walls of Beechworth and Melbourne gaols. It'd given him a ghoulish disposition, as he later wrote: 'I took delight in the gallows and all its hideous appurtenances, animate and inanimate, from the hangman, Gately, who was my particular friend ... and from the rope, renewed for each execution, to the soap wherewith it was greased.' Jack would sit in the burial ground and imagine the gallows victims beneath his feet. But his most cherished activity was visiting the men who were about to go into their quicklime graves.

On the night before Weachurch was to hang, Jack slipped out of the family quarters and – not stopped by the bored warders, who were all his friends – wended his way to the condemned cell. He was so little he could slip through the bars.

'Ain't you frightened of me, little man?' Weachurch asked.

Jack climbed up on his knee.

Weachurch asked: 'D'you know what is to be done to me?'

Jack nodded.

'Do you know why?'

Jack shook his head.

'It is because I sought justice. Never seek justice, my boy. Let people do what they like to you. If you don't you'll only be hanged like me.'

Jack said of their farewell: 'The miserable wretch pressed my boyishly soft, small hand in his, rough and so often less gently used. Then he kissed the top of my head, leaving it wet and warm with tears.'

Weachurch's hanging the next morning merited detailed coverage. Gately, 'hideous and repulsive', was spied peering from the cell adjacent to the gallows. On the signal, he crossed to the condemned cell, pinioned Weachurch and shook his hand before leading him onto the drop. There, Gately whispered for Weachurch to raise his head so he could position the noose correctly. Weachurch appeared to adjust the knot himself before giving a short, graceful speech, saying he had only ever wanted the injustice he suffered made public. Gately lowered the hood. Weachurch's long sufferings were mercifully over in an instant.

Hairdresser-phrenologist James Doubleday took his cast and pronounced Weachurch a 'very dangerous person' among other things obvious to anyone who'd been following the extensive coverage. But

Melburnians could make up their own minds a few days later, when Weachurch proved the biggest Boxing Day attraction at Kreitmeyer's, though the crowds were surprised that this 'human tiger' had been such a puny fellow.

~

Gately was released in mid-February 1876. At £5 per execution, and £1 per flogging, he'd amassed a kitty. A week after regaining his freedom, he was in Little Collins Street, drunk, chasing children and attacking pedestrians. No one dared intervene; one hotel's staff barricaded their establishment's entrance for safety and there wasn't a constable in sight.

An hour into this rampage, Gately was in a hotel yard, smashing things, lashing out with a pot and gashing a man's head. A brave citizen tackled him and cracked him on the noggin. Only then did the police show up. With help from other punters, and after furious resistance, they handcuffed the berserker. Gately was sent back inside for six months.

*The Mount Alexander Mail* thought it lucky no lives had been lost. But if he were allowed run amok again, 'Who shall hang the hangman?'

# CHAPTER NINETEEN

# A Hangman in Love!

No-one was going to hang the hangman. But Gately was going to keep hanging other men. In May 1876 he went to Castlemaine to turn off the rapist John Duffus. He did the pinioning like a 'professional dancing master'. Then the bungling began. Duffus wore a collar. Gately put the noose over it. He was told by the gaol governor and the deputy sheriff to remove it. Then he adjusted the knot so badly that he was told to reposition it. Finally, all was ready. Duffus dropped with a thud – and his white cap turned red with blood.

Had he hit the scaffold? Had a vein popped as he strangled? Opinions varied. *The Bendigo Advertiser* said the body hadn't clipped anything. But *The Mount Alexander Mail* said Gately put him too far forward and he suffered a terrible wound when he hit the edge of the drop, the knot slipping so badly it nearly severed an ear. There was plenty of time to consider the matter, because Duffus convulsed for eight minutes and it was another three before his pulse stopped. *The Mail* believed 'he was strangled, but not hung'.

'Peerybingle' was sickened that Gately's bungling had seen Duffus 'battered against the scaffold, and at last strangled like a puppy'. If we had to hang criminals, it should be done deftly, he argued; the bungler should be dismissed. He had no doubt that Melbourne had dozens of men better at 'the art of scragging'.

It's hard to think there could have been anyone worse. But Gately kept his job.

~

Gately flogged his way through late autumn and winter. Reporters provided blow-by-blow accounts of how some men suffered and smiled at the end, while others screamed for it to stop and slumped into unconsciousness upon being untied from the triangle. When a Chinese man collapsed and had to be carried away, *The Herald* noted: 'During the ghastly scene, Gately looked on unconcerned, and after he had deliberately collected and bound up his hideous instruments of torture into a bundle, left the yard, saluting those present.'

Soon after he was released from Pentridge, Gately got himself 'well primed with liquor' to perform floggings back out at the prison, and then continued drinking at a Coburg hotel. A crowd gathered to gawp and guzzle the nobblers he paid for with the blood money.

But the mood soured when Gately insisted his proper title was 'the public executioner', and he should not be insulted as the 'common hangman'. Sober souls tried to get him onto Sydney Road and on a course for the city. Gately fell down at the old toll gate and wouldn't get up.

When the police arrived, he was shouting obscenities at the growing crowd of onlookers. Constables and citizens grabbed him roughly as he kicked, snarled and bit like a beast. Gately was bound hand and foot and thrown into a cab to be taken to the lock-up, the conveyance followed by a crowd of jeering larrikins as his roars and curses echoed around Coburg.

The magistrates were tempted to sentence Gately to fifty lashes. Instead they gave him the maximum punishment for his charges: six and a half months in gaol. But Gately could avoid doing time by paying fines of around £17. Having been paid for so many floggings and hangings, and having had so little time free to spend his earnings, the hangman was still cashed up. Gately coughed up and walked free.

*The Kyneton Observer* thought he had a sweet set-up. To work, he only had to remain sober-ish a few days a month – and when he did get drunk and disorderly, he had more money than most to pay the fines and stay free. 'Who wouldn't be a hangman?' the paper asked.

Gately's next spate of floggings went a long way to refilling his coffers. He'd get another £5 for tending to rapist James Ashe on 21 August at Ballarat. Gately used his own belt to pinion the man, gave him nine feet of rope and what was reported as an instant death. Bumpologist barber James Doubleday then did his thing, while Gately gathered Ashe's clothes and carried them to a cab that awaited to take him to the railway station. *The Courier* correctly predicted: 'These clothes will probably be found upon an effigy of Jim Ashe in the Melbourne waxworks a day or two hence.'

A crowd awaited Gately that night at Geelong station, surrounding the train to gaze in at the rough-looking character. But when this man stepped from his carriage, fans were disappointed because they'd been admiring the wrong fellow. Gately had actually passed through on the midday train. But a few days hence, Melburnians could gaze on the hangman at their leisure.

With *Lee's Pictorial Weekly Budget Police News: Tales, Trials, Sports and Events*, publisher Richard Egan Lee did for Melbourne newspapers what Sohier had done for waxworks. Launched in August 1875, this high-circulating and eye-popping forerunner to modern tabloids offered stories of sex, scandal and slaughter that were infinitely splashier for their nightmarishly rendered amateur illustrations. Readers could salivate over graphic yarns like 'Death of a Schoolboy, Caused by Furious Driving', 'A Fanatical Fool Saws His Right Hand Off' and 'Horrible Deeds of a Mad Chinaman'.

The 21 August 1876 issue of the *Police News* offered up Michael Gately on the front page. The picture was of James Ashe on the gallows, the hangman lowering the white cap. By the paper's standards, it was tame and not much more than a stick figure and happy face; the article was also straightforward and mostly plagiarised from a mainstream report. But inside this issue, readers could revel in a shocking view of Gately giving child rapist James Trevarrow the first fifty of his 150 lashes. The engraved image showed torrents of gore pouring from the man's back as the flagellator stood nearby, cat-o'-nine-tails in hand, smiling widely, eyes filled with delight.

The accompanying article – this one reading like an original report – told how Gately had thrown down sand on the grass to ensure his footing and then insulted the man as he laid in, sending blood and flesh flying. After his victim was untied and collapsed unconscious, the hangman went through his little ritual: 'Gately bowed to the officers, took up his cats in his arms with a tender solicitude which showed how much he loved them, and retired, evidently regretting that the horrible duty of flogging, which he so much revels in, was over.'

The pictures in the *Police News* were so crude that any resemblance to Gately was purely coincidental. But his name, habits and brutality were now before the paper's large readership, which – as the establishment newspapers sniffed – comprised the lower classes. Many were members of the city's army of larrikins.

Around the time Gately first appeared in the *Police News*, he was sitting on the steps outside Inspector-General Duncan's office waiting for his pay when he got talking with a young woman. Mary Jane Parsons was girlish at four-foot-nine, with grey eyes, brown hair and a fresh complexion. Born in Victoria in 1860, she was an orphan by March 1874, when she and another girl were arrested for misbehaving with boys at Flemington. Mary was sentenced to a year in gaol for vagrancy. Released with remissions in January 1875, she got a job as a domestic servant with a gentleman at Windsor. While society shuddered at Gately, this girl was taken with him. And that made him – *them* – comically newsworthy.

Mary soon quit her job to shack up with Gately in a house they'd managed to rent in Hotham. The happy couple would even get a dog called Smoker. All that was left was to make it official. But Mary was nineteen and still a minor, so it was up to a magistrate to permit her to marry.

In early September, the couple sought out the famed charity worker and gaol evangelist Dr John Singleton. Would he write a recommendation? He obliged, and Gately and Mary took his referral to the magistrate Mr Sturt. Mary told her orphan story. Gately explained how they'd met. But Mr Sturt had recently been unsympathetic to the hangman when he howled about his hair being hacked off. There was no way he was allowing this unholy matrimony.

Gately protested that the law shouldn't put up obstacles to him mending his ways. Mr Sturt asked if he'd renounce his profession as hangman. Gately said he wouldn't. He said he'd rather scrag one man than flog a dozen, because the latter was hard work and didn't pay well enough. Mr Sturt told the lovers to get lost. Gately and his fiancée left in disappointment. Reports said some people present tried to persuade her away from the executioner, while others wanted him locked up as a means to set her free. But Mary stood by her hangman.

The *Police News* relished the court scene, giving it a big illustration, making it one of Australia's earliest tabloid love scandals. The mainstream newspapers also couldn't resist the hangman wanting to tie the 'matrimonial noose'. *The Herald* called it 'a startling revelation' of Gately's domestic life. *The Hamilton Spectator* offered: 'Love, we know, takes strange directions at times ... but who would have thought a very nice-looking and respectable young woman of eighteen, employed in good service, should have thrown herself upon and now desire to marry ... a repulsive-looking hangman of fifty years of age.' Yet the often vitriolic *Ovens and Murray Advertiser* said that although he was 'one of the lowest of his species ... there is no reason why a hangman should not get married'. The story was picked up around Australia, running in Sydney's *Evening News* as 'A Hangman in Love!'

*The Herald* had an update about Gately loitering around the Supreme Court, hoping to argue his case. But there was no need. Magistrate Henri J Hart gave permission for the marriage. On 7 September, at the Independent Chapel in Collingwood, the Reverend John Strongman of Adelaide married the lovebirds.

In the wake of this wedding, *The Australasian* struck a rare reflective note to say that just as hangings were private, so should be the personal life of the hangman. Further newspapers should stop referring to his job as a 'repulsive office', because without him the sheriff would have to hang people. 'Ought we not rather to regard the executioner as the avenger of justice, and in that sense the protector of innocence?'

This sentiment evaporated when Gately pushed things too far by claiming recognition as a civil servant. He sent a letter to Premier James McCulloch, published in *The Herald* on Saturday 16 September 1876:

Having acted as the public executioner since the death of Bamford, and as the nature of the duties preclude me from obtaining other employment, I beg respectfully to ask that you will take into your consideration, this, my application, vis., to be paid in future by salary instead of by fee for each execution, with quarters in the neighbourhood of the gaol, or wherever the Government may deem it most expedient to locate me, as is done in the neighboring colonies of Tasmania, New South Wales, and Queensland. I have difficulty in obtaining lodgings, and consequently have frequently to sleep in the scrub on the banks of the Yarra, which results in the police locking me up, and my being convicted for vagrancy. Trusting you will take my application into your kind consideration, I have the honor to be, sir, your most obedient, humble servant.

Gately was only asking for fair play – and indeed for what Jack Harris had got thirty years earlier. But *The Herald* now mocked him for not spending his honeymoon 'in idle dalliance'. It warned he'd probably also want a nice suit to go with his salary and house. Gately might then expect invitation to official balls so he could appear with rapier, cocked hat and blushing bride on his arm. Marriage had spurred 'his "vaulting ambition," which perhaps may end in his "falling on t'other side"'.

*The Herald* may have mangled its *Macbeth* a little, but its prediction would prove right by the following night.

~

Sunday was supposed to be a day of rest. But as night fell on the newly-weds' nest in Hotham, a crowd of larrikins gathered and started pelting the house with stones. When Gately stepped outside, he was bombarded. Chased by the missile-throwing mob, he bolted for the one place he thought he'd be protected – Melbourne Gaol. The hangman holed up there for three hours before he felt safe enough to go to the Russell Street police barracks to make a complaint. Then he returned to Mary.

The attack was reported in the next morning's papers. *The Argus* helpfully informed readers that the Gatelys lived in a right-of-way off Bedford Street. *The Age* splashed fuel on the fire by saying he left Mary 'in the house at the mercy of the mob had they wished to do her any harm', even though it was evident that his running had drawn them away.

That night, a larger larrikin army staged a bigger assault on the house.

*The Herald* belatedly saw sense in Gately's request of the premier. While the hangman shouldn't be a public servant, he deserved protection like any citizen, and while his work was shocking and repulsive, the service he provided was indispensable. So if people wouldn't rent him rooms or serve him food, the authorities should, in the interests of 'our reason and our humanity', provide both 'where the dread of hourly assault may not disturb him'.

These were calming words. Yet *The Herald* concluded its compassionate new approach by bringing Mary into the imagination of readers in a new and repulsive way. If the couple was made safe and comfortable, the paper suggested, they 'might favor the Government with a race of hereditary hangmen'.

With the police providing no protection, the authorities not offering accommodation and the newspaper coverage fanning the flames with visions of hangbabies, the Gatelys forfeited the rent they'd paid and fled to hide out in a rough hut on the banks of the Yarra.

The following Friday night, they were spotted at the corner of William and Little Collins streets and chased by a mob of thirty larrikins. They sought protection from Constable Stewart but this didn't deter the thugs, who threw stones that hit the hangman and his wife and also wounded the policeman. Gately and the constable went on the offensive. The officer chased down one larrikin, while the hangman ran down another, hauling the offenders to the lock-up.

The next morning, *The Age* reported this latest larrikin attack and said Gately and Mary had narrowly escaped serious injury and that they had been singled out since their marriage. The paper also reported that the hangman was to testify against the two larrikins that morning. When he and his wife arrived, the city court was surrounded by a huge crowd, who stared, stalked, besieged and abused the couple. Inside the court, Mr Sturt, who'd precipitated this chaos by turning Gately's matrimony into a controversy, gave the larrikins a reprimand and fined them ten shillings each.

As the Gatelys left under police guard, the hooting crowd of 500 men, women and children followed them through the streets and tried to provoke a fight. With violence set to erupt, Superintendent Frederick

Winch ordered Inspector William Montford to use a small party of police to clear the thoroughfare. A constable tried to usher Gately and Mary through a laneway at the back of the post office, but a red-coated official refused to let them pass. The crowd howled and unleased fresh abuse. *The Argus* recorded the action: 'Gately became perfectly enraged, sprang forward and seized one man by the cravat, and proceeded to drag him to the watchhouse ... The crowd became excited, and a disturbance of a serious nature seemed imminent.'

A constable persuaded Gately to release his prisoner, and the hangman and his wife were escorted back to the watch house as the larrikins booed and vowed harm. The police took the besieged Gately back before the court, hoping to charge him with vagrancy and have a reason to lock him up. The magistrates – usually so happy to toss a hangman in gaol – for once refused.

Mr Sturt said it was only boys outside: the police should go and beat them with sticks. If anyone brought assault charges, he added, he'd only fine the constables a farthing. Superintendent Winch and some men were able at least to clear the crowd from Swanston Street, where the traffic was almost at a standstill of impatient pedestrians and banked coaches. But Gately and Mary remained in the watch house for hours until the mob eventually melted away.

Late that night, Gately, Mary and another woman were crossing the Falls Bridge. Mary said her boots hurt. Gately told her to cut them, presumably to make them looser. It's unclear why, but she went under the bridge to do so; at this point, a young sailor named James Ryan threw her to the ground and tried to rape her. The hangman caught him and dragged him to custody. On Monday, Gately testified in court. But the magistrate concluded, as *The Argus* reported, that he had 'subjected his wife to degradation for the purpose of entrapping the prisoner. The evidence was quite unfit for publication.' The circumstances of the boots and the bridge were odd. But exactly why Gately would want to entrap this man wasn't explained. Nevertheless James Ryan was free to go.

An *Age* writer would later recall another attack on Gately from around this time. A heavy storm had turned the streets into raging streams. 'The state of the surroundings provided evil suggestion to the larrikins, who tied a rope around Gately's middle and threw him into a gutter. He was borne, rolling over and over, a considerable distance, and was only rescued, half suffocated and severely bruised, by the intervention of a policeman.'

Such chaos led *The Herald* – which had mocked Gately's entreaty to the premier – to say the government urgently needed to solve 'The Gately Difficulty'. It reported that he'd vowed to keep his head down if he was allowed to live in a cottage inside the gaol which was then standing empty.

*The Age* – which had helped put a target on the hangman's back by alleging his ungallant cowardice – said it was best now for the newspapers to just ignore him, because all this publicity had made him think he was 'a man of some importance'.

*The Australasian* – which had so recently called him an 'avenger of justice' and a 'protector of innocence' – agreed that 'Mr Gately mistakes the position altogether'. While it had argued for the dignity of his office, it now said he should live in the scrub, do his job for casual pay and only be seen in in public when he faced court.

*The Argus* – which had published Gately's address – said the government shouldn't give him a salary and lodgings due to his notorious character. It claimed that the authorities believed a 'quieter, less obtrusive, and altogether more eligible man for performing these functions could be procured'. If that was true, where was he?

In its reporting, *The Herald* had helpfully mentioned that Gately and Mary were hiding in a hut by the Yarra. On Sunday 1 October, larrikins came on him in 'his lurking place' and a foul-mouthed stand-off ensued on the South Wharf. The paper said that if the government didn't find a 'habitat' for the hangman, more 'disgraceful scenes' would follow and 'possibly terminate in bloodshed'.

A few days later, *The Herald* took up his cause again in an article headlined 'Give the Hangman a Home'. Gately didn't deserve 'to be hunted like Cain, and almost driven to brutal acts by brutal treatment'. Solving the problem was not a Herculean one. It could be done at the stroke of a pen. The chief secretary just had to write a letter to Inspector-General Duncan, telling him to provide quarters and rations. Yet in this very same editorial, *The Herald* further demonised Gately as a 'very ill-conducted hangman', a 'disgraceful nuisance', an 'unmitigated scoundrel' and a 'repulsive animal'.

There's a good chance the government knew it didn't have to act because Gately would solve the problem himself. After all, the man was a criminal drunkard who'd been in gaol almost continuously since arriving in Victoria. Two days after the wharf scene, Gately obliged with a double assault.

In the Botanic Gardens, Gately, his wife and a companion street wastrel named Mary Greenwood got into a fracas with a carter named James Walsh, the hangman delivering a severe beating to the man. Later that day, near the Immigrants' Home, Gately assaulted a man named William Buck, then lashed out at constables and swam across the swamp near the governor's palace, where he further resisted arrest.

The next day, in court, victim William Buck didn't show up to testify against Gately. But constables sustained the charge against him, and the mayor sentenced him to three months with hard labour. His Honour also gave a startling legal opinion that Gately 'was a savage brute, and that he would best serve society by hanging himself'. The more serious assault charge against Gately couldn't be heard because the victim was still too injured to appear.

Public excitement over the hangman – of whom *The Age* said 'there exists no man in Victoria of such bad repute' – intensified with his committal hearing on 9 October. The Prahran Court was crowded to suffocation, its yard packed. In the surrounding streets, *The St Kilda Telegraph* reported, 'two or three thousand people of all class gathered'. The paper got an eyeful of the unlovely couple: 'His features are anything but attractive, in fact a more morose or degraded-looking creature could scarcely be imagined, and his better-half, though infinitely his superior in facial development, is the picture of debasement.'

Victim James Walsh testified that he'd been leading his horse and cart through the Botanic Gardens when Mary Gately and Mary Greenwood had asked him for some tobacco. When he said he didn't have any, Gately jumped from behind a bush, demanded tobacco and then tried to hit him on the head with a fence paling. Walsh had protected himself with his arm, which was paralysed by the blow, and he fell to the ground. Gately kicked him, and shouted, 'You ———, I'll eat you!' He pinned Walsh down and 'worried' a chunk from the man's cheek.

The carter was so stunned, he didn't know how he got free. Next thing he knew, he was running after his fleeing horse while Gately and the women pelted him with rocks. The victim said he'd been under medical care since the attack and had been unable to work. Gately was committed to stand trial.

The Marys, 'a couple of dirty-looking creatures', were next brought up. The bench heard from the police that they'd previously been turned out of the Botanic Gardens for 'preying upon persons', and Gately was 'always lying in ambush to assist them in their designs'. The Marys were each sentenced to six months with hard labour.

Outside court, the threatening mob remained at the ready. The police waited for an hour before they hurried their prisoners through the town hall to a horse cab to whisk them away. As the conveyance rushed off, the crowd sent up a 'deafening chorus of groans'. At Melbourne Gaol, Gately and Mary were separated to go to their respective cells in the men's and women's sections. They had been married one month.

When Gately went to trial for malicious wounding and assault, Mary Greenwood testified that Walsh had provoked him by calling him a loafer. She said it'd been more of a fair fight than a cowardly ambush. There were reports that Walsh had a 'mark' on his face, rather than a chunk of cheek missing. In his statement, Gately said he'd acted in self-defence, for he was under continual attack from the larrikins.

Justice James Stephen told the jury that Gately's reputation and persecution had no bearing on the case. He offered: 'If people had the misfortune to be disliked, the best thing they could do was to keep out of the way.' The judge reminded them that Gately had admitted he had 'thrust himself' upon Walsh, who, His Honour noted, was 'small and weak', while the accused was 'strong and powerful'.

Gately was found guilty. The judge gave him the maximum punishment of three years with hard labour.

*The Mercury* – a recently launched Fitzroy paper – naively commented that 'Wanted: A Hangman' advertisements would soon run in *The Age* and *The Argus*. But there was no need. Victoria had solved the 'Gately Difficulty'. The hangman would be sober and available for work in Pentridge and Melbourne Gaol for the next three years.

# CHAPTER TWENTY

# The £20 Gang to Hang

Justice James Stephen had put Michael Gately back in gaol. Two months later, in December 1876, His Honour sentenced Swiss-Italian Basilio Bondietti to go to the hangman for the murder of his mate Carlo Comisto at Sandy Creek.

This was another controversial case. Comisto may not have been dead – he might've merely taken off, as the accused had claimed. No body had been found, just calcined bone fragments and bloodstains that both a doctor and chemist believed were human. Yet they might equally have come from game butchered and eaten by the men over the past year. Bondietti barely spoke English. So testimony from witnesses about supposedly contradictory claims he'd made in the wake of his friend's disappearance could well have been lost in translation.

The jury found Bondietti guilty but recommended mercy on account of his being old and a foreigner. Before sentencing, the convicted man made a rambling statement about having had an argument with his mate and not seeing him afterwards. Justice Stephen cut him off and sentenced him to death. The Executive Council refused the jury's recommendation. The impending execution was vigorously debated in parliament, with critics saying the government had to be certain a murder had been committed before hanging a man.

Days before Bondietti was due to die, 150 people gathered at the Town Hall and resolved to petition the governor to respite him for one month. Among the delegation to His Excellency was a jury member who said he and his fellows believed Bondietti was guilty of killing Comisto in the heat of a quarrel and this was why they'd recommended mercy. But their foreman had failed to explain this properly in court when delivering the guilty verdict.

Dr LL Smith, still an opponent of capital punishment, told His Excellency there was no evidence Comisto was dead, and the public believed this hanging would be 'judicial murder'. Solicitor David Gaunson – recently elected to parliament, and a leading light in the liberal opposition to the McCulloch government – was another Bondietti supporter. His leader, Graham Berry, who by then had already briefly been premier, also argued in parliament that a miscarriage of justice was about to be done. But the Executive Council wouldn't budge and the governor refused to exercise the royal prerogative.

On the morning of the execution, Sir George Stephen – a QC, eminent British anti-slavery activist and father of Justice Stephen – handed a protest letter to Sheriff Wright arguing that the execution shouldn't go ahead until the petition he'd sent to London was considered by the secretary of state for the colonies. The sheriff would do no such thing.

Gately pinioned Bondietti and led him to the drop. The man was asked twice in Italian if he wanted to say anything. He didn't reply. '[H]e did not appear to understand one word ...' *The Herald* reported. 'It appeared as though he were oblivious of all around him save the horrible reality of his doom'. Gately was told: 'Do your duty.' He did, but didn't lower the white cap, and so for once the witnesses saw what a man looked like as he hanged. Fortunately, this death, as *The Argus* wrote, 'was almost instantaneous, there being very few writhings of the body and the features did not appear much discomposed'. Bondietti was cut down after half an hour, rather than the customary hour.

~

Among those present at Bondietti's doom was John Stanley James, then thirty-three, an English journalist who'd changed his name to Julian Thomas but who wrote under the sobriquet 'Vagabond'. He'd arrived in Victoria around October 1875, and in the vein of Marcus Clarke sought to show the side of the city most never saw. His angle was going undercover in places such as the Immigrants' Home and the Kew Lunatic Asylum. The mystery of his identity added to the sensation his articles were to cause. 'Who is Vagabond?' would be the oft-repeated question.

Vagabond had likely written the straightforward account of Bondietti's execution that appeared in *The Argus*. In any case, he privately credited Gately with the 'neatness' of the hanging. But he also noted that 'the man's brutal appearance corresponded with his vocation, and I could well believe that he enjoyed his work, and that he was guilty of the atrocities for which he is now undergoing punishment'.

Just a month later, Vagabond got a much closer look at that face, when he went undercover at Pentridge for a month by claiming enough medical knowledge to be hired as an assistant to the doctor. Within half an hour of arriving, as Vagabond was being shown around by prison surgeon Dr Reed, a warder came to the hospital and said: 'I've just come up from A Division, and there's Ballyram wants a tooth out. Will you go down there, sir?'

Vagabond asked who this 'Ballyram' might be. When told it was one of the nicknames for the hangman Michael Gately, the fake medical assistant was enthusiastic: 'I did not mind giving him a little pain.' He stood ready, he said, to pull every tooth from Gately's head. The warder took him to A Division and led him to cell 93. The hangman sprang to attention as the door was unlocked. Vagabond's description of Gately appears touched by phrenology:

A frightful animal – the immense head, powerful protruding jaw, narrow receding forehead and deficient brain space, seemed fitly joined to tremendous shoulders and long, strong arms, like those of a gorilla, which he resembles more than a man. All the evil passions appeared to have their home behind that repellent, revolting countenance.

Vagabond stayed in character, ordering Gately to open his foul jaws. He then set to work, joking to the warders that they should bang the patient's head against the wall if he struggled too much. 'I took out the largest and strongest pair of forceps, which would pull a tooth out of a crocodile,' Vagabond wrote. 'One grip, a roar from Gately, a twist of the wrist, and out came the tusk.'

The journalist, who was amused Gately had cynically converted to Judaism so he could partake of Passover cake, did reflect on the hangman with some compassion, writing that the man once had some good in him, which had led him to save the guards back in 1859; those who knew him said his conduct had deteriorated since he became the executioner.

Poor Gately. All the world is down on him, and when free he had not a place to lay his head. A natural brute, he is as God, or the devil, made him, for it is hard to believe that any spark of aught Divine can rest in such a frame.

Vagabond also had a scary run-in with Frank Neville, 'an outrageous ruffian ... and the terror of his fellow prisoners'. The murderer accused the undercover reporter of attempted poisoning because he believed a similar attempt had previously been made to kill him. After Vagabond told off Neville, he was advised by a warder that it was better to humour the homicidal maniac as he couldn't be held back by half-a-dozen men and was 'nearly mad sometimes'. Such reporting made Senior-Constable Arthur Steele's various Rowdy Flat tangles with the brute more impressive for resulting in arrests rather then the policeman being torn limb from limb.

In contrast to Gately and Neville, Vagabond believed that 'Harry Power, the renowned bushranger' was something of a saint. 'It was worth while spending a month in Pentridge to make the acquaintance of this man, the last and the best of the class of criminals who made themselves feared throughout the land,' he enthused.

Power was then seriously ill, but not too sick to talk the under-cover reporter's ear off, and Vagabond lapped it up. Unlike other petty prisoners, this 'king of men' had risked his life 'hundreds of times against overwhelming odds'. But Power lamented the lonely life of the bushranger – and that a partner he had taken on had turned out to be a junior Judas.

> I always was stuck for a want of a mate. There's young Kelly was with me for a time, but he was no good, and helped to sell me at last. They say that he or one of the Quinns was dressed up as a black tracker to deceive me. God will judge them for taking the blood money.

Power's belief about Kelly dressing as a black tracker was wrong, but he still regarded his old accomplice as a black snake. So did Vagabond, who predicted of Kelly and the Quinns: 'The measure they meted out to Power will be meted out to them at last, for the "friendships" they have formed are not likely to remain proof against the temptation to earn the "blood-money" which may be won by a word.'

~

'A Month In Pentridge' was reprinted in pamphlet form in series three of *The Vagabond Papers*. The articles were also widely syndicated, including in *The Ovens and Murray Advertiser*, which circulated in Wangaratta, where now-Sergeant Arthur Steele had been transferred a few months earlier. It's likely the lawman would've been pleased to read of Frank Neville's paranoias. Similarly, Steele surely enjoyed Kelly's reputation being poisoned by Harry Power and Vagabond's prediction the outlaw would himself be betrayed for 'blood money'. All of that was because the Sergeant was on Ned's trail.

After three years of living lawfully – or at least not getting caught – Kelly and the 'Greta mob' – who dressed in flash larrikin fashion, itself an echo of the old Ribbon and Jew Boy gangs – were running a massive horse-stealing operation that straddled Victoria and New South Wales. Among their number was Dan Kelly, Joe Byrne, Steve Hart, William 'Brickey' Williamson, William Skilling/Skillion, Aaron Sherritt, Isaiah 'Wild' Wright and even Ned's old bushranging hero Allen Lowry. Now Sergeant Steele was trying to bring them down – and this involved keeping surveillance on Ellen Kelly's home at Greta.

In mid-July 1877, Sergeant Steele scored a victory when he nabbed Steve Hart for horse stealing. The lad received two sentences totalling twelve months in Beechworth Gaol. In September, Ned got drunk with Constable Alexander Fitzpatrick, who'd befriended him, and was subsequently taken to the Benalla lock-up for being disorderly. On his way to face court, he got into a brawl with Fitzpatrick and three other police, including Constable Thomas Lonigan, who allegedly 'blackballed' Kelly by gripping his testicles and squeezing them violently. Refusing to yield to the police, Kelly surrendered to a miller and Justice of the Peace named McInnes. The story went that in the wake of his wounding, the larrikin had supposedly said: 'Lonigan, I never shot a man yet, but if ever I do, so help me, you will be the first.' For this affray, Kelly received fines of just over £4. But his balls, he'd say, would cause him excruciating pain for years – until, that was, he happened on a bloody cure.

Soon after, Ned's brother Dan and cousins Tom and Jack Lloyd were on the run from charges of breaking, entering and theft during a home invasion. Kelly, understanding from Fitzpatrick that they weren't facing serious trouble, got the boys to surrender. Even though the trio were acquitted of the main charges, they were dealt a harsh sentence for destroying property: three months' hard labour each.

~

During this period, in March 1877, Michael Gately hanged wife-killer William Hastings. This was the first Melbourne Gaol execution supervised by Robert Rede, appointed sheriff after the sudden death of his old Eureka contrarian Wright the previous month – deputy Louis Ellis having been passed over yet again for the top job. Rede had nothing to complain about this time: Hastings' death was reported as instantaneous. The new Melbourne sheriff also kept the numbers down so that only thirty or so people were present, all of them officials, medical men or reporters.

The *Police News* went all-out with a special 'execution' edition, its front page displaying a comic book-style series of images depicting the doomed man's last moments. A circular centre panel featured Gately, with his ghoulish smile, lowering the cap before the drop. 'Gateley [*sic*] Performs His Office' read the cheerful banner. The final image showed the hanging body with the caption: 'It Is Finished'.

Gately had finished Hastings, but the hangman still had two years to serve, which made it surprising when he was found propping up a bar in Cootamundra in New South Wales. Strong, powerfully built, six feet tall, about fifty years old and with a most forbidding countenance, he was attired in torn and filthy old clothes. As he guzzled beer, his lips loosened and he told several other drinkers that yes, he was Gately, the Victorian finisher of the law. Someone in the bar *did* recognise him – just not from down south but from due east. This fellow asked 'Gately' if he'd ever been to New Zealand. He said yes, in fact, he knew more of that place than he did of New South Wales. Further questions brought the truth: this wasn't Gately, the hangman, but Joseph Sullivan, the Maungatapu murderer. Once he'd been identified, the killer vamoosed and vanished into the night, his destination as mysterious as his motivation for claiming to be Melbourne's hangman. But the fiend's whereabouts would remain on the minds of many, including Ned Kelly.

If Gately learned of this imposture, he might have been pleased by the homage. But he would have been less happy at other news. In November 1877 *The Herald* ran an article headlined 'The Hangman's Bride' that reported that Mary, her sister and 'two other wood nymphs' who haunted the timbers of the wharves had been found 'guilty of amorous dalliances with some mariners'. The paper thought this disgrace might mean that she'd face 'mild chastisement' when her 'loving lord' was released from gaol, if he were of 'jealous disposition'. Mary got a month in gaol from old friend Mr Sturt. In February 1878, she'd get another three months for vagrancy.

Gately's monotonous gaol sentence was at least broken up by his trips to Pentridge to serve up scourgings. In April 1878, *The Age* reported a double, saying he 'performed his work with great vigor, and seemed to enjoy the exercise'.

~

In the middle of that month, when Constable Fitzpatrick visited the Kelly homestead to take Dan Kelly into custody on a horse stealing warrant, he was hit on the head by Ellen and shot in the wrist by Ned, before being sent on his way to claim he'd been the victim of attempted murder. The Kelly version was that Ned hadn't even been there, and later the story was to be that Fitzpatrick had made drunken advances on young Kate Kelly. In this account the constable had simply been shown the door by Dan and Ellen, before wounding himself to fit them up.

Conflicting stories aside, this was the flashpoint. Sergeant Steele watched the Kelly household for a few hours, then rode in to question Ellen and Kate. He and Senior-Constable Anthony Strahan would soon arrest Ellen, then looking after her three-day-old baby Alice, as well as next-door neighbours and Greta mob members Brickey Williamson and William Skilling/Skillion – who'd married Maggie Kelly in 1873. Ned and Dan were now on the run, and would be joined by Joe Byrne and then Steve Hart when he got out of gaol.

By the end of April, Ned had a £100 reward on his head. *The Ovens and Murray Advertiser* a month later reported:

We know Ned Kelly to be a lawless desperado, who, if driven into a corner, would stop at nothing, and who, now that he is wanted, must sooner or later do something serious, and therefore in the interests of public safety, it is incumbent upon the Government to do everything in their power to effect his capture.

Sergeant Steele would be central to that hunt. He knew the Kellys and their type, and had already put some of them behind bars. Patrick Sheehan had swung. Frank Neville was inside Pentridge for twenty-one years. Steele usually got his man. But according to *The Herald*, Ellen Kelly's parting words to her son had been: 'Ned, be sure you are not taken alive.'

~

Governor Castieau wanted to make Melbourne Gaol a more pleasant place. This included gardens with flowers and vegetables. In July 1878 it meant planting trees out on a street frontage. Some specimens had already been put in by Judge Barry, but had died. Nevertheless, His

Honour arrived to boss Castieau around.

The amused governor noted that, as the pompous jurist approached, 'Sir Redmond's continuations were a little disarranged & I notified the fact to him by a pantomime action & whisper of "buttons your honor".' Barry quickly did up his flies and thanked Castieau – before holding forth at length about how to plant the trees, what to name them and the art of pruning the vines growing inside the gaol.

By the time Castieau resumed his diary years later, some of Melbourne Gaol's flowers had reportedly given Ned Kelly his last moment of beauty.

~

On 9 October 1878, at Beechworth, Ellen Kelly, Williamson and Skilling/Skillion were tried for aiding and abetting an attempted murder. Back in May, during the committal, Fitzpatrick had testified that after three shots and a scuffle, with the others in the room pointing revolvers, Ned Kelly had said, 'That will do, boys.' Then he'd turned to 'Skillion' – who was in fact Joe Byrne – and said: 'You ——, why didn't you tell me who was here?' To the wounded constable, he said: 'If I had known it was you, Fitzpatrick, I would not have fired, but none of the other —— would have left here alive.' Then Fitzpatrick had fainted.

When he came around, Ned was talking to Williamson. Ned was supposedly saying that Skillion/Byrne would have shot Sergeant Steele the other day if he – Ned – hadn't intervened. To which Skillion/Byrne reckoned 'he had a pill for Sergeant Steele one of these days' – a 'pill' as in a bullet.

But in October, at the trial, Fitzpatrick testified that 'Kelly said to Skillion, "Bill would have given that fellow a pill who passed to-day." Skillion replied, "What, the Benalla cove." "No," said Ned, "Sergeant Steele: but I've got one for him yet."'

Fitzpatrick's version had questionable elements. For one, why he'd been shot by a man with whom he'd been on reasonable terms, and yet been allowed to live and leave. *The Ovens and Murray Advertiser*'s view was Fitzpatrick had fallen 'into a trap designed not for him, but for someone else who has made himself particularly obnoxious to the Kelly family'. Kelly had heard a policeman was at the house to arrest Dan, 'and imagining the arresting Constable was a man against whom he had special hatred, he rushed in and fired, with the deliberate desire to commit murder. He shot the wrong man ...'

This incident would ever after be subject to claim and counterclaim. While Kelly had plenty of police enemies, Fitzpatrick's testimony made it seem Steele had been foremost in Ned's mind that crucial day.

Ellen, Williamson and Skillion were found guilty. Three days later, Justice Barry sent Ellen Kelly to gaol for three years. The men got six years each. In sentencing, Barry said he hoped 'this would lead to the disbanding of the gang of lawless persons, who have for years banded themselves together in that neighbourhood against the police'.

Just over a week later, two parties of plain-clothes police were secretly despatched to catch the Kelly Gang. One was from Greta, composed of five men to have been commanded by Steele, but he was called away on court business and was replaced by Senior Constable Anthony Strahan. The other, from Mansfield and heading north into the Wombat Ranges, was led by Sergeant Michael Kennedy and comprised Constables Thomas Lonigan, Michael Scanlan and Thomas McIntyre.

Being out bush could be boring. Reading would help pass the time. McIntyre had recently bought the *Vagabond Papers* pamphlet containing the Pentridge article and found its revelations about Kelly and Harry Power intriguing. Now he gave it to Lonigan to read during their trek.

On the morning of 26 October 1878, at Stringybark Creek, Kennedy and Scanlan ventured out from camp while McIntyre and

Lonigan remained behind. In the middle of the day, McIntyre baked bread and shot some birds for dinner, while Lonigan engrossed himself in Vagabond's undercover report of 'Ballyram', Frank Neville and Harry Power.

Around 5pm, after the two police constables had made a big fire, Kelly and his gang suddenly rushed the camp. In a few desperate moments, Ned shot Lonigan dead and then the outlaws bailed up McIntyre. While the bushrangers and their captive awaited the return of Kennedy and Scanlan, Kelly said Fitzpatrick was the cause of all of this, and that his mother had been unfairly gaoled. He asked McIntyre to get his comrades to surrender when they returned, and in return he'd let them all live. Kelly said if they had been the other party – which he mistakenly believed was still led by Steele – they would not have been so lucky. As McIntyre would initially tell it: 'He made enquiries about four different men, and said he would roast each of them alive if he caught them. Steele and Flood were two of the four named.' Constable Ernest Flood was the married man who in 1872 had been involved with Ned's older sister Annie, her own husband then in gaol. Annie died days after giving birth to Flood's child – a tragedy that met Ned when he was released from Pentridge. Flood was also, according to Kelly, deeply involved in horse-stealing.

Later, McIntyre's testimony would be expanded, with McIntyre testifying as to what Kelly had said:

> At first I thought you were Flood, and it is a good job for you that you are not, because if you had been, I would not have shot you, but I would have roasted you upon that fire. There are four men in the police force, and if ever I lay hands on them I will roast them. They are Fitzpatrick, Flood, Steele and Strahan. Strahan has been blowing that he will take me single-handed.

Kelly then interrogated McIntyre about the weapons the other party was carrying. When told, he said, 'Well, that looks very like as if they came out to shoot me.'

McIntyre said they were just obeying orders.

Kelly replied: 'They are not ordered to go about the country shooting people.'

His story would be that – despite the earlier 'blackballing' – he had only shot Lonigan in self-defence and because he had believed him to be Strahan. Kelly would claim that what happened next was also a kill-or-be-killed fair fight.

On 27 October 1878, Melbourne learned that Lonigan and Scanlan had been foully murdered at Stringybark Creek. Kennedy was missing, presumed dead, and his body would be found soon after shot in cold blood while lying wounded against a tree. McIntyre had survived to tell the tale by galloping off on a horse and then hiding in a wombat hole.

Among the police equipment and possessions taken by Kelly, McIntyre would say, was his copy of the *Vagabond Papers* pamphlet. When the excitement died down and the boredom of being a bush fugitive set in, Ned could at leisure read how Harry Power still thought him a blackguard after all these years and how Sergeant Steele's infamous adversary Frank Neville was seemingly mad as he approached a decade in Pentridge. Not that Kelly had to worry about seeing his old mentor or going insane behind bars; if he was caught with the blood of three police on his hands, he'd end up in the hands of the man the Vagabond had called a frightful animal with a face of pure evil and a soul devoid of any divine spark. If Ned Kelly hadn't known much about Michael Gately before, he now had a pamphlet containing the only detailed portrait of the man whose job it would be to hang him.

~

The Stringybark murders were terrible news for everyone – except Michael Gately.

If the Kelly gang lived to see trial, then he'd be looking at a payday of some £20. The hangman hoped that was how it went. As 'Peerybingle' wrote in *The Weekly Times*, 'Mr Gately … must take a close interest in the matter, as one who knows that the capture of the miscreants means four fees and four suits of clothes.' This made it sound like a good deal. Yet the dead-or-alive reward for all four Kellys would soon skyrocket from £500 a head to £2000 per man. That was a lot of the sort of blood money Vagabond had predicted would induce a betrayal. Yet if the gang was captured and Gately hanged all four members – finishing the law on behalf of the colony of Victoria – his fee would be just one-quarter of one per cent of the reward that others would carve up.

'The Mansfield Murders' generated bushranger press not seen since the days of Mad Dan Morgan and Ben Hall. These endless stories led *The Colac Herald* to fume that the Kelly thugs were being romanticised with a 'Newgate Calendar style of literature' that was 'demoralising the minds of young Victorians', especially those with 'larrikinish proclivities', by sensationalising the 'abnormal development of the vanity, ignorance and folly of youth into criminality'.

It was now that Professor Nimshi's claim he'd analysed Ned's head back in 1874 was reprinted in the Melbourne press, with all the apparently prescient phrenological details. And anyone wanting to get a look at the face and head of this sudden criminal celebrity only had to step into the waxworks, with Max Kreitmeyer in early November advertising:

WAXWORKS
JUST ADDED,
Life-like Tableau of
The Fatal Encounter Between
Constables LONIGAN and McINTYRE
With the Bushranger, KELLYS and their Gang.

While Michael Gately bided his time, the Kellys and their gang excited further admiration in some quarters with their daring raid at Euroa on 10 December 1878. They didn't use violence, and even their temporary hostages said the four outlaws were handsome, daring and courteous. Soon afterwards, Ned sent the 'Cameron letter' to politician Donald Cameron and Police Superintendent John Sadleir, which set out his side of the story, arguing police persecution and claiming that he'd acted alone and in self-defence at Stringybark Creek. On 9 February, Ned Kelly, who'd written or dictated another version of his autobiographical missive, commanded his gang in an even more daring raid on Jerilderie.

Five later, Gately was released from Pentridge. He'd earned £47 during his time inside. Determined to lead a sober-ish life, he deposited all but £7 in the bank. Gately then called in at the Russell Street police barracks to tell Sub-Inspector James Larner that he stood ready for 'finishing the Kellys' as soon as they were caught. This had to make Gately even more of a larrikin target.

That same month, George Wilson Hall, proprietor of *The Mansfield Guardian*, published the first book about the bushrangers. *The Kelly Gang or the Outlaws of the Wombat Ranges* described the undisguised sympathy and admiration of the 'larrikin class' for their heroes: 'This is more noticeable among the youth in various large centres of population, where, not content with openly avowing their feelings in simple conversation, they congregate occasionally at street corners and elsewhere to sing ballads – hymns of triumph, as it were – in their praise.'

While Gately awaited his duty, he asked Sub-Inspector Larner whether he might have police protection from the larrikins. The answer was still no. Risking limb and life, Gately went to search the city for his wife. After all, it was Valentine's Day.

# CHAPTER TWENTY-ONE

# Where Is Ned Kelly?

Mary Gately had been in the news recently. In October 1878 *The Herald* reported she had been 'on the war path to an alarming extent' in Melbourne and it'd taken three constables to haul her into the lock-up. She was fined. A fortnight later Mary was picked up with a 'harridan named Annie Snowden'. *The Herald* wrote: 'It appeared that the couple had been engaged during the last few nights in accosting men in Bourke street west, and otherwise misconducting themselves.' Mary was fined forty shillings. Tellingly, in court she said her name wasn't Mrs Mary Gately but Mary Jane Parsons.

Two nights after he was released from gaol, Gately found his estranged wife at a lodging house. Mary was woken in her bed to some bad news: her hangman husband was outside and surrounded by a mob of abusive larrikins. This was not a happy reunion. Mary refused to acknowledge him. They argued. He summoned the constables and had her charged with insulting behaviour. A woman couldn't dishonour her husband, even if he was the hangman.

Appearing in court, Mary promised that if dealt with leniently, she'd leave Melbourne immediately for her sister-in-law's place in Gippsland. She was fined ten shillings. Gately was also in court for drunkenness, blaming his lapse into insobriety on the trouble with Mary. He too received a minor fine and, after nipping out to Pentridge to serve up some lashes, was back out, looking for his wife and to cause more havoc.

*The Age* reported Gately's antics on Tuesday 18 February. As colourful as they were, the story paled beside the big feature on that page headlined 'Ned Kelly's Letter'. While the 'Jerilderie Letter' wouldn't be published in full in his lifetime, the newspaper carried closely paraphrased excerpts of its self-justifying defences and allegations, right down to Kelly having written he was 'a widow's son outlawed, and his orders must be obeyed'. It also contained his withering assessment of the police, which held up colonial youth as formidable even when persecuted and downtrodden: 'With regard to the constables in Victoria, he had seen eight or ten who could not take one half-starved larrikin without the aid of a civilian.' The bushranger stood for the larrikins. The hangman made himself their target.

The next afternoon, as the foundation stone of the Exhibition Building was being laid ahead of 1880's Melbourne International Exhibition, and as the city was still buzzing about the revelations in Kelly's letter, Gately was making a pandemonium of Bourke Street, flourishing a great stick, endangering passers-by and plate-glass windows alike. He hit one boy but didn't do much damage, though a swing at another citizen would reportedly have been fatal if it had connected.

It took four constables to subdue Gately, and he tried to kick and bite them as they dragged him to the lock-up. They were followed by a crowd of about 300 men and women, boys and girls, which suggests his rabid behaviour was in part response to larrikin provocation. The senior constable in charge of the lock-up, as the *Portland Guardian* reported, 'narrowly escaped feeling the ugly fangs of the brute in the calf of his leg'. Inspector Montford said the next day in court: 'He is a nuisance and a danger to the whole community; a wild beast, and utterly unfit to be at large.' Gately was ordered to find two sureties of £25 each and to keep the peace for twelve months. As he couldn't come up with two men foolish enough to stand for him, he went back to gaol for the time being.

The hangman was on hand now for finishing the Kellys, if they could be caught. But there was plenty of mockery about the manhunt.

A week after the Jerilderie Letter, *Corowa Free Press* commentator 'Q Vive' penned witheringly sarcastic commentary on the police pursuit of the outlaws. He said Chief Commissioner of Police Frederick Standish was leading the hunt from behind, and was guarded at Benalla by elite constables who were expert trackers in the wilds of Little Collins Street, had got most of their riding experience in Collingwood brothels and disguised themselves so well that a blind man couldn't tell they were troopers from a distance of fifty yards.

Three weeks later, Q Vive published a lengthy fictitious interview with Ned Kelly, in which the outlaw breezily recounted how he and the boys were roaming free and unworried. Q Vive noted that 'Gately is growling at Standish not running you in', and that the hangman claimed the government was defrauding him of fees and wanted them to pay interest. 'Kelly' replied: 'Well, yes, I think Gately has a good action for damages against the Commissioner of Police. However, I'll sling him a tenner to keep him quiet. Let's change the conversation. Talking about Gately gives me a crick in the neck.'

There was other fun at this time. A Beechworth wheelwright advertised his fast coaches as being the surefire way to catch the Kellys and get the £8000 reward, and a racehorse was named Ned Kelly because he was sure to outrun all comers as surely as the outlaw was furlongs ahead of the police.

The chase seemed a bigger joke still on April Fool's Day, with the premiere of the comic extravaganza *Catching the Kellys* at the Theatre Royal. Ned and the gang were all on stage, bailing up the bumbling police and making them sing a silly song. *The Sydney Mail* said the performance would delight the 'natural enemies' of the law – the larrikins and outlaw sympathisers. *The Weekly Times* thundered that the 'Kelly atrocities are not a proper subject for mirth', while *The Argus* said the show deserved 'severe condemnation' because it had been written 'for the purpose of ridiculing the police at a time when they most require the moral support of the community'.

The public thought it hilarious. As did *The Herald*, which said there was 'nothing objectionable in it, nor is there anything offensive or bad; for the whole thing is a joke, and full of fun'.

During the show's two-week run, Commissioner Standish got word that Ned's sister Kate was in town, and he sent his detectives out looking for her. The flatfoots had no luck. They ought to have been at the Theatre Royal, because she'd come to Melbourne especially to see *Catching the Kellys*. Kate attended without trying to conceal her identity, and left the city without the police catching up with her. Or at least that was the story, widely reported at the time, which had to add to the general mirth.

~

Michael Gately was out of gaol by June and, though again a private citizen, was accompanied by a Melbourne Gaol warder when he went up to Beechworth Gaol to hang Thomas Hogan for fratricide. Castieau sent a letter to the Beechworth governor saying that while the hangman was legally free to roam, there'd likely be trouble if he did, because he'd drink and might not be able to carry out his duty. But Gately, who drew a crowd at the railway station, surprised them by taking advantage of the gaol quarters and keeping himself sober, and the hanging went off without a hitch.

It turned out he'd been saving his 'customary revels' for Melbourne. When he returned, he cut loose and got fined five shillings. Two hours after Gately walked out of court, he turned his fury on King Street and had to be captured by constable and citizens. They tied him hand and foot and transported him in a cart back to the lock-up. Mary had by now resurfaced, also drunk and savage in the city, attacking a constable who accosted her.

The Gatelys were reunited in court. During the proceedings, it was established that the government owed him £90. For his disorderly conduct, the hangman got three days in gaol.

Immediately upon his release, he was at war with the larrikins on William Street. When the police arrived, he turned from the mob and attacked the constables. In the lock-up he was found to have forty sovereigns, a gold watch on a chain that he'd bought for Mary, a bundle of cigars and a pound of tobacco. Revoltingly, he also had a lock of hair which had belonged to Hogan, *The Ovens and Murray Advertiser* explaining that 'the scoundrel stated he cut [it] from the head of the Beechworth convict after his execution'.

In court the next day, Gately, looking like a wild man, was 'designated as being a vile brute' by the magistrate, who fined him £10 and ordered him pay another £2 to cover the damage he'd done to police uniforms and a cab during his arrest. Gately paid and walked out. *The Herald* was impressed at his 'development into a man of capital'.

Although Mary was reportedly given a month in gaol, no record of this sentence appears in her prison file, which suggests Gately paid a fine to have her go free. A week after their double court appearance, the twosome reunited in Richmond for a pub crawl, before kicking on with more drinks at the house of some mates. Emerging onto the street in the evening, Gately and Mary were larrikin magnets. When constables reached the scene, they told the couple they'd take them into protection. But on arriving at the watch house, Gately was arrested for insulting behaviour and Mary for drunkenness.

Enraged, Gately pulled out a pocket knife and tried to cut his own throat, and was only prevented from doing so by a senior constable. The hangman, *The Argus* said, 'roared and fought more like a wild animal than a human being', before being handcuffed and thrown into a cell. Late in the evening police allowed 'some gentlemen from the Town Hall' into the watch house to gawp at him. Gately's 'rage and fury then knew no bounds; he used the most horrible oaths, and wanted to know why he was to be made a puppet show,' reported the *South Bourke and Mornington Journal*. He attacked the sergeant who'd admitted the audience, the officer escaping and locking the door on the 'now raving maniac'.

No one doubted that Gately was a violent, unbalanced and self-destructive being. But the incident showed how various officials provoked him and escalated his behaviour. Seeking protection from larrikins, Gately and Mary had been arrested under false pretences and charged with offences that would land them back in gaol. Then, after Gately tried to kill himself, he was offered up to punters as a real live Jack Ketch from a Punch & Judy show.

In court, Gately accused the government of robbing him of his liberty and his money, and declared he'd resign and quit the colony. But if he was to do that, he'd first have to be freed. While Mary was discharged on her promise to get out of town, Gately was remanded for a week and then charged with attempting suicide. He was ordered to find £50 in sureties and pay a £50 bail, in default of which he'd serve three months. Back to gaol he went.

Having failed to leave town, Mary was arrested in the city one night for trying to spirit a man away; she had then offered the constable a measly sixpence as a bribe. She got three months in Melbourne Gaol. *The Herald* mocked that 'the loving couple are once more under the same roof, which is to them a home'.

Gately had been unable to quit Victoria. He'd still be on hand to hang Ned Kelly and the gang – if the police ever got their act together. Approaching the first anniversary of Stringybark Creek, the outlaws were nowhere and everywhere. In July 1879 alone, Ned was reported to be comfortably holed up caves in the Buffalo Ranges, flitting about in Castlemaine, exchanging nods with an official in Oxley Shire, outside

Jerilderie and about to launch another raid, and laid up with a severe illness and being nursed by members of the Kelly clan.

Then, in the middle of August 1879, there was excitement at Lancefield when Ned and Steve Hart strode into a bank, pulled out their revolvers and announced, 'We are the Kellys; put your hands up; we have secured the police.' They made off with about £750. But the loss could've been greater – the bushrangers had left £3000 behind!

The only problem was that the Kellys hadn't committed this crime. After other robbers were arrested, *The Herald* had a lark by printing a new 'letter' from Ned in which he protested that he and the boys were hopping mad they'd been mistaken for such amateurs: 'Mr editor, I put it to you, as a man has watch our kareer pretty closely all through, and many a thousand papers we've sold for you, you well know – is it not a vile shame that we should be villyfide in this slanderous way.'

A Kelly letter appeared in September when an Echuca selector came home to find his place broken into. A note on his table read: 'This is the poorest place we have entered since we turned out. Next time you go away leave more tucker, as we can't always live on eggs. We have taken your best horse, which will be returned in three weeks' time.' It was signed 'Ned Kelly and Co.' But the selector's horse hadn't been stolen; and his eggs hadn't been eaten, but instead pelted all over his house. Clearly, country larrikins were having some fun.

Another report soon afterwards said that Ned had escaped from Adelaide aboard the steamer *Chimborazo*, and had left the ship when it reached the Suez Canal. The outlaw might as well have been visiting the pyramids, for all the good the law seemed to be doing in north-eastern Victoria. *The Benalla Standard* reported:

> Regarding the Kellys, there is scarcely a whisper – in fact, the police only laugh when they are jocularly asked, 'What about the Kellys?' or 'You've not caught the Kellys yet?' There are no parties out in search of the

murderers, and a general impression prevails that no further action will be taken by the authorities until the gang break out again.

Although Ned and the gang were dodging the noose, parents and children had some hangman laughs at a Punch & Judy show at Hamilton Carnival in November 1879. Given it was a 'real London-style' production, it would have included the plot that always pleased the crowd. After Punch bashes a policeman to death, he's sentenced to hang by the judge but then induces Jack Ketch to put the noose around his own neck. Once he's finished off the finisher of the law, Punch is carried off to hell on a pitchfork by the Devil.

Would Ned Kelly be like Mr Punch? Would he outwit and outlive everyone? Certainly that was the hope in an 1879 four-page broadsheet of songs celebrating the gang. 'The Ballad of the Kelly Gang' began:

Oh, Paddy dear, and did you hear the news that's going round
On the head of bold Ned Kelly they've placed two thousand pounds
For Dan, Steve Hart, and Byrne, two thousand each they'll give,
But if the sum were double, sure the Kelly boys will live.

~

Gately was released on Christmas Eve. He went to Inspector Montford and asked for a police bodyguard to protect him from the larrikins. The senior officer thought this highly impudent, which can't have filled Gately with seasonal cheer. Nor did running into his wife a few days later. *The Weekly Times* reported:

The ruffian half throttled and twice knocked down his youthful spouse early on Tuesday morning, and on being arrested he, according to Constable Griffin, who was assisted by Senior-constable Drum and

Detective O'Donnell, fought, bit, and kicked like a demon. The officers eventually managed to knock him down, and on the way to the watch-house he drew a knife, with which he attempted to stab Constable Griffin.

Mary told the court she lived in fear of her husband, who'd threatened to kill her several times. Charged with vagrancy and assault, he was sent back to Melbourne Gaol for six months. Life and work went on, and he'd flog up to six men in a single session, the Melbourne *Punch* saluting him in 'Gately's Song':

Great grow the gashes, O!
Larrikins I mashes, O!
The 'biggest licks'
That I go in
Are those amongst the lashes, O!

The same week 'Gately's Song' appeared, *The Benalla Standard* had a new Kelly story. A 'reliable informant' had recently been at local railway station when he saw a young woman he thought one of the Hart family. Wanting to be sure, he asked a little girl nearby if she knew the lady.

'Yes,' the child said, 'that is Miss Hart, Steve's sister.'

The man asked the kid if she'd ever seen Ned Kelly.

'Oh, yes, often; he is at our place sometimes twice a week; he was there last Monday for provisions.'

No sooner had the child spoken than an older girl came and dragged her off, telling her to 'shut up'. Turned out the little dobber was the daughter of the town's storekeeper, and it'd been one of the family's servants who'd silenced her.

*The Benalla Standard*'s report – carried in all the major papers – said that this 'appears to be undoubted proof that Ned Kelly is not only in the district, but located somewhere near Glenrowan'.

# CHAPTER TWENTY-TWO

# Murder Most Fowl

If you were unwell in Ballarat during the late 1870s and in possession of money and education, you might consult the respected Dr Fyffe of Sturt Street. But if you were poorer and had less schooling, you might see Mrs Thursfield in Armstrong Street for a bottle of her 'Synovitic of Stimulating Liniment', the 'never-failing cure for all cases of Rheumatism, Sprains, Lumbago, Asthma, Sore Throat, Diptheria, Enlarged Glands, and in fact any disease that requires an external stimulant'. If Mrs Thursfield's stuff wasn't up to snuff, then 'Raynham's Entericon' was also available around the town, for the 'Immediate Relief and Speedy Cure' of everything from 'Wind in the Stomach' to 'Spermatorrhea'. But should you have more serious problems than excessive farting and unwanted immoral orgasms, it might be time to seek out the nightman-turned-launderer-turned-herbalist Elijah Upjohn.

The years since 1871 involved no serious trouble for Upjohn. But his lower-middle-class life hadn't been without a few newsworthy dramas.

Elijah's son Charles was arrested in November 1873 for loitering in a public place, suspected of being about to commit a felony. His defence was that he was out late because he'd been seeing some ladies home. The court discharged him with a caution.

Three years later, in October 1876, Elijah's youngest son Ernest was playing an accordion in the yard when his music attracted a diamond python. The lad ran for his mother, but when she arrived the snake was gone. Ernest resumed playing, the reptile returned and was killed by a neighbour. This curious yarn about the accidental child snake charmer made news as far away as Sydney and Rockhampton.

But Ernest was in a different sort of trouble the next winter, when he was truant and his father was fined five shillings. Eldest son Alfred, meanwhile, achieved a measure of local fame as a talented skittles player, winning a competition trophy for six weeks running.

In March 1879, magistrate Henry Glenny, who also wrote for *The Star* under the pen-name 'Silverpen', was on the bench when it dismissed an abusive language case Upjohn brought against a neighbour. Minor matter though this was, Glenny, who'd lived in Ballarat for many years, would have known Elijah at least by reputation. Neither could've imagined the circumstances that would put them in the same room the following year.

Elijah's notoriety in Ballarat was increased by his purveying of quack remedies, promoted in a flyer as 'E. Upjohn's cures'. The ingredients weren't reported. Likely they were harmless – ginger, mustard, peppermint, clove, aloe and the like – and when boiled up in combinations might taste medicinal and act as a placebo to relieve minor symptoms. But there were dangers. Some herbalists, for instance, used foxglove for heart troubles – which was good because it contained digitalis, but bad because an overdose caused severe side-effects and even death.

Upjohn didn't kill anyone. In fact, he saved a lot of lives, and the proof was on his flyer. The paper listed the names of a dozen of his patients – ten from Ballarat and two from Geelong – who'd been given up by doctors as hopeless cases. The case histories were wonderful. Number five was breast cancer, which he'd cured in fourteen days. Then there were cases of diarrhoea, rheumatism, blindness, heart and lung disease. All cured! Additionally, the flyer claimed, he had saved many other people at the Ballarat and Geelong hospitals.

Despite the miracles his medicines performed, Upjohn didn't appear to enjoy sustained success with his quackery. So it was that he set himself on the path to his final career as a purveyor of the 'hempen cure'.

~

On Tuesday 27 April 1880, getting on towards midnight, Mr IJ Jones, manager of the Ballarat Banking Company, was with his son in their residence above the bank when they heard a noise. It wasn't the Kelly gang come to break into the vault; it sounded more like someone was out back meddling in the chicken coop.

Jones Junior went down to the yard and called out to see if anyone was in the fowl house. From the clucking darkness came the reply: 'If you try to stop me, I'll stick you.' Although young Jones was slightly built, he had plenty of pluck and picked up a brick and hurled it in the direction of the voice. A large man ran out into the moonlight and took off across the yard, before escaping along a right-of-way. Jones chased the behemoth and caught him near the Victoria Hotel, providing, as *The Ballarat Courier* reported, 'the interesting spectacle of a rather short gentleman taking captive to the lock-up a tall and powerful man'.

Lo and behold, the trespasser was none other than the redoubtable Elijah Upjohn.

Back at the coop, it was discovered that Upjohn had delivered the *coup de grace* to thirteen birds. The fowl criminal had wrung their necks and lined them up ready to be taken away. Elijah had apparently been about to scrag more when he'd been interrupted.

In court the next day, Upjohn told the presiding judges he'd been drunk. But they heard he'd been seen hanging around and pretending to be intoxicated. Further, he used to take laundry from the bank for mangling, so he knew the layout of the yard and how to access the chook house. This had been no drunken crime of opportunity: it had been a planned chicken heist and massacre.

Upjohn now admitted his guilt but offered a miserable excuse. His wife and son were the cause of his troubles! Consciously or not, he'd just done what his father had when Henry had been caught stealing and blamed Elijah for his transgressions. Upjohn's ungallant claim didn't put the bench in a better temper. He was sentenced to twelve months in Ballarat Gaol.

Back in Governor Arthur Phillip's day, he might have hanged for this crime. But another case that morning did make him being punished with a year in prison seem out of proportion. The same night Upjohn was in the coop, a man came home in a drunken rage and turned his wife and their young children out into the cold, rainy street in their nightdresses. Then he assaulted a policeman. But this offender only got a twenty-shilling fine – in default of which he'd spend a week in gaol. *The Star* commented on the disparity in sentences: 'Verily, law and justice are wide apart as the poles.'

Upjohn's sentence was harsher because he had a wife and sons who were his legal dependants – and such circumstances were one of the reasons that men who *beat* their wives often *weren't* gaoled. Further, he'd had a clean record for the past decade, and for the two decades before that had been convicted only of relatively minor offences. By comparison, Michael Gately was then serving just six months for *choking* his wife. Before that, he'd been in Victorian gaols nonstop for the past thirty years, and had served many long sentences for serious and sometimes violent crimes.

If the men's situations had been reversed – Upjohn getting six months for killing chickens and Gately a year for throttling a woman – then history would have been different.

Upjohn got no compassion from a correspondent to *The Courier* because it had been so shameful for him to blame his family; the letter also hinted that he'd neglected them, much as Henry had neglected Elijah as a small child in Shaftesbury:

> I have known Mrs Upjohn for a long time, and can truly say I believe her to be a most honest and excellent Christian woman. She had had to support her children almost from their birth. With regard to her sons, I believe them to be good and industrious. Hoping that Mrs Upjohn will receive all the sympathy she so much needs at the present time.

How much sympathy, if any, Ann Upjohn had for her husband isn't known. But his incarceration was the end of whatever was left of their relationship. Elijah's own mother had called herself a widow after Henry was transported to Tasmania and never returned. Now Ann was on her own with their boys.

Like father, like son.

Elijah Upjohn had his gaol photograph taken. Despite what was later written about his monstrous visage, the image showed a man whose deflated air, snow-white hair and fleshy face made him look like a disappointed grandfather. His prison file gave his occupations as 'Herbalist' and 'Nightman', and now labelled him a 'Rogue & Vagabond'.

Upjohn began his sentence on 28 April 1880. Two months later to the day, Ned Kelly would be in custody and awaiting the dread punishment of the law.

~

Michael Gately looked rather different to his grim mugshots when he was released from Melbourne Gaol on 7 June 1880. The hangman had dyed his red hair and beard black so that the larrikins wouldn't recognise him. Now he wanted to find Mary. But he soon learned some disturbing news: she'd taken off to Sydney with another man. Gately wasn't letting her go that easy, and booked a ticket on the steamer. He was smart enough to leave it in the care of a publican before he went out and drank himself into oblivion.

By late the next morning, Gately was in his usual state in Bourke Street in the company of Mary's 'harridan' friend Annie Snowden. His new look didn't fool anyone. Word spread, and soon they were surrounded by a horde of larrikins. The thugs stalked the pair and hooted to goad him into violence. Gately pulled his knife but the police arrived before he could use it. He and Annie were taken to the lock-up, followed by a procession of larrikins, who, as usual in these circumstances, seemed beyond police control.

As Gately slept off his debauch, another official was granted a peek at the hangman. The man was surprised by his new black hair and beard. The *Herald* judged his face 'one of the most awfully repulsive ever bestowed on mortal man'. But another writer for the paper was kinder when the hangman appeared in court the next day, saying 'he does not look so villainous in his black hair and whiskers as he did in the auburn'.

Gately's hair might have helped him argue that he'd tried to stay out of trouble. Facing a vagrancy charge, he told the court he had dyed it to 'go about unmolested'. That he had a steamer ticket also went in his favour. All he wanted to do was find his wife. The *Herald* vaguely recalled old Jack Harris clearing out for Sydney after hanging John Price's murderers for fear of retribution. It said Gately could be forgiven for doing the same, because he was being hunted by larrikins and the government had done nothing to protect him.

The bench remanded Gately for a day. Then the magistrate set him free.

Usual form would dictate Gately get drunk and get himself thrown back in gaol. Instead, he collected his ticket and boarded the steamer for Sydney. There's no record of how his fellow passengers felt about being cooped up with a hangman for the duration of the journey. But *The Ovens and Murray Advertiser* was glad to say goodbye: 'I should rejoice if he never returned to Victoria, although I cannot congratulate New South Wales on the accession to her population in the person of so horrible a creature.'

Gately was now Sydney's problem. He was also Mary's. Based on recent experience, he would murder her if he found her. The Melbourne magistrate either hadn't thought of this when he released Gately or didn't care.

Luckily, he didn't find Mary. Sydney's *Evening News* reported his arrival in the city, and a few days later Gately and a 'married lady of the mature age of 36 summers' drank their way through Paddington and Moore Park. They were arrested, hauled into court and both fined five shillings. The paper noted that Gately had £15, which was plenty of money to keep him in drink. New national magazine *The Bulletin* also had its wry eye on him. In its Saturday 26 June 1880 issue, a wag punned that the only way to account for Gately's visit was that 'business in Victoria must have all dropped off'. But business was about to pick up.

That night, Joe Byrne murdered Aaron Sherritt, the Greta mob member who had walked an uneasy path as a police informant. This assassination was Ned Kelly's bid to lure Melbourne's finest to Glenrowan, where the gang was holding townspeople in the pub, so they could derail their train and unleash bloody havoc on any survivors.

During the bail-up of the Glenrowan Inn, Kelly learned the surname of the platelayer hostage who, with another railway worker, he'd forced at gunpoint to rip up the rails for the grand slaughter – Sullivan! In an exchange much like the one in that Cootamundra pub a few years earlier, the outlaw asked him if he'd ever been to New Zealand. The man said he had. Kelly asked: 'How long ago?' Sullivan answered: 'Ten or twelve years ago.' Ned asked more questions and Sullivan clarified that it had been a little longer ago than that. Yes, this Sullivan had been in New Zealand in 1866, when the Maungatapu murders were committed; no, he wasn't the Sullivan who'd killed the five men, dobbed in his mates, escaped the noose and then been set loose by Victoria's rulers.

Kelly accepted this. As he should have because his hostage Sullivan was some thirty years younger than the killer. Nevertheless the outlaw continued on his track. '£8000 has been offered for our capture,' he said. 'I promise to give you a similar amount if you tell me where that Sullivan is to be found.' Joseph Sullivan hadn't been seen in Victoria for years; why this young country railway worker would know his whereabouts was anyone's guess. Kelly's next offer was even odder. He'd give Sullivan another £8000 for information regarding where he could find 'Quinlan, the man who shot Morgan'. 'Mad Dan' had been killed in 1865, when Sullivan was about eleven. Then Kelly supposedly launched into a lecture about Joseph Sullivan, saying the authorities who had branded him a murderer were themselves accomplices to the same crime because they had let such a maniac go free.

Whatever Kelly was on about, the time for talking was soon over when Joe Byrne told him: 'The train is coming'.

Kelly responded: 'No one leaves this house now.'

Not long after that, the shooting began.

# CHAPTER TWENTY-THREE

# Such Is Fame

Sergeant Arthur Steele arrived around 6am, armed with a double-barrelled shotgun. As the shooting entered its third hour, it was unclear who was alive and who was dead inside the Glenrowan Inn. Around 7.15am, by the early light, Steele was confronted by the sight of a strange, armed figure in an iron helmet and breastplate, this spectre staggering and firing a revolver as police bullets pinged off his armour.

When Steele saw his chance, he rushed in and aimed his shotgun low, blasting the man twice in the legs. The outlaw fell and the sergeant grabbed him by the throat with one hand, holding his wrist to keep the revolver clear as the man fired one last shot.

Railway guard Jesse Dowsett, civilian volunteer Charles Rawlins and Senior Constable John Kelly helped Steele overpower and hold the outlaw. They took off his helmet.

'My God,' Steele said, 'it's Ned Kelly.'

Pulling out his own revolver, Steele was about to kill Kelly, saying: 'You bloody wretch, I swore I would be in at your death, and I am!'

Kelly replied: 'That's enough: I have got my gruel.'

Constable Hugh Bracken was credited with preventing Steele from cheating the hangman by standing over Ned and threatening: 'I'll shoot any bloody man that dares touch him.' But Senior Constable Kelly would also claim he'd stopped the sergeant.

Steele was to deny this version of events, saying that he'd been the one to prevent a constable from shooting the outlaw in cold blood. However it had played out in those fraught and frantic moments, Ned Kelly had survived capture.

This was one of the biggest stories in Australian history, flashed by telegraph all over the colonies. Newspapers put out extraordinary editions, with armies of newsboys running them hot off the presses to breathless readers. In Sydney, *The Evening News* was up early. Its second edition updates read:

The Capture

The Fight with the Police

Melbourne, 10:32am

Ned Kelly has been caught. He was wounded in the thigh.

He wore an iron breastplate.

Melbourne, 11am

Ned Kelly was taken alive, shot in the leg, at Glenrowan railway station, about 37 miles from where they shot Sherritt. The rest of the gang are inside an hotel about 80 yards from the station. The gang are barricaded in, and encompassed by a large number of police, with whom they are exchanging shots rapidly.

Will advise further as soon as anything fresh to hand.

What was soon fresh to hand was that Joe Byrne had been shot dead inside the Glenrowan Inn, his corpse pulled clear before the building was burned to the ground by police. Dan Kelly and Steve Hart were also dead – apparently committing suicide before the flames charred them beyond recognition. Two civilians were killed by police bullets. One fleeing hostage had been shot and wounded by Sergeant Steele.

An *Evening News* update answered the most vital question: 'Ned Kelly is still living. Although he is wounded seriously, and is very weak, the doctors are confident that he will recover, and that the hangman will not be cheated of his due.'

There would be some angst in the press that the police at Glenrowan had fired on a hotel filled with innocent people. Vagabond was to say their lack of judgement was 'criminal'. His own was open to question when he celebrated the Kelly Gang's last stand as 'more wonderful than the wildest dreams of fancy indulged in by the authors of boys' novels. Truth is indeed stranger than fiction.' Echoing the demonisation of Weachurch, there was greater editorial joy that the three outlaws – 'men-wolves' and 'human tigers' – had been slaughtered and their leader caged ahead of his own certain execution.

Gately might have had mixed emotions upon hearing the news. If he wanted to 'finish the Kellys', as he'd said the previous year, there was a chance he could still make his name by pocketing £5 to launch Ned into eternity. Gately could have sent a telegram to Sheriff Robert Rede to say he'd be back on the next steamer. Yet this would return Gately to the city where he'd been denied police protection despite being persecuted by an army of larrikins. If he went back to Melbourne, he might not live to hang their hero.

Even if Gately had volunteered his services, Sheriff Rede may not have been interested. Having him in the city would present an extreme provocation to the larrikin horde. Kelly's hanging had to go as smoothly as possible, and Gately was no guarantee of that. If Kelly's head was split open during the drop and he suffocated in a bloody hood while grasping at the noose, his sympathisers would be even more furious and the wider public might even be outraged. On a personal level, Rede also needed to ensure that his role on the fatal day remained hands-off.

For decades Melbourne had moved glacially – if at all – in making decisions about its public executioner. But Rede had already solved the problem. The colony's new hangman was named four days after Glenrowan: Elijah Upjohn.

~

Despite the selection of Upjohn for the role, *The Herald* was more interested in an older incarnation of Jack Ketch, whose story was suddenly deemed relevant and newsworthy.

Back in Tipperary in 1848, two brothers and their red-haired mate had been regularly thieving sheep in the mountains of Slievenamon. An aggrieved farmer tried to catch them in the act and got a deadly bullet from one of the brothers. When the trio were arrested for murder, the government offered a reward and free pardon if one gave evidence against the other two. The red-haired mate turned dog.

But he did more than that. The brothers went to the gallows with caps already over their faces. As he placed the noose around one man's neck, the hangman's own black hood fell off. In the crowd, a sister shouted to her condemned brothers that their former mate was now their scragger. One of the doomed men lunged and tried to throw the bastard from the drop, but the sheriff and a warder saved the finisher from being finished. This ignominious Irishman soon after fled to Australia.

His name? John 'Red' Kelly.

This story – which *The Herald* headlined 'A True Narrative of the Outlawed Kellys' Father' – was reprinted in other papers. For the Kelly family, it was another example of their demonisation. It had indeed been a neat trick Red had pulled off in Ireland in 1848 given that by then he'd served his time in Van Diemen's Land and had moved to Victoria.

Yet the story did have a kernel of truth. Red had informed on a criminal accomplice, leading to this man being shot by the police during his arrest and soon afterwards dying in prison. Whoever the new and improved story came from, it might have been payback for Kelly writing in the Cameron letter that the police were 'worse than cold blooded murderers or hangmen'. It might also have been intended to revive memories of Kelly as Harry Power's snitching black snake.

Like father, like son.

~

Elijah Upjohn arrived at Melbourne Gaol on 1 July 1880. *The Herald* said he 'had not long ago' expressed a wish to be a hangman, and had volunteered after Gately's departure. The wording suggested he'd asked for the job shortly before the events at Glenrowan. If so, his timing was extraordinary. Upjohn lent that credence by later saying he put his hand up when he heard the government was 'took short for a scragger and flagellator'.

Just as Elijah's surname had been oddly suited to his work as nightman, the *Weekly Times* columnist Peerybingle commented on the new nominative determinism: 'Upjohn ain't a bad name, anyhow, for a hangman. It's the sort of signal the sheriff would give when the rope is wound round the criminal's neck.' Peerybingle didn't point out the obvious about the timing of his appointment. But *The Ovens and Murray Advertiser* didn't shy away: 'His first client in that case, will, of course, be the murderer, Kelly. Such is fame – to defy the whole police force of the colony for twenty long months, and be finished by a miserable chicken-stealer.'

What did Kelly think about the prospect of being hanged by a 'robber of hen-roosts'? There's no record. Nor do we know if he knew Upjohn had formerly been a filthy shoveller of shit. The newspapers were coy about his profession; in Ballarat, *The Star* referred to it as 'an unsavoury but necessary occupation'. Though Kelly was largely kept incommunicado in Melbourne Gaol, he also had months and months ahead in which to interact with the police and his gaolers. It seems likely someone would have let slip – or even gloated – that his hangman was once a nightman.

~

As a crime scene, Glenrowan offered ghoulish delights.

Seven hundred years earlier, William Fitz Osbert, the self-proclaimed saviour of the poor with the abundance of facial hair, had been wounded in a siege and then captured to become the first recorded victim hanged at Tyburn. Longbeard's followers had souvenired everything related to the man, even scraping his blood from the road as a relic. Now *The Herald* reported that a thousand spectators had gone to Glenrowan and carried off anything they could get their hands on, from bullets embedded in the stockyard fence to burnt cutlery found among the ashes of the inn. 'On the spot where Ned Kelly fell some leaves spotted with blood from his wounds were found, and these have been all taken away and preserved, as if they were of great value.'

Following on from Mad Dan Morgan's posthumous treatment, Joe Byrne's body had been brought out of the lock-up, slung up on a door and photographed by Arthur Burman of Melbourne. One of his fellow city artistes, John William Lindt, took a panoramic photograph of Burman making his pictures, the image also including the artist Julian Ashton, who'd just made a pen-and-ink drawing of the corpse, and a couple of boy spectators, one still in short pants.

Newspapers and magazines weren't yet able to reproduce photographs, with *The Bulletin* on 10 July carrying a reproduction of a wood engraving made from Burnam's image. Lindt's image would be credited as Australia's first news photograph, capturing as it did an important moment as it happened, rather than a portrait, staged scene or landscape. Other journals gave readers pages of excellent illustrations, such as the iron outlaw blazing away with his guns and Sergeant Steele and a constable wrestling him to the ground. The *Police News* had by then closed, denying readers what would doubtless have been a crazed visual interpretation of events.

But the public would be able to get up close and personal in vivid colour. The Kreitmeyers had been at the scene fast. Joe Byrne's head cast was taken by Max, while his wife moulded the body. The couple also secured his bloodstained boots, which were displayed in their window while they finished his face and figure. By 3 July the waxwork was ready for the public. Two days later, they had a visit from Ned's sister Margaret and Wild Wright, who, as *The Argus* reported, 'inspected the figures and tableaux relating to the Kelly gang with evident interest'.

~

Victorian premier James Service claimed credit for catching the Kellys. But it did him no good with the voters, who tossed him out on 14 July 1880 and gave Graham Berry his third term as leader. The election was a landmark because the results were conveyed in real time by the miracle that was the telephone, which had just arrived in Melbourne – a first for any Australian city.

The morning after this remarkable technological achievement, Elijah Upjohn was sent out to Pentridge in a cart for his first work assignment with the cat-o'-nine-tails. The new flagellator – himself lashed as a child and young adult – was now to whip three offenders. Upjohn may have experienced conflicting emotions at the prospect. But when the job was done, *The Age* had a more definitive feeling: disappointment: 'Upjohn, who is unacquainted with the work, was not so severe in his infliction of the punishment as his predecessor.'

The next day, Upjohn, who'd for the moment remain at Pentridge, had another five customers. All had previously suffered instalments from Gately. But now *The Herald* complained they got off lightly from 'an old man'. The paper pined for his predecessor's style and severity, 'who, at each blow, would step backward to twirl the cat, bringing it down with a cut stroke on his victim's back'. By the end of the month, when another felon got an Upjohn tickle, *The Argus* worried that 'if the punishment of the lash is to be inflicted by this man, it is thought it will lose the desired effect'.

~

Ned Kelly was spirited from Melbourne Gaol and taken by special train for his hearing at Beechworth. Sergeant Steele had charge of the guard – which included Constable McIntyre – watching the prisoner. In the carriage, near Beveridge, the outlaw stuck his head out the window and said: 'That's the place where I was born.' But as they neared Glenrowan, he became agitated and aggressive. *The Ovens and Murray Advertiser* reported that he 'offered to fight any member of the police single-handed, selecting Sergeant Steele (whom he advised to go to India, for safety) as the butt of his contemptuous and altogether uncomplimentary remarks – even going so far as to throw his coat into Steele's face.' Other reports said Kelly's challenge happened before they boarded the prison train, and was the result of Steele making disparaging remarks about Steve Hart having been a mere boy and none of the gang being able to shoot straight.

Either way, Steele had no need to fight. Later that evening, *The Ovens and Murray Advertiser* representative asked him if Kelly had really asked for mercy after being shot. Steele claimed the outlaw had pleaded in a piteous voice: 'I'm done; I'm done; for God's sake, have mercy and don't shoot.' The reporter asked if he'd been tempted to kill Kelly. 'I had for the moment,' Steele admitted, 'but I afterwards considered that, having the fellow at my mercy, it would be a cowardly thing to do, although he certainly deserved that I should have extended not the slightest mercy towards him.'

Kelly had wanted to roast Steele alive on a campfire. The sergeant could now slowly cook the outlaw's reputation in the press and courts.

At his committal, Kelly was represented by David Gaunson, the solicitor and Victorian parliamentarian who'd agitated for Bondietti's reprieve. Usually the Kelly family was defended by William Zincke, also a solicitor and MP, but the Kellys believed they'd have a better chance with Gaunson, who was allied with the Berry government.

In an 'interview' with Gaunson that was published in *The Age*, Ned said all he wanted was the chance to put his side:

> If I get a full and fair trial, I don't care how it goes; but I know this – the public will see that I was hunted and hounded on from step to step; they will see that I am not the monster I have been made out. What I have done has been under strong provocation.

In their next interview, Kelly would claim that Constable Fitzpatrick may have drugged him that time he was arrested for being drunk and disorderly in Benalla in 1877. Far stranger, the outlaw said that killing Lonigan, who'd blackballed him back then, had immediately cured his aching testicles. As Kelly put it: 'It may seem strange, but it is as true as I am here that from that time up to the time of Lonigan's death I suffered excruciating pain and inconvenience from his treatment; but from the day of his death until now I have been free from that pain and the ill-effects I before experienced.' What would be more remembered from this interview was Kelly musing about his legacy: 'If my life teaches the public that men are made mad by bad treatment, and if the police are taught that they may not exasperate to madness men they persecute and illtreat, my life will not be entirely thrown away.'

Whether Kelly realised it or not, he was echoing the defence, justification and hopes that Weachurch had offered before he was hanged.

Such an outcome was naturally on Kelly's mind. During the hearing, he was kept in Beechworth Gaol, where seven men had been seen off by Tom the Devil, William Bamford and Michael Gately. He'd probably

299

be the eighth – necked by new hangman Elijah Upjohn. Gazing at its gallows, the outlaw said: 'What a pity that a fine fellow like Ned Kelly should be hung up there.'

But it wasn't to be. The trial was ordered moved to Melbourne, where a jury would be less likely to include sympathisers. If Kelly was to hang, he'd hang from the same beam as Weachurch and so many others who had said they were innocent to the last.

~

In Melbourne, Elijah Upjohn was suddenly in favour with flagellation aficionados. Like Bamford, it seemed that all he needed was a little time to warm to the task. *The Herald* said his latest victim's cries 'were heard for a considerable distance from the place of punishment'. The same went a fortnight later, when he dealt with three prisoners. *The Bulletin* called him 'a complete success'. But the man's true test lay ahead.

~

Ned Kelly's trial for the murder of Lonigan began properly before Judge Barry in the Supreme Court on 28 October 1880. The accused was likely to be convicted. Yet the Eureka Rebels, Captain Melville, Harry Power and even the 'human tiger' Weachurch had all been acquitted in this court. However, what they had in common was they had all been defended by Richard Ireland QC. While he'd spoken against the abolition of the death penalty in 1862, he was also the colony's most brilliant criminal defender when it came to saving clients from hanging. But he'd been dead three years.

Instead of getting a man of Ireland's calibre, David Gaunson instead chose junior barrister Henry Bindon. This man – who was making his criminal trial debut – had been out of the country while much of the

Kelly saga played out. Though advised by Gaunson, Bindon initially knew little about the case or the evidence.

Constable McIntyre testified that Kelly had murdered Lonigan. Then Sergeant Steele's evidence assassinated Kelly's character. He said the captured outlaw had said, 'Don't kill me; I never hurt any of you.' Then Kelly had confessed he'd meant to shoot everyone who escaped the police train. Further, he supposedly admitted being responsible for the whole outbreak, and had said of Fitzpatrick: 'Yes, it is true; I shot him.'

Steele had been stopped from killing Kelly at Glenrowan. But his testimony was now to help finish him off.

Bindon's central argument was that McIntyre had possibly misidentified Kelly. He didn't raise his client's contention that the police had wanted to kill him and he'd thus acted in self-defence. The barrister's cross-examination was largely ineffective – and he refused to let Kelly question witnesses. Bindon also successfully objected when the Crown tried to introduced the Jerilderie Letter, arguing it was a copy and not in Kelly's handwriting. Letting it be read would have meant the accused's by now well-known claims of police persecution and self-defence could have been heard by the jury in something like his own words. But the contents also made it clear McIntyre had *not* mistaken another man for Kelly – and that Ned admitted shooting Lonigan thinking he was Strahan. Why Gaunson – who had a far better idea of the case – had not instructed Bindon to argue self-defence is open to debate.

Ultimately, all that mattered was that the strong prosecution case and weak defence saw the jury convict Ned Kelly of murder on 29 October 1880.

Judge Redmond Barry would now pass sentence. Asked if he had a statement to make, Kelly admitted it was a little late to say much, other than that he wished he'd examined witnesses because it would have thrown a different light on the case. He reckoned he'd been reticent because otherwise it would have looked like 'bravado and flashness'.

Kelly didn't blame Gaunson or Bindon, though he noted that the latter knew nothing about the case, and he agreed that, based on the evidence heard, 'no juryman could have given any other verdict'.

What followed was the famously heated exchange between Kelly, who hadn't spoken his piece during the trial, and Barry, who through his career had specialised in bloviating to captive condemned men. The bushranger said, 'My mind is as easy and clear as it possibly can be.' This caused a court uproar.

Barry thundered: 'It is blasphemous of you to say so. You appear to revel in the idea of having put men to death.'

Kelly's immediate response – 'More men than me have put men to death' – seemed aimed at this hanging judge, who for over a quarter of a century had been sending men to their executioners, ignoring jury recommendations for mercy and guiding the Executive Council to let the law run its course. Kelly continued to deny he was a murderer, and Barry said he was a liar for saying so.

Unbowed, the condemned man taunted that 'the day will come when we shall all have to a bigger court than this. Then we will see who is right and who is wrong.'

Their argy-bargy continued. But Barry was going to have the final say. Early in his career, he'd cried when undertaking this solemn duty. Not today. He donned the black cap. 'I have now to pronounce your sentence,' he said. 'You will be taken from here to the place from whence you came, and thence on a day appointed by the Executive Council to a place of execution, and there you will be hanged by the neck until you are dead. May the Lord have mercy on your soul.'

Ned Kelly's riposte was perhaps spontaneous, perhaps prepared, but either way it was to ring in eternity: 'I will go a little further than that, and say I will see you there, where I go.'

## CHAPTER TWENTY-FOUR

# Such Is Life

On Saturday 6 November 1880, an iron man was walking around in circles in Melbourne. It wasn't Ned Kelly. It wasn't even human. This was 'Frankenstein, the Steam Man', promoted as 'the most wonderful mechanical construction ever exhibited in the world', and for a shilling you could see this automaton – '[b]uilt to as closely resemble a man as any figure in the Waxworks' – shamble about as vapour clouds rose from his black coat. It was a strange sight in what had been a big week for the city.

On Monday, the ongoing Melbourne International Exhibition had attracted more than 8000 people – one of them being Governor George Phipps – to enjoy the displays and amusements beneath the marvellous new dome. That night there was more going-around-in-circles fun with a 'Go-As-You-Please' tournament on a track at the Hippodrome, the audience cheering on pedestrians and runners who were trying to cover 150 miles in forty-eight hours.

But as far as racing in a circle went, there was nothing to compare with the following day's fixture. The city emptied out in a way reminiscent of the gold rush as the biggest crowd on record gathered at Flemington hoping to strike it lucky at the Melbourne Cup. Grand Flaneur won the big race. The nag named Ned Kelly didn't compete. His race seemed run.

The unluckiest punters that day were those on Upjohn's triangle, as *The Herald* noted: 'Cup Day 1880 will no doubt be remembered in a very unpleasant manner by three inmates of the Pentridge Prison.' They brought his flogging total that week to six. Now the paper contradicted its recent appreciation of his predecessor by saying it was pleased he didn't display 'that coarse brutality and gloating disposition of Gately'.

On Wednesday, Upjohn was put in a cart and transferred from Pentridge to Melbourne Gaol. Any who witnessed this had to think it predicted the outcome of that day's Executive Council meeting to weigh the fate of Ned Kelly, who since sentencing had been in the condemned cell, number thirty-eight, in the old wing of the gaol. Graham Berry, the man who'd once spoken of the abolition of capital punishment, now headed the cabinet, whose members were guided in their deliberations by Judge Barry.

Barry wasn't recommending mercy. How could he? How could they even consider it? The evidence was compelling and the defence flimsy. Kelly's crimes were more abhorrent than those committed by any number of men who'd gone to the gallows. Intractable convicts Weachurch and Richard Rowley, bank robbers Woods and Carver, bushrangers Condon, Dixon and Jackson: they'd all hanged for *attempted* murder, or even lesser crimes.

Then there were so many – such as Edward Feeney, Ah Cat, Basilio Bondietti, Long Poy and Christopher Harrison – whose death sentences had seemed unjust but had been upheld. To reprieve Ned Kelly – as had been argued after Laurence Shanklin's commutation twenty years earlier – would make them and so many others hanged in Victoria seem victims of judicial murder.

Let Ned Kelly live and they might as well abolish capital punishment altogether.

The Executive Council set his execution for 11 November 1880. Governor Castieau went to the condemned cell with the unhappy news. Kelly said: 'It is very short.'

On Friday, Melbourne crowds gathered to celebrate the 275th anniversary of Guy Fawkes being foiled in his plot to blow up the British Houses of Parliament. This traitor had been convicted in a star chamber and sentenced to be tortured, strangled and quartered while alive. Fawkes escaped the last part due to the hangman's bungling, the executioner's inattention giving him the chance to fall or jump from the scaffold so his neck was broken. But Fawkes had been cut up post-mortem and his body parts distributed around the country as a warning. Melbourne recalled this grisly slice of history with festive hillside bonfires as fireworks exploded in the night sky.

That evening, a massive public meeting in support of reprieving Ned Kelly was held at the Hippodrome. Some 3000 to 4000 people were inside, with perhaps same number again out in the street. Describing the crowd, the city's conservative papers used the same language they had employed to portray those who used to gather for public executions and who now clamoured outside gaol walls when a hanging was on. These protestors weren't genuine supporters or principled opponents of capital punishment. They were the lower classes: thieves, prostitutes and larrikins.

But the luminaries who'd organised this meeting would also come in for a press beating.

David Gaunson, who had form as a Ned Kelly defender and opponent of capital punishment, was pilloried because he was an elected member of the Legislative Assembly and yet was now going in to bat for a convicted constable killer.

Gaunson was supported by his younger brother, William, who was characterised as a fame-chaser who'd tried to ride his sibling's coattails into parliament. William had first run in 1876, aged just twenty-seven or so, and had been mocked as 'the boy politician'.

John Caulfield, who'd inherited the 'boy politician' label from William, was also campaigning for Kelly to be reprieved. The precocious seventeen-year-old had come to prominence the previous year, giving speeches as a Berry supporter. But by November 1880, Caulfield – like Gaunson – was opposed to the premier and his government.

More risible still was the chairman of the meeting: Professor Sohier's old phrenological rival Archibald Hamilton. In the past quarter-century, this bumpologist had followed a bumpy path. In 1860, in Maitland, New South Wales, he'd stood trial for trying to induce a sexton to dig up graves so he could steal a couple of celebrity criminals' skulls. Hamilton's long-winded defence was that everyone was doing it and people who came to his lectures to see such heads were aware of their provenance – besides, the brain boxes he had hoped to score only belonged to a murderer and an Aboriginal man. Hamilton was acquitted. Three years later in Maitland, he unsuccessfully stood for the NSW parliament, with abolition of capital punishment one of his many policies.

Hamilton had another bumpy legal moment in 1866 in New Zealand, where he stole the casts of the three hanged Maungatapu murderers from local phrenologists. The magistrate ordered him to return the casts but dismissed the charges because he thought a case argued by bickering headcases would be laughed out of court by a jury. But Hamilton used the illicitly obtained information to bolster his reputation with a book about the murderers, in which he also claimed to have examined Joseph Sullivan back in the 1850s and presciently concluded he was a violent time bomb.

After returning to Melbourne for a few years, Hamilton went back to Maitland and again stood for parliament in 1872, speaking once more against hanging. The winner of the East Maitland election polled 316 votes, beating the next candidate, who scored 278. There were 12 informal votes. Hamilton got five. Undeterred, he immediately declared his candidacy for West Maitland, where he did a little better but still polled a distant third. After another unsuccessful electoral stab in 1874, he moved to Sydney and advertised himself as 'the Only Legitimate Practical Phrenologist in the Southern Hemisphere'.

By early 1880, Hamilton was back in Melbourne and reading heads. Among those whose bumps he felt was Alfred Deakin. The phrenologist advised this young fellow – perhaps a man after his own heart because he had recently been defeated in a couple of elections – not to give up his political dreams because he really was meant for parliament.

While Hamilton's opposition to the death penalty was part of his phrenological beliefs, he didn't appear to have been publicly vocal about the issue for years, and even then it had been in Maitland rather than Melbourne. Nevertheless, he now spearheaded the campaign to save Ned Kelly, and was the first to address the crowd to say he was an advocate for the abolition of capital punishment, and that they should listen to the speakers as if their very lives depended on it. Hamilton's courage failed him when some larrikins lobbed crackers onto the stage and he grabbed his head in fear and fretted that someone was shooting a revolver. David Gaunson displayed more fortitude – though the fireworks interruptions continued – as he reiterated that Kelly should be reprieved because he'd been persecuted, had acted in self-defence and so on. The meeting ended with Gaunson proposing a successful resolution to beseech the governor to exercise the royal prerogative of mercy. Hamilton would lead the deputation.

On Saturday, as Frankenstein the Steam Man was clanking around his patch of Melbourne, Kate Kelly accompanied Hamilton, the Gaunsons and Caulfield to see Governor Phipps. They were politely told there was no hope. David Gaunson bowed out of the fight, but the others weren't giving up. Using the Robert Burns Hotel as their headquarters, they started collecting signatures across the city, helped in this work by Jim Kelly, Tom Lloyd, Wild Wright and others. *The Australasian* would claim this was a farce, saying they had obtained signatures by 'the most flagrantly unscrupulous devices' – and besides, they were working on 'behalf of one of the most bloodthirsty criminals ever known in Australia'.

By Monday 8 November, they had more than 34,000 signatures and presented the petition to the governor's secretary just before the Executive

Council met at 2pm. There was no reprieve. As *The Weekly Times* reported: 'On looking over the sheets of the petition, it was found that in many instances names representing eight or ten persons of one family had been signed by one and the same person. Numerous other signatures were found to be in the same handwriting, and there was scarcely the name of any representative person to be found in the sheets examined.' This was both true and misleading. Adult males would have felt entirely justified signing on behalf of their entire families, and the likes of Wild Wright would have felt no compunction scribbling down the names of supporters who couldn't write their own names and perhaps adding a few phoneys for good measure. But the petition sheets also contained thousands of seemingly genuine signatures in different handwriting.

The Kellys continued to collect signatures in public. Of course, many – perhaps most – refused to sign. An example was given by Henry Glenny, the Ballarat magistrate who had come to Melbourne to witness the execution and to cover it for *The Star* under his nom-de-plume 'Silverpen'. On Wednesday 10 November, on Bourke Street, Glenny spied the rather attractive Kate Kelly stopping a gentleman and presenting her petition. The fellow responded: 'Ned Kelly's reprieve! Why, I would hang the scoundrel myself if they were short of a hangman, rather than allow the monster to go unhung.'

That same day, a last-ditch attempt saw Kate, Archibald Hamilton, William Gaunson and John Caulfield meet again with the governor. Caulfield told His Excellency that the majority of people – which *The Australasian* interpreted as 'meaning the seedy, unkept, and detested mob' – wanted mercy for Kelly. But it was the phrenologist who delivered the 'coup de theatre' when he brought Kate forward and asked if the governor wanted her to beg on her knees. His Excellency was mortified and said the meeting was over. Not unreasonably, the paper said this final scene had the 'character of shabby tragedy and extravagant burlesque'.

If Ned Kelly had known what Hamilton had tried to make his beloved sister do, he likely would've wanted the opportunistic phrenologist's head for his own 'study'. The outlaw's temper wouldn't have improved if he'd learned the bumpologist's next move was making an application to Premier Berry. This wasn't a request for a reprieve. Hamilton wanted access to Kelly before he hanged so that he could read his head and shine 'the light of science upon the character of the condemned man'. He also offered to make the post-mortem cast. These requests – from a fellow who'd hardly endeared himself to the government in the past week – were curtly denied by Graham Berry.

Castieau went to Kelly's cell to say there was no hope for reprieve and he must prepare himself. The outlaw dictated his third and final letter to Governor Phipps. He made a last request: that his body be given to his relatives for burial in consecrated ground. This was refused. It was against the law. Besides, even if an exception could have been made, no one wanted to see Kelly's body propped up in an oyster shop or his grave become a magnet for troublemakers and souvenir hunters.

But Kelly could leave his family a photograph. Charles Nettleton took Australia's most famous criminal portraits in the gaol yard, the doomed man looking defiant with his steady gaze and huge beard, one hand in a fist and the other holding a rope to his leg irons, in order to disguise the weakness and withering he'd suffered these past months on account of his bullet wounds. Kelly said his goodbyes to his mother, to Jim, Kate and Grace, and to Tom Lloyd. *The Weekly Times* reported 'his mother's last exhortion to him was "to die like a Kelly".'

That afternoon, Ned had another visit from Castieau, who'd brought his thirteen-year-old son Godfrey. Through the bars, Kelly put his hand on the lad's head and said: 'Son, I hope you grow up to be as fine a man as your father.' At some point Kelly also had a secret visit from Jack Castieau, now eleven and too big to slip through the bars. While the lad had been impressed by Weachurch, all he'd write of Kelly was that he was 'historically heroic, literally commonplace'.

After a restless last night, Kelly rose around 5.30am on Thursday 11 November 1880. He knelt and said prayers, before resting on his bunk until around eight. Kelly refused breakfast so he could receive last Holy Communion. He sang a few songs before the blacksmith came to remove his leg irons.

How Elijah Upjohn had spent the night isn't known. He'd been a pretty criminal as a child, an unruly convict in Tasmania and an occasional gaolbird in Ballarat. But his only recorded violence had been against chickens. It's reasonable to assume that the prospect of hanging Ned Kelly was unsettling. Did he have instruction and training? As had been the case with Bamford after Harris, and Gately after Bamford, Elijah's predecessor wasn't around to show him the ropes.

Yet in a striking piece of timing, given how long hangings had been more or less random acts of fatal legal violence, Sheriff Rede should have been able to ensure that Ned Kelly's execution was carried out as humanely and efficiently as possible under new guidelines from 'Home'.

In London, on 27 June 1880 – right as the shootout at the Glenrowan Inn was unfolding – the secretary of state for the colonies had issued a 'Memorandum upon the Execution of Prisoners by Hanging with a long drop'. The three-page pamphlet was meant to 'prevent by every possible means' the 'revolting circumstances' that had attended the execution of some criminals. It instructed rope lengths based on weight, and adjustments that should be made if the prisoner had a strong neck. It specified that the knot had to be placed 'just in the front of the angle of the jaw-bone on the left side, so as to run up behind the left ear when the man falls and receives the jerk ... If the rope is adjusted the other way there will be less certainty of breaking the man's neck.' It even included a helpful diagram. This wasn't where Dr Barker had been saying it should be placed. And, in addition to pinioning the arms, the convicts' legs were now to be strapped tightly.

The memo listed everything a sheriff should ensure from the moment a culprit was sentenced. This included how a hangman was chosen and instructed:

> The executioner should be a trustworthy and intelligent person, and on the first occasion of his employment care should be taken to ascertain that he knows fully and accurately what he has to do, and in what order he is to do the several acts which constitute his duty.

Did this memo reach Rede in time? Ships by then could do the London–Melbourne run in two to three months. The memo should have arrived by 11 November. But if it did, many of its provisos were about to be ignored – and would remain unimplemented for years.

At around 9am, according to *The Sydney Daily Telegraph*, when Castieau came to say it was time for Kelly to move to the condemned cell, the outlaw responded: 'Such is life.' But as reporters weren't actually admitted for another half an hour or so, this, like so much about the last hours, seems to have come from what the reporter was told by gaol officials or heard from other newsmen. But 'Silverpen' *was* allowed into the gaol early – or so he'd claim – thanks to his status as a Justice of the Peace. He reported the blacksmith removing the irons, yet he didn't mention this first supposed utterance of the famous last words. But he did describe what happened next, as Kelly 'was then removed to the condemned cell, and walked along without the slightest sign of fear, the priests and their aide following'.

During this last walk, Kelly saw what awaited him: the death cart Upjohn would use to wheel his corpse to the deadhouse. He also took in a last moment of beauty, courtesy of Castieau's ongoing efforts to make the gaol more pleasant. 'Oh, what a pretty garden,' he said. Or, in another account, 'What a nice little garden!'

Since early that morning, as in 1842, a large crowd had been gathering outside the gaol. As had been the case since Melbourne's first executions, the press wasn't sure of its number, the estimates ranging from 3000 to 6000 people. Nor was there anything like agreement over who they were.

*The Herald* said all classes were present, including many women who were 'young, well-dressed, and apparently respectable'. *The Argus* saw that 'a large proportion of them were larrikin-looking youths, and nearly all were of the lower orders'. *The Weekly Times* reckoned they were a 'mob of nondescript idlers' enslaved to their 'morbid and depraved tastes'. Yet there was agreement that they were well behaved – thanks, perhaps, to the large police presence. A *Herald* reporter felt it was actually reverence, and 'could not but contrast the quiet orderly assemblage of today with the hideous concourse of all that was vile that used to throng Newgate street on Hanging Monday'.

Those in the crowd weren't sure what was happening inside. To help them, a young man 'of a decidedly legal appearance' described the corridors, the floors, even the beam around which the rope was coiled. He also pointed out the skylight under which the hanging took place. A widely expressed sentiment, summed up by one man, was that it was horrible what was about to happen to Kelly, 'but he'll die game'.

By now, Elijah Upjohn would have been waiting in the cell adjacent to the gallows. If he'd been properly instructed, he should already have ascertained Kelly's weight and how strong his neck was, allowed the correct length of rope for the drop, and ensured it had been stretched so it wouldn't lengthen further. He should also have soaped the noose so it would snap tight and break Kelly's neck. But from what Castieau later said, it seemed Upjohn wasn't given training and barely knew what was expected. At around a quarter to ten, noises would have reached this unprepared hangman as people began to arrive.

Sheriff Rede had kept tighter control over who'd be admitted than some of his predecessors. Although there were twenty-seven witnesses listed, some forty or fifty people were present, though few if any were ordinary citizens. People were admitted from around 9.30am and assembled in small groups, nervously pacing around the yard, discussing the merits of the case and previous hangings they had attended. One of them was Alfred Deakin, by now elected to parliament, working as a journalist and subject to much mockery as president of the Victorian Association of Progressive Spiritualists.

Ten minutes later, Castieau led them deeper into the gaol, through a gate, along a corridor, and through another gate where they confronted the gallows. *The Herald*'s reporter noted that it was where the corridors branched right and left 'in the shape of a cross', and that all was 'silent and grim' as he and other visitors stood gazing upwards at the huge beam with its long rope that reached down to the platform and ended in the running noose.

But from where they stood, 'breathlessly gazing up', what they could see and hear was limited, as Castieau had made clear in his diary entry about Edward Feeney's execution in 1872. The perceptions of reporters would have been further distorted by the dreadful anxiety of this moment. They wouldn't all see the same thing. First Fleeters had recorded different versions of Thomas Barrett's death in 1788, and journalists had been doing likewise ever since.

In his condemned cell, Kelly was receiving his last consolations from the priests, including Dean Charles O'Hea, who it's believed had baptised Ned a quarter of a century earlier. Just before 10am, Castieau, Sheriff Rede, Deputy Sheriff Ellis and Dr Edward Barker ascended to the first floor. With the religious rituals continuing, at 10am the post office tower clock tolled and the last part of the legal ritual began. Silverpen quoted the formal colloquy:

Rede: I demand the body of Edward Kelly.

Castieau: By what authority do you make this demand?

Rede: By virtue of this warrant, signed by his Excellency.

[Rede handed it over.] Castieau: Bring forth Edward Kelly.

313

This was the signal for Elijah Upjohn to step upon the stage, leather pinioning strap in one hand and, according to one report, carrying what looked like a small white bag. Different eyes saw him differently. *The Argus* called him 'an elderly, grey-headed, well-conditioned looking man'. *The Weekly Times* said he was 'by no means the typical hangman of current literatures ... his worst expression of countenance is that of sulk doggedness.' But it was *The Herald*'s account that would endure:

> He stepped across the scaffold quietly, and as he did so, quietly turned his head, and looked down upon the spectators, revealing a fearfully repulsive countenance. Those who have seen Gately know how dreadfully forbidding were that miscreant's features. If it be possible his successor is even more repulsive in appearance.

The paper said he was closely shaved and in the prison uniform. Yet the other reports had him in civilian clothes with shirtsleeves rolled up. *The Herald*'s nightmarish description continued:

> Were it not for the prison cropping he would probably have a heavy crop of hair, for thick bristles, of a pure white, stick up all over his crown and give him a ghastly appearance. He has heavy lips and heavy features altogether, the nose being about the most striking and ugly. It is large in proportion, and appears to have a huge carbuncle on the end. Altogether the man's appearance fully sustains the accepted idea of what a hangman should look like.

Silverpen – who had to know Upjohn from Ballarat – didn't make any comment about him. Perhaps he didn't want to alienate his hometown audience by reminding them of the shame of supplying the colony's new Jack Ketch. Instead, he wrote: 'The hangmen then walked across to the cell, and pinioned the prisoner.'

But it didn't happen as simply as that. Upjohn entered the cell. Kelly is reported variously to have said, 'You need not pinion me', 'There is no need for tying me' or 'There's no need to pinion me, I'll go forward quietly'. Apparently in response to being told it was indispensable, he reportedly added, 'Ah well, I suppose.'

Upjohn pinioned Kelly's arms behind him at the elbow. Then he placed the white cap on his head. The priests emerged from the cell, their attendant ahead of them carrying a large crucifix. They recited the sacrament of the dying, and Kelly made the appropriate responses as he stepped firmly from the cell and onto the drop.

*The Weekly Times* now had Kelly saying, 'Ah well, I suppose.' The paper said it probably meant 'he supposed this was the last of it, or this was what it had come to, but the expression was never concluded'. *The Herald* said Upjohn 'came forward and placed the fatal noose of the rope, which was pendant from a strong beam overhead, round the neck of the condemned man, who looked calmly at the priests in front of him the while, without paying any apparent attention to anything round him'. Kelly winced at the touch of the rope but then moved his head to make the hangman's work easier.

*The Herald* admired that it had been arranged there were no final words now, crediting Castieau with 'anticipating the possibility of a scene, or of a breakdown, either on the part of the criminal, or the executioner'.

In Kelly's final seconds, *The Argus* claimed his calm might be about to shatter: 'his face was livid, his jaunty air gone, and there was a frightened look in his eyes as he glanced down on the spectators'. This paper reckoned it was 'his intention to make a speech but his courage evidently failed him'. *The Argus* here ignored the well-known fact that clergymen often exhorted prisoners not to speak but to focus themselves on eternity. The paper continued that as the rope was being fitted to Kelly's neck, he said: 'Ah, well, I suppose it has come to this.' *The Sydney Morning Herald* caught Kelly's last words as: 'Ah, well! It's come to this at last.'

Melbourne's *Herald* claimed that this was when he said: 'Such is life.'

Sergeant Anthony Trainor, a witness, reckoned Kelly's last words had been a murmured response to a question. Similarly, Silverpen heard – or rather didn't hear – what Kelly said: 'After the noose was put over his head, he said something in a low tone of voice to the hangman about the placing of the rope.' If Silverpen's version was right, Upjohn alone may have heard Kelly's final words, which were practical and intended to give him a measure of control over his death.

Dr Edward Barker watched closely. He was reported to have told Upjohn to place the knot under the left ear, which wasn't quite where the memo had ordered, just as Kelly's legs had not been strapped. Satisfied, Dr Barker stepped back.

Kelly looked up at the skylight. Upjohn lowered the cap, his face the last Kelly would see on this earth. As the priests prayed, the hangman stepped back.

But Dr Barker had seen something that didn't please him. As he reached – 'as if to adjust the knot' – Upjohn pulled the lever that withdrew the bolt that opened the trap.

Kelly dropped eight feet and was brought up with a terrible jerk. The thud was heard around the gaol, and the prisoners supposedly let out a roar. The reporters looked up at Kelly, whose boots were four feet above the floor.

*The Weekly Times* told readers that 'death must have been instantaneous, for there was but the slightest muscular contraction, the natural result of the sudden shock received by the system. Beyond a slight lifting of the shoulders and a spasmodic quiver or two of the lower limbs, no motion was visible after the drop fell.' *The Argus* had it that 'his neck was dislocated and death was instantaneous; for although muscular twitching continued for a few minutes, he never made a struggle'. Sergeant Trainor was to say of the hanging: 'Except [for] some muscular action after he fell there was not much movement of the body which I walked around and so far as I can judge if he suffered any pain it was of the shortest duration.'

But the Melbourne *Herald*'s man did not see it this way:

There was for a second or two only the usual shudder that passes through the frame of a hanged man but then the LEGS WERE DRAWN UP for some distance, and fell suddenly again. This movement was repeated several times, but finally all motion ceased, and at the end of FOUR MINUTES ALL WAS OVER.

Silverpen, too, said muscular twitching lasted several minutes. *The Herald*'s reporter worried Kelly had suffered. But he was informed by doctors that death was 'absolutely instantaneous'; the raising and falling of the legs were simply 'post-mortem involuntary contraction of the extensor muscles'.

Had Ned Kelly been given enough rope for a quick and painless exit? Whether received and read or not, the memo had stipulated: 'A man of 10 stone and under requires a drop of 8 feet, a heavier man requires a slightly lesser drop in proportion to his weight over 10 stone.' Kelly's weight – as recorded in his prison file – was eleven stone and four pounds. The memo had continued: 'If the man's neck and shoulders are very hard and muscular, he should have an extra foot or so beyond the normal drop of his weight.' Given Kelly's reported strength, they – Upjohn, Rede, Barker, Castieau and whoever else had input – by hook or by crook had come close to getting the drop right. Falling eight feet, Kelly's neck should have been broken. Yet if it had, he was also unlikely to have moved much at all. So it came down to which report you believed as to whether he died in an instant, in a matter of seconds or over minutes.

Outside the gaol, when the post office clock struck ten, a silence had fallen on the multitude. *The Herald* wrote: 'The idlest, the most ignorant, the most dissipated realised at that moment the solemn fact that a fellow-creature had been passed from this world to the unknown in obedience to the just dictates of the outraged laws of his country.'

That morning of 11 November 1880, outside the gaol, Silverpen said that when he emerged, he was rushed by hundreds of people who wanted to know every little detail. They also wanted to confirm that Ned Kelly had really hanged, because up to that last minute they'd expected he would be reprieved or cheat the hangman. Even on hearing he was dead, there was disbelief he was actually gone.

*The Herald* reported: 'Each exodus from the gaol was watched as if the gazers expected to see the ghost of the criminal stalk forth in his now famous armour.'

Ned Kelly was dead. Long live Ned Kelly.

~

Kelly remained hanging for half an hour – not one hour, as had been stipulated in the memo from London. Upjohn lowered the body, cut it free and took it to the deadhouse. When the cap was removed, Kelly's eyes were said to be bright, his features not distorted; one witness even claimed Kelly had something of a death smile. The only mark was where the knot had been behind his left ear.

At midday, the formal inquest was held to confirm he'd been hanged. Despite depredations to come, the results of a minor autopsy weren't revealed to disclose whether Kelly's neck had been broken or whether he'd strangled.

Dr Barker, his morning work done, hosted a luncheon at his house, where the guests included Dean O'Hea. True to form, the conversation around the hanging doctor's table was about methods of execution.

Sheriff Rede – who'd created the Eureka martyrs – was the one to give official notice to Premier Graham Berry, who had once argued the abolition of capital punishment was the mark of a modern civilised society. The sheriff wrote: 'Sir – I have the honor to report that Edward Kelly was executed at 10 a.m. – everything passed off satisfactorily.'

Compared with so many previous hangings, even if Kelly was alive and struggling for a few seconds or longer, Rede probably felt justi-fied in saying that. Yet Castieau – though he didn't keep a diary at this time – reportedly said it could have been far less than satisfactory. Upjohn, he reckoned, 'did little more than pull the bolt and had it not been that the warders helped him in a variety of ways, there would prob-ably have been a scene'.

Had Elijah Upjohn nearly bungled the most famous execution in Australian history? If that was the accusation, he, like Jack Harris all those years ago, was hardly solely – or even mostly – to blame. His supe-riors had known for more than four months that he'd likely be doing this work. Where did responsibility rest? With establishment figures paid handsomely and whose job it was to oversee hangings, or with the lowly convict they had appointed as a scragger at £5 per job?

*The Herald* was Melbourne's afternoon paper, and its extensive, colourful and contestable coverage became the first draft of history on 11 November 1880. It led with a headline that created a legend:

The Execution

of

Edward Kelly

the

Notorious Bushranger,

for the

Police Murders

at the

Wombat Ranges.

The Last Scene of All.

How the Convict Died.

'Such Is Life'

# CHAPTER TWENTY-FIVE

# Such Is Death

Max Kreitmeyer shaved Kelly's beard and head and made the cast. Despite being turned down by Graham Berry, Archibald Hamilton was on hand to take measurements of the head. Sheriff Rede gave the corpse to doctors and medical students. They sawed off Ned's head, which was souvenired, like other parts of him. *The Bendigo Independent* described this *Grand Guignol* as:

> A nice mess ... It was a ghastly sight – indeed hardly ever paralleled. I am told that portions of the corpse are now in nearly every 'curiosity' cabinet in Melbourne medical men's places. The skull was taken possession of by one gentleman, and it is probable that he may hereafter enlighten us in the peculiarities of the great criminal's brain. The medical men call these things 'preparations,' and, therefore, the public can imagine what has become of Kelly's body.

Did Archibald Hamilton steal Ned's head? He's the most obvious suspect. He had form as a body snatcher, yet if he souvenired this skull he kept silent. *The Bendigo Independent's* writer intimated that – as with Sohier's 'Queensland Mummy' – another part of Kelly had been souvenired in the manner of Napoleon: 'As a matter of fact, I know, and indeed, I have seen a part of the body although it was supposed that it was consumed in the quick lime which is thrown into the grave.'

~

For hanging Ned Kelly, Elijah Upjohn had earned £5 to add to the money he'd already made from floggings. But he didn't appear to get the dead bushranger's clothes. As for his last outfit, Sheriff Rede was hardly going to hand over the iron armour to the hangman. The outlaw had gone to the gallows in a prison uniform, which would have remained the property of the gaol. As for how Upjohn fared inside Melbourne Gaol, the story was that later that day he was knocked down by a prisoner who'd thundered: 'Take that, you ———, for hanging Ned Kelly.' While apocryphal, there's every reason to believe he would have been subject to such treatment in gaol if an opportunity arose. Upjohn was fortunate to have four months left to serve. If he'd been thrown back on the street like his predecessors, there's a good chance he would have been killed.

On the night of the execution, Silverpen went to the Apollo Hall, assuming the flyers he'd seen advertising a show featuring Kate and Jim Kelly were a hoax. But there they were, on stage, sitting in armchairs, Kate with Ned's watch and chain, and Jim with his dead brother's coat. Jim, he said, looked like he was trying not to laugh. Over the next four hours they sat and talked with all comers.

Silverpen wrote: 'This was without exception the most disgraceful exhibition ever placed before the Melbourne public.' The ghosts of any number of people horrifically executed in public and 'private' – not to mention the scarred flogging survivors who'd suffered before the 'connoisseurs' – might have disagreed with that particular claim. *The Weekly Times* said that it could only have been more disgraceful if Gaunson, Caulfield and Hamilton had been there handing out handbills and 'doing the "crying"'. The Kellys were quickly banned and would take their show to Sydney.

Exploitation of the dead Ned Kelly was best left to those who'd long been in the trade. The next day, Max Kreitmeyer had his ad lodged with *The Herald* before its 1pm deadline, announcing he had:

> just placed in the Waxworks a wax cast from a mould taken from the face and head of Edward Kelly after death. The face is quite calm and composed, and is reproduced with great fidelity. The artist is engaged on a full-length figure, which will be proportioned from actual measurements.

Whether Archibald Hamilton had Ned's head or not, he certainly tried to use the access he had gotten to elevate himself to the sort of official status he had so clearly wanted in the 1870s in NSW. So much so that a cynic might have believed this had been his real reason for inserting himself into the reprieve efforts. Hamilton penned a letter to *The Herald* that set out 'The Phrenological Character of Edward Kelly'. He prefaced his commentary by saying he was 'willing to make a personal examination of the heads of all prisoners' then confined in Melbourne Gaol and Pentridge. Hamilton was essentially making a public application to be made the official penal bumpologist. It seems doubtful he would have worked *pro bono*.

Lest he jeopardise his chances by incurring the wrath of the chief secretary who had refused him permission to make the cast, Hamilton explained that he'd made his careful observations while Kreitmeyer did the excellent plaster work on Kelly. The phrenologist detailed the outlaw's measurements, which were 'remarkable' because the 'head is scarcely of medium size for so big a man'. Kelly scored a 'perfect' twenty out of twenty for destructiveness, acquisitiveness and self-esteem. He ranked nineteen for combativeness, eighteen for secretiveness, seventeen for alimentiveness, sixteen for philoprogenitiveness, et cetera.

While Hamilton said Kelly's general bumps were no worse than many of the low types on Bourke Street, there was 'not one head in a thousand of the criminal type so small in caution as his and there are few heads among the worst which would risk so much for the love of power'. His problems also came from his enormous self-esteem and large love of approbation, qualities that made him dazzling, charming and heroic to people who couldn't see through his vanity, et cetera. Hamilton closed his observations – which any newspaper reader with a passing knowledge of Kelly and phrenology might have offered – by saying he would soon deliver his views on capital punishment in *The Herald*.

That article appeared two days later and it was another public job application. Hamilton's remarks were far less about his moral opposition to the death penalty than a claim that Kelly's outrages might have been prevented by phrenological *intervention*. Contradicting what he'd written previously, Hamilton now said that there were 'hundreds of heads of a lower type than that of Edward Kelly among our juvenile population', and so it was 'desirable that Government should employ an expert in phrenological science to select the worst types, with a view of putting them under a system of physiological and phrenological training'.

Hamilton's offer to snatch up wrong-headed larrikins on Bourke Street to save the colony from crime wasn't taken up by Graham Berry. As a final indicator of the phrenologist's commitment to the abolition cause, he wouldn't be heard from again when men came to be hanged in Victoria. If he had Ned's head, his secret went to the grave with him in 1884.

Kelly's hanging had been 'private', but that didn't mean the public couldn't 'see' what had happened. These illustrations were far more sophisticated than the *Police News* engravings of penal punishments. The definitive one appeared on the cover of *The Australasian Sketcher* on 20 November. It showed the pinioned Kelly, white cap on head, noose not yet placed, facing Upjohn, looking like a military figure rather than a monstrous freak, the men flanked by priests and warders, and watched by Castieau, Rede and Dr Barker. It was a sombre image.

*Punch*'s full-page cartoon – 'Sooner or Later – the Unerring Arm of Justice' – was more energetic. This depicted Kelly in the shadow of the gallows, his face in a surprised rictus as he was grabbed by a giant fist, whose arm wound back miles and miles into the distance of the country-side – and, presumably, across the seas, given that the long arm of the law and the rope that hanged him belonged to Her Majesty, Queen Victoria, ruler of the British colony of Victoria.

~

Ned Kelly had famously told Redmond Barry that he'd see him 'there, where I go'. People naturally wondered where the outlaw had gone. The city's spiritualists were on the case. This would almost certainly have included Alfred Deakin.

They soon revealed that while Kelly had been counting down the days to his doom, seances across the city had gone quiet because the good spirits were busy making a big ethereal web to cast over Melbourne Gaol. They'd succeeded in nabbing Ned just in the nick of time. As *The Ballarat Courier* related, 'a troop of bad djinns swarmed round the place and banged up against the net in a vain endeavour to get at what they considered their own'. Ned's soul was saved and taken to the good place:

> The first spirit Kelly recognised in the land of the disembodied creatures was that of Constable Lonigan. Lonigan did not attempt to ambush and make reprisals, but welcomed the soul of the outlaw, expressing his pleasure at the good spirits having gotten him instead of the bad "uns".

But how would Ned and Barry get on there, where he went? The question became relevant sooner than anyone could have imagined. By 15 November, the judge, who suffered from diabetes, had developed a carbuncle on his neck. His homeopathic physicians advised him to rest and recover, but Barry knew better and soon the boil had grown to an immense size. Taking to his bed, the restless sufferer continually flung off his coverings, leading to lung congestion from 'exposure'. On 23 November, *The Argus* reported the good news: Barry had for the past few days been unable to take his seat in the Supreme Court but 'happy to say ... the latest reports are favourable'. By the time Melburnians read this article, Sir Redmond Barry was dead.

Flags flew at half-mast and the Exhibition Building's bunting was lowered. *The Telegraph* said the 'feeling of regret was universal'. Not quite. Soon it was overheard on Bourke Street that Barry's carbuncle had been in the *exact* same spot as the knot mark on the outlaw's neck. So perhaps he'd been cursed. Another rumour said he'd been poisoned by the gang's sympathisers. Now the question was: how would Kelly and Barry get on in eternity?

On the day the judge died, *The Herald* promised: 'Spiritualistic circles are arranging for an account of the interview in spirit land.' There was no immediate follow-up report. But in May 1881, Ned would make contact from beyond, only to say he was in the 'second sphere', which as *The Hamilton Spectator* informed, was 'a very respectable portion of the spiritualist heaven'. As there was no word on Barry, it might have been taken to mean that the outlaw and the judge hadn't ended up in the same place.

~

Four days after Elijah Upjohn hanged Ned Kelly, he was transferred from Melbourne Gaol to Pentridge to serve the rest of his sentence. Although he was safely tucked away, his name and likeness were known in Melbourne. A few days after the execution, a performance of *Romeo and Juliet* at the Theatre Royal was interrupted by larrikins, who noted that the actor playing Friar Lawrence bore a resemblance to the hangman. Every time he appeared, a 'knot of small boys in one corner of the gallery, composed of sympathisers with the murderer just executed', cracked up and called out: 'Upjohn!'

*Punch* knew where Upjohn now fitted into society, and its satire 'The Almanac Procession' – which set out the order in which notables would make an imaginary march through the city – put the hangman last, alongside do-gooder David Gaunson and boy politician John Caulfield. This trio was flanked by Kelly sympathisers, Chinamen-murderers, police smashers and larrikins, and tailed only by 'Burglars, Bruisers, Blackguards, Card-Sharpers, Magsmen, Thieves, Bullies, Roost-robbers, Snow-droppers, Welshers, Picketpockets, *et hoc genus omne*'.

Elijah Upjohn was thus the lowest of the high – or the other way around.

~

In early March 1881, a *Herald* journalist went to Pentridge to see Upjohn administer floggings, reporting that he wasn't flashy like Gately but that his punishments were very severe. That day a young lad about to be whipped began yelling in fear when he saw Upjohn.

'Quiet, my boy,' the flagellator said, 'it will do you good.'

The youngster wrestled so much that two warders had to hold the triangle. *The Herald* thought Upjohn's comment and the boy's fruitless struggle 'afforded a rather amusing scene'.

Just over a week later, Upjohn's sentence was served. He was released with the money he'd earned. If he wanted to, he could get a train to Ballarat and try to resume his old life. But in reality, that was impossible. At the best of times, an ex-hangman couldn't get work or lodgings in Melbourne. Ballarat, where he was already well known, was far smaller – and now he had the blood of Ned Kelly on his hands. It was also likely Upjohn's wife and sons didn't want him back, given what he'd said about them in court, and that they'd be tainted by his presence.

Instead, Upjohn stayed on as Victoria's Jack Ketch. But he'd have a new deal. Upjohn had spent decades as a small businessman dealing with government officials and he wasn't backwards in demanding fair compensation; Sheriff Rede and Premier Berry had witnessed what insecurity and impermanence had done to the colony's hangmen during that same period. Now Melbourne was again to have a salaried executioner.

Upjohn would be paid five shillings per day, enjoy his own quarters in Pentridge with food and fuel rations, and be free to roam as he pleased. What he negotiated was exactly what Gately had for years been denied. Yet they were the same conditions Jack Harris had briefly enjoyed in 1847. Victoria had stepped backwards three decades in order to move forwards.

Although it had now been months, Upjohn still had to answer the question: 'What was it like, hanging Ned Kelly?' On one occasion he gave a startling answer. In May 1881, Upjohn, warming to his new salaried station in life and calling himself a 'civil servant', was 'under the verandah' at the Supreme Court, which was where plaintiffs, defendants and minor legal functionaries gossiped. Several men took the opportunity to introduce themselves to the infamous figure in their midst. *The Herald* reported: 'Mr Upjohn at once exhibited a condescending affability, which ripened into communicativeness.' One of his new friends suggested he must have felt the weight of the responsibility of his office when called on the hang Ned Kelly.

Upjohn cracked a ghastly smile, as if pitying the fellow's ignorance, and replied: 'Why, I didn't hang Ned Kelly at all; it was the sheriff that hung him. I only pinioned him, and put the white cap over his face, but the sheriff drew the bolt.'

Upjohn's audience 'exhibited extraordinary surprise' at this revelation. A bailiff cracked a joke along the lines of, 'So that's why you didn't get a portion of the reward!' A few days later, a *Herald* columnist wrote a commentary that took the claim mock-seriously beneath the headline 'Who Hung Ned Kelly?'

Was Upjohn being candid or canny? Despite the variations in newspaper coverage, none had reported that Sheriff Rede had pulled the bolt; indeed, Castieau's account said this was pretty much the only thing Upjohn had done. But the hangman was now on the outside, and he might have thought he'd be safer from the larrikins if he sheeted home the actual hanging to someone else. Rede can't have liked being named as that someone else. This perhaps wasn't quite 'affronting a sheriff' – the offence that had got the original Jack Ketch sacked back in 1686 – but clearly it wasn't good to be tainted in the press in this way.

Upjohn wasn't given the flick. Right then, Robert Rohan was being sentenced to death in Beechworth for murder. A month later Upjohn was there. *The Herald* reported it went the way it was meant to, the hangman giving this heavy man just the right short drop so he died instantly.

With hangings now less frequent – Victoria was coming more into line with the rest of the colonies – Upjohn was in the papers most regularly for wielding the cat under the all-purpose headline 'The Lash'. Men fainted, begged for mercy, screamed, 'Murder! I'm dying!' Others took it with a smile, handing off the leather they'd ground between their teeth to the next in line. One hardened crim, upon being offered water afterwards, said sarcastically, 'Give it to Upjohn, he's exhausted.' Some complained he was striking too low. Some vowed revenge on everyone when they were released.

~

Melbourne hadn't forgotten Ned Kelly, but the tragedy became comedy and history was rewritten when *Ostracised* debuted at the Princess Theatre in August 1881. Written by EC Martin, an *Age* employee who'd been at Kelly's hanging, the production came with musical interludes that saw the gang do Irish jigs and sing songs like 'Slap, Bang, Here We Are Again'. The audience hooted the police and roared with approval at every appearance of a Kelly gang or clan character.

*The Ararat and Pleasant Creek Advertiser* asked why, if Kate Kelly had not been allowed to have her show, should EC Martin and the producers be allowed to make money catering 'to the morbid curiosity of the evil disposed'? Handbills were pasted all over town and the show was a hit that ran for five weeks. Upjohn would've been aware of *Ostracised* and – if he wanted to distance himself from the Kelly hanging – might have been pleased that this 'Grand Moral Drama' omitted the execution, and instead had the outlaw giving a speech before exiting the stage on a barrow.

But Melbourne had not forgotten Upjohn. A few days into January 1882, he was stoned in the street, knocked down and brutally kicked. When he prosecuted his two assailants, the magistrate said there was 'no question' of their guilt, before fining them just five shillings each – what you might get for the most minor drunkenness offence. It was hard not to see this as a message.

Just as Bamford had been interviewed by Marcus Clarke, and Gately had been profiled by Vagabond, Elijah Upjohn got to have his say when a *Ballarat Post* reporter sought out him out in his Coburg environment near Pentridge in February.

Upjohn was clean, clad in light-coloured trousers, a tweed coat, a white vest and a broad-brimmed Panama hat with a flowing head scarf. The reporter thought he looked 'remarkably well – in fact majestic, towering as he does far above those around him'. He was 'more like a quiet old farmer, or other easy-going personage, than that "officer of her Majesty," whose functions, of all others, are the most loathsome and repulsive'.

Their chat started on a testy Gateley-esque note, the hangman insisting that his correct title was 'paid executioner ... to Her Majesty's

Government of Victoria'. As for how he viewed his role: 'Obedience to authority', Upjohn said, was the first law of discipline, and this was how he framed accepting the job when the government was 'took short for a scragger and flagellator!'.

The interviewer explained for readers the hangman's pay, lodgings and freedoms, Upjohn agreeing he was 'very comfortable'. Even so, daylight wasn't 'altogether favourable to his walking abroad'. The reporter got a taste of this as they strolled a street and were met by a number of lads who shouted something like, 'It's the hangman!' and then continued 'yelling and hissing in most pronounced and venomous manner'. Upjohn took little if any notice, walking on with his 'measured military steps' and drawing on his pipe contemplatively, as the reporter had seen him do back in Ballarat when he was carting washing back to the missus.

Asked how he liked his present business, Upjohn bristled: 'Business – what d'ye mean by business? I am a paid officer of the Queen, and a necessary one too; and there ai'nt a man in the country as can say I'm any the worse for faithfully doing what I'm paid for, sir, that's – obey orders.'

Upjohn talked about how he had obeyed orders as a prisoner back in the day: 'I've done it afore I saw Australia, and seen many a better man nor you and I shot like a dog, for refusing to do what them as called themselves gentlemen ordered them to do.' Now it was different only in that he was on contract rather than a convict: 'Her Majesty's officers orders me to do what I'm paid for, and when I agrees to do a thing, and don't, then disobedience and breach of agreement begins – things that never pay – not in the government service.'

Upjohn saw himself strictly as a functionary. And now he wanted to change the subject: 'But don't talk "shop",' Upjohn said. 'How's things looking at Ballarat?'

Things in Ballarat weren't so good for his family. In March 1881, Elijah and Ann's now adult son Alfred – the tinsmith, former murder witness and skittles champion – had been charged with violent assault. When he and his co-accused appeared before Henry Glenny and other magistrates, the alleged victim was still too ill or injured to attend, so they were remanded on bail. A week later, Alfred was free after the case was settled out of court. On 3 January 1882 – the same day his father was being stoned in a Melbourne Street – Alfred was confined to Ballarat hospital with pneumonia. He died two weeks later – six weeks before Upjohn pontificated with his pipe for *The Ballarat Post*'s reporter. If this sad development was discussed, it didn't make it into the article.

While their chat had appeared amiable, the reporter didn't really believe that Upjohn's talk about only following orders made a moral difference. His silvery head bore the stain 'of having, from choice, often shed the blood of fellow creatures'. When death came for this old man – as it must come to all – few would regret his passing.

The journalist had neglected to include an important question: how did it feel to hang a man? It'd be a few years – and a few more executions – before a *Herald* reporter put this to Upjohn. Then he'd reply: 'I take no notice. In fact it takes no effect on me.'

Was Elijah Upjohn the antidote to the poisonous personages that had been Jack Harris, William Bamford and Michael Gately? *The Ballarat Post* reporter's 'An Interview with the Hangman' made it seem so. Here was a man who was clean, sober, respectful and sane. Given what Melbourne had endured with his predecessors, readers might have been forgiven for thinking they at last had a fellow along the lines of the 'gentlemen' executioners of London.

But of course it wasn't true that finishing lives had 'no effect' on Upjohn. Being the hand that delivered men to horrific deaths or that ripped the flesh from their backs had a mental, emotional and spiritual cost. And the results could be fatal.

Up in Sydney, Alexander Green had been sent to Tarban Creek insane asylum in 1855, and died there, forgotten, well over a decade later.

Even in places where hangmen were respected, it was a career that could send you mad. A London hangman haunted by the ghosts of his victims would come within moments of suicide before being saved by a Christian evangelist. Another one would succeed in killing himself – and this was a fate that also awaited a Victorian executioner.

But even before that future bloody day in Melbourne Gaol, there was no denying that for half a century the city's Jack Ketches had quelled their demons in spectacular alcoholic obliteration. Their 'profession' had thrown them into lives of squalor, into the path of violent persecution and into paupers' graves.

Elijah Upjohn might have looked and sounded like a gentleman executioner. But he was, like his victims, merely a dead man walking.

~

By June 1882, Upjohn's final slow slide was underway. *The Weekly Times* put it to readers that Upjohn's services were only needed every couple of months and he spent the rest of his time wandering the streets and 'using offensive remarks to females and children'. He would do the same when taking transport. 'A few evenings ago he got into one of the omnibuses at Brunswick, in which there were four young ladies, and his conduct was so insulting that the driver had to stop and order him out, as the other occupants refused to remain with him in the omnibus.' That he was getting a salary of £90 a year – with quarters in Pentridge – meant 'he should be subjected to some regulations which would compel him to conduct himself in a proper manner.'

Upjohn's big boss, the inspector-general of penal establishments and superintendent of Pentridge, John Castieau, who'd taken these roles in 1881, was already aware of these complaints. Upjohn's behaviour inside the prison was no better. His quarters were filthy, he treated warnings with contempt and officials felt repugnance at having to let him in and out of the prison. What was perhaps the last straw was Upjohn smuggling goods to the prisoners.

Castieau's patience was at an end and he kicked Upjohn out of Pentridge. Warders were relieved; the local villagers less so. On 5 July, *The Herald* reported: 'A strong feeling exists against Upjohn wandering about Coburg and Brunswick, and unless he alters his conduct he may rest assured he will be summoned, the result of which will be the meting out of very severe punishment.'

But ever the negotiator, Upjohn argued that he should get a pay *increase* to compensate for the loss of his quarters and rations. The government agreed, and he was henceforth to be paid an extra shilling a day, 'on the understanding that he conducts himself properly in the future'.

Upjohn didn't do himself any favours in this regard. When ordered to go and see Castieau, he didn't turn up. The next time Upjohn was at the prison, he received a severe dressing-down. Also concerning was the increasingly 'reckless manner' of his floggings. Men on the triangle would swear at him between their screams because his lashes hit high on their necks, or wrapped low around their loins to the 'woodwork'.

Something had to be done. The government cancelled its deal with Upjohn – but he only lost his salary. He could work on a per-job basis and be paid £5 per hanging and 10 shillings for each flogging. Upjohn, *The Weekly Times* reported, 'stated that he will neither hang nor flog till he is paid his full salary.' Then came news the executioner role would soon be advertised. With Upjohn's bluff called, he backed down.

What choice did Elijah have? As Jack Harris's miserable years had shown, no-one would hire a former hangman for other work. Though Melbourne strode into the future in many areas of life – there were now so many telephones, for instance, that people were complaining about the unsightliness of the overheard wires – on the hangman question it took a big step back into the darkness.

Upjohn's behaviour worsened. In September 1882 he had a beer at a Carlton hotel and exposed himself in the presence of two women and a child. Indecent exposure was a flogging offence. But in court it sounded more like he'd been going to the toilet outside, and a lesser charge was substituted. Even so, he was fined £10, forty times more than his recent violent attackers had been slugged. Upjohn couldn't pay and went to gaol for three months. Such a severe sentence might have been intended to put him back under strict control and save the community further unpleasantness.

*The Herald* dragged out the old drum and gave it a beating, saying Upjohn's disgrace presented an opportunity for a hangman 'who prides himself on his sobriety, bringing up a family in respectability, besides going to church, and occasionally giving newspaper interviewers his opinion on the theological questions of the day'. This was a reference to William Marwood in London, who'd succeeded Calcraft and become respected as a social commentator. The paper said: 'Seriously, the hangman need not be a person who outrages society, as has been the case with Bamford, Gately and Upjohn.' In Melbourne, this argument was now thirty-five years old.

But *The Herald*'s problem with Upjohn was resolved in October 1882 when he served up a good lashing with the cat-o'-nine-tails. It reported that he was now 'flogging better than when he was knocking about drinking'. Castieau was in a forgiving mood too, with Pentridge officials regaling Upjohn that same day with a post-flagellation lunch before they put him back on his cart to Melbourne Gaol.

Just after Christmas, Upjohn was released from gaol with a 'nice little sum of money to draw'. He'd keep earning sporadically as flagellator. But the man – who forever seemed to be trying to wrestle his demons and attain respectability – in mid-1883 returned to spruiking his quack medicines. He even used his old pamphlet from Ballarat.

Upjohn's new profession saw the wags have fun with this

embodiment of Jack Ketch as the 'excellent physician' with the axe and rope saying, 'Here's your cure, Sir.' *The Herald* said the pamphlet would 'if perused by some of our medical men rather astonish them', but allowed that 'his remedy with "hemp" has no doubt been efficacious many times'. *The Bulletin* said it was true that his 'celebrated drop mixture' had relieved Ned Kelly and others from 'all earthly pain', and no customer had written to make any claim otherwise.

As previously, Upjohn's quackery didn't change his fortunes.

~

As for the fate of his predecessor? Garryowen's 'The Chronicles of Early Melbourne' series had appeared in *The Herald* from the middle of 1882, and at the end of the year its epilogue gave a potted history of the city's hangmen. With Upjohn then in gaol, Garryowen had wondered whether Michael Gately might return, saying the man recently 'had the astounding audacity to write to one of our members of Parliament, beseeching the employment of some political influence to reinstate him in his former position'.

It wasn't to be. Even before Ned Kelly hanged, Gately had gone from Sydney to Brisbane. He hadn't exactly landed on his feet so much as behind bars at St Helena, the Moreton Bay island prison, where in August 1880 he assisted Queensland's Jack Ketch in the hanging of an Aboriginal bushranger convicted of rape. After Gately got out, he got up to his usual tricks and got a six-month gaol stretch in Toowoomba. Then he moved on to Roma, where in April 1883 he enjoyed a week behind bars for resisting arrest.

But that was the end of the line. Gately died in Roma in August, aged about fifty-seven. *The Queensland Figaro* offered a pun-obituary that was bleakly accurate:

[W]hen he wasn't scragging a felon, [he] was engaged in either of the delightful occupations of getting drunk or kicking his wife. Gately died up at Roma the other day, and the doctors 'cut him up.' (By-the-way, Gately, in his official capacity as Flogger for the Victorian Government, as well as hangman, had often *cut other men up*!) At the inquest there was no rope found. Nary a '*drop*!'

Jack Ketch was dead. Long live Jack Ketch.

~

The next month Elijah Upjohn went up to Ararat to hang the murderer Robert Francis Burns. This father of six had the previous year been charged with killing a man and cutting off his head. His protestations of innocence were eloquent and heartfelt and he was acquitted. No sooner was the verdict in than he was re-arrested for an earlier murder. Burns pleaded not guilty again but the jury wasn't convinced.

In the lead-up to his date with the gallows, he wrote a statement – but his priest convinced him not to make it public. Then Burns wanted to make a speech on the scaffold – yet the priest prevailed on him not to. Now, as Upjohn was doing the pinioning, he asked the condemned murderer if he had anything to say. Burns did, and spoke quietly to Upjohn.

Moments later, appearing very nervous, Upjohn led Burns to the drop where he placed the noose loose around his neck, with the knot beneath his chin. This was strange, and not Upjohn's usual method – nor anyone else's. The senior warder noticed and told the hangman to do it right. But Upjohn was so 'nervous' that the warder had to make the adjustment. Upjohn pulled the lever and Burns died instantly. The papers noted that if not for the warder, the man would have strangled.

But maybe that was what Upjohn had wanted. The next day, at

Pentridge, the hangman made a statement to reporters to reveal what Burns had said to him on the gallows. But first he wanted to set the record straight: his shaking was due to a natural infirmity he'd suffered all his life, and the warders had interfered with his work on the gallows. He wasn't a drunk and he wasn't a bungler.

Having justified himself, Upjohn now spilled what Burns had said before he swung: 'I cooked eight, five in Victoria, and now you're going to cook me.'

Burns had apparently confessed to *eight* murders.

Upjohn was called a liar by *The Argus*'s reporter, who said that if anything had been said, the sheriff and gaoler would have heard it too. But *The Herald* believed the hangman. Burns, it thought, had said his piece, 'gratifying his vanity or love of notoriety, or whatever else it might be, and at the same time keeping his promise to the priest'.

*The Herald* sent out a 'special reporter' to investigate. By the following March, the paper believed it had confirmed the gallows confession. From 1876, Burns had been luring workmates to their bush deaths, smashing their skulls and in some cases beheading the bodies. Upjohn had been in the right place at the right time – or the other way around – to help expose one of Australia's earliest and worst serial killers.

~

Upjohn flogged his way into 1884. One old man suffered immensely but when it was over said, 'Thank you, Mr Upjohn', to which the flagellator replied: 'Quite welcome, until the next time.' Another man, receiving his final instalment, said, 'That squares you and me, Upjohn.' Offered a wet rag for his back, he refused the comfort with: 'That's apt to give a man a cold.' A boy of seventeen, convicted of sodomy, was terrified when he saw Upjohn in his skullcap. He pleaded to be dealt with gently. Upjohn told him: 'My lad, I have to do my duty the same as any other servant of the Government. You should have thought of this before.' *The Fitzroy City Press* said what came next was 'terrible to witness'.

During this period, a truly wretched convict came to the triangle. This man – listed in the *Police Gazette* as Thomas Jones, alias William Perrins – had indecently assaulting a nine-year-old girl he'd lured into the Treasury Gardens. Not so long before, men convicted of such crimes had been hanged, their death masks displayed by Sohier and Doubleday. But this fiend had only been sentenced to one year and to fifteen lashes. Jones/Perrins took his flogging with relative equanimity. But he would be back at the triangle in extraordinary circumstances before the end of the year.

Upjohn had been keeping himself out of trouble in public. But trouble found him in the first week of April 1884. In a pub on Little Bourke Street, he offered to shout a man a drink, only for the man to tell him to keep his 'blood money'. Insulted, Upjohn said he hoped to one day have the pleasure of flogging the ungrateful wretch. When the hangman walked from the hotel, the man smashed him in the skull with a piece of timber, then kicked him repeatedly in the head as he lay on the ground insensible. Upjohn was taken to hospital by police. His assailant was fined twenty shillings. Such a paltry punishment could be seen as yet another message from the bench that the Upjohn was fair game.

*The Herald* worried about what might happen next – and sided with the larrikins. Yes, it was proper to try to protect Upjohn, but his appearance in public was 'an almost unavoidable temptation, if not an absolute excuse for members of the criminal class to commit a breach of the peace'. *The Bulletin* agreed: Upjohn 'delights to be heroic' in being out and about but was asking to be put in a 'hero's grave'.

Upjohn was damned even when he tried to do his work well. Going up to Ararat to turn off child rapist-murderer Henry Morgan in June 1884, he and a warder spent the evening testing the rope with various weights. This was how it was supposed to be done. Yet even as *The Ovens and Murray Advertiser* described this 'perfect rehearsal of his apparatus' to 'obviate bungles', it was still outraged: 'Heaven save us! Hath this fellow no other feeling than that of his calling, that he can go through such grim preparations with such calmness?' Reports of the hanging said Morgan died almost instantaneously. Including Ned Kelly, the hangman was actually four from four in delivering what were considered 'quick' deaths, attended by a minimum of struggling and other discomfort for the viewers. Somewhat less to his credit was that he was reported to have pissed out a train window during his jaunt up to Ararat.

A few days later, back in Pentridge, Upjohn was at the triangle. The hangman was hungover, red-faced and shaking from the debauch funded by the £5 for Morgan. Castieau was watching, concerned about recent erratic floggings. Under this pressure, Upjohn was more careful, and his boss had no cause for complaint.

At this time, Melbourne was complaining about a man who *wouldn't* be sent to Upjohn for flogging. Philip Leucy came before the court for a dreadful assault on his wife, Catherine. Even though he'd tried to cut her throat, the magistrate let him off with a caution – the beaten woman, who depended on her husband's labouring wage to feed their two children, having asked for mercy for him.

Three days later, Leucy beat her again, hit her with an axe and was about to kill her when her stepfather intervened, wresting the weapon from him and running for the police. Leucy continued to bash Catherine and was strangling her when a constable arrived and hauled him off. Leucy broke free, punched her in the face again and then bloodied the constable's nose.

In court, one of the five magistrates judging the case said it was clear 'you will certainly kill her some day', before they set him free on a six-month bond of £50 to keep the peace, to what *The Age* described as 'the evident astonishment of everyone in court'. That night Leucy beat and tried to strangle Catherine again. This time he went to gaol for six months – but only because he couldn't find the £50 and two new £25 sureties.

*The Age* said this scandalous parody of justice was all too common, and the government needed to weed out imbecilic magistrates like Mr Call, who were in effect telling men that such crimes didn't count. 'If every act of aggravated assault like Leucy's was followed by flogging and a year or two of penal servitude, a few women would escape sudden death, and many hundreds more would be saved from a daily or weekly purgatory and death by inches,' the paper wrote.

The issue was raised in parliament. Solicitor-general Alfred Deakin – who'd fulfilled phrenologist Archibald Hamilton's belief in his political capabilities – admitted there had been a failure of justice but said it wasn't his place to interfere with magistrates. He did promise – as Victorian government ministers had previously – that a bill would be introduced to give magistrates the power to order wife-beaters flogged.

It wasn't, and men continued to beat their wives with impunity. This injustice was to help put a hangman in his grave.

In July 1884, Castieau was feeling the heat over problems at Pentridge. These ranged from his being too lenient with prisoners to his being too lenient with drunken warders. After thirty-two years in the penal establishment, Castieau took six months' leave before retiring.

Just a month later, Elijah Upjohn also reached the end of his career.

James Hawthorn had been convicted of the murder of his brother. The jury believed him guilty, but was also troubled that some of the evidence wasn't as strong as they would have liked; they recommended mercy. The Executive – which included ex-premier Graham Berry and rising star Deakin – allowed the law to take its course.

Upjohn's performance was severely criticised in the press. *The Geelong Advertiser* said he had to be 'captured' and lodged in the gaol. *The Portland Guardian* had him 'trembling from the effects of a recent drinking bout'. *The Star* reckoned he was barely able to perform his duties: 'The cap was drawn down, but two warders had to assist the hangman in adjusting the noose. Upjohn then proceeded to pull the bolt by means of a switch-like handle, but even in this simple matter he bungled, and had to make a second attempt.' According to *The Age*, which came to a curious conclusion given how long spasms had been dismissed as meaningless, he had 'failed to adjust the rope properly, the result being that death was not instantaneous, spasmodic contortions of the lower part of the body indicating the presence of life for nearly a minute after the drop fell'.

The three hangings following Ned Kelly's had taken place outside the city, under the supervision of deputy sheriffs, but Hawthorn's execution was in Melbourne Gaol, and thus directly under the watch of Sheriff Robert Rede. The widespread coverage of Upjohn's alcoholic bungling can't have pleased him. Rede wrote to the chief secretary that day about Upjohn:

> He is in no way fit for his position for his nerve is gone; in fact before an execution he has to be wound up by giving him spirits. I have no hesitation in saying, that the execution this morning, although effectual as the neck was dislocated, was done in a bungling manner, and Upjohn in dress and general appearance was simply disgraceful and revolting in the extreme.

Of course, all of that might also cast doubt on Rede's judgement. If Upjohn had been a problem previously, why had he been allowed to continue? If he was in such a shocking state on the day of the hanging, why had the sheriff not stepped in to take over?

Ever uppity Upjohn made things worse when, rather than taking his gruel and vowing to do better, he instead channelled Jack Ketch's sorry-not-sorry *Apologie*. In a statement to *The Herald*, he said he hadn't needed to be captured before the hanging; following the usual procedure, he'd been at home in Coburg waiting to be picked up. When a 'new chum' from the prison had come to get him, he was taken to the new inspector-general of penal establishments, William Gore Brett, and 'the head man in Mr Castieau's place began to blow me up because I did not go up and report myself. I never was told to do so.' Sent on to Melbourne Gaol, Upjohn was met by its governor, William Magee, a former Ballarat Gaol governor who surely knew him, and he 'blew me up because I did not go to the gaol. I had no orders to do so'.

Upjohn said he had *not* been drunk or hungover: 'I have not been drinking more than I usually do at my meals, and nobody has seen me in an hotel since last Friday until yesterday afternoon after I hung Hawthorne, and all I have had since are four nobblers of rum.'

As for Hawthorn's hanging:

It was not me that fumbled the knot after placing the rope round Hawthorne's neck, it was the head warder of the gaol. I kept telling him, 'that's not the place to put it,' but he would put it where he liked, and he has not been a witness when any one has been hanged before. I wanted to put it where I did, when I hanged the others, with the knot more at the back of the neck, so that it would have been broken directly he fell.

A knot at the back of the neck wasn't in the memo. But neither was what anyone else was suggesting. Upjohn's previous work had been judged fine. After Upjohn made his long self-justifying statement, *The Herald* reporter asked questions, to which he replied:

There was nothing wrong with the bolt, but it ought to have been oiled or greased so that it would slip free. It is not my place to see to the bolt, it is those in the gaol. I don't go and see to the drop or anything connected with it; this is all done before I go there. The knot was even tied, but it was shown to me, and I was asked if it was all right, and I said 'Yes'.

All of that sounded reasonable. But back in 1686, Jack Ketch, who hadn't been fired after his worst atrocities, had eventually been gaoled for 'affronting a sheriff'. Upjohn had now committed his version of this unforgiveable offence. The hangman's job wasn't just to do the dirty work: it was to be the sin-eater for society. A society whose representative on the gallows was the sheriff. Now, rather than meekly absorbing the blame, Upjohn had tried to throw his betters under the omnibus. He'd specifically said William Gore Brett and governor William Magee had treated him unfairly, and suggested they were incompetent. He'd claimed it had been the head warder who bungled the hanging. None of this reflected well on Sheriff Rede, with whom the buck stopped when it came to executions.

Elijah Upjohn had acted like the pissed-off nightman he'd once been, lashing out verbally and in print to dump shit on everyone.

Even so, the newspapers only reported that Rede had 'suspended' Upjohn. The sheriff was said to have received two fresh applications from men who'd first applied for the job when Gately cleared out. One wrote that he had a wife and child to support and so was 'desirous of obtaining some respectable employment', and that he had the 'high moral character' that 'every Civil Servant should possess'. *The Ovens and Murray Advertiser* reported that Rede was considering another option: that a gaoler should take over and be paid the £5 fee in addition to his regular salary. 'The warders are in a state of the utmost consternation, lest the loathsome office should be forced upon one of their number'.

Yet Elijah Upjohn had lived in the colony during the reigns of Harris, Bamford and Gately – nearly forty years of hangmen who'd behaved themselves far worse than he had on the gallows and in the streets. They'd kept their jobs. He probably didn't have to worry.

In a sign that Upjohn believed Rede was bluffing, he went to Pentridge on 1 October because he knew a man was due for an instalment at the triangles. But on his arrival he was told there would be no flogging, and he was sent away. This was reported as mysterious – the prisoner wasn't ill, which usually was the only thing that would save a man from being flagellated.

On 6 October, *The Geelong Advertiser* reported that three or four applications had now been received. Rede was putting applicants before the inspector-general, with Mr Brett reported to have 'selected one whom he considers suitable for the post in the event of Upjohn's services being dispensed with'.

Dispensed with they were. Sheriff Rede had finally done what his predecessors could not or would not do.

Jack Ketch had been fired.

On 24 October, the Victorian newspapers reported that a newly appointed hangman would execute murderer William O'Brien that morning in Melbourne Gaol. At 10am the condemned man stepped from the cell, and a couple of minutes later was dead at the end of the rope with a broken neck. As *The Star* remarked, the new finisher 'proved a great improvement on the clumsy Upjohn'.

Victorian newspapers soon agreed to keep the hangman's identity secret, referring to him only as 'Jones'. But at the time of his debut, this anonymity hadn't yet been conferred. Reports called him an 'ex prisoner' and named him as Thomas Jones. What they didn't say was that the colony had just given the job of hangman and flagellator to the child rapist William Perrins – aka Thomas Jones – whom Upjohn had flogged earlier the same year.

Long live Jack Ketch.

~

Elijah Upjohn was out of a job and out on the streets. No one would give him work or a place to stay. The threat of larrikin attack was constant. But there was one organisation that might protect him.

Since the Salvation Army had arrived in Melbourne three years earlier, its leader, Major James Barker – assisted by Dr John Singleton, who'd facilitated Gately's marriage – had set up the 'Prison Gate Mission'. This offered food, lodgings and employment to men and women upon their release from gaol. It was lauded as good, practical, Christian work.

But the 'Soldiers of the Cross' were most visible and audible when they held their loud musical street marches and open-air services. Testifying in the name of temperance had earned them the hatred of many, and the Salvos were often abused, pelted with rotten eggs and even assaulted. In March 1884, a female member was picked off from a procession in Brunswick, beaten, strangled and dumped in a waterhole. Her murder would never be solved.

In such a warlike atmosphere, the Salvos didn't need to make themselves more of a target. Yet on Sunday 23 November 1884, Elijah Upjohn presented himself as a penitent at the Temperance Hall. Several members objected to him being accepted into the congregation. But Major Barker insisted that all were welcome.

Upjohn's recruitment was even funnier to columnists than his previous calling as a quack. *The Ovens and Murray Advertiser* chortled that he'd traded his 'plurality of pinions' for a 'pair of shining wings'. *The Bulletin* reckoned he'd be popular in a congregation of dipsomaniacs: 'They say that when he opened his mouth to pray, it's as good as having a drink.' A columnist in the short-lived *Federal Australian* weekly newspaper worried that if 'Saint Upjohn' was to testify to the congregation, he'd spill the secrets of his victims, these revelations 'scarcely calculated to improve the minds of a mixed audience'. The ever-punning *Punch* headlined its piece 'Up John and At 'Em': 'They don't want him but he wants them, and they have got themselves into a knot over the affair ... Could he not edit the *War Cry*? Just the man for a noosepaper.'

It's not known whether Major Barker offered Upjohn a job or a place to stay. He may not have qualified because he wasn't a recently released prisoner. Instead, Upjohn hovered about the major's Bourke Street office for safety during the day. When night fell, he hid and slept in any outhouse that kept him out of sight of the larrikins.

Bamford had lived in the outer darkness. Upjohn lived in shitholes like the ones he used to empty.

~

Now officially retired, John Castieau on 31 December 1884 bought a new diary and some paper to commence his memoirs. The latter promised to be lively reading – especially the part about Ned Kelly, whose hanging had occurred in period in which he'd apparently neglected his journal. In his entry that day, Castieau noted that his son Godfrey, now eighteen, was being disagreeable, while young Jack was worrying about his exams. He finished: 'I close this careless kept book. May I do better & be better if I live to close one for 1885.'

Castieau died on 25 January 1885. Godfrey would go on to be an actor, producer and director of early Australian silent films, and at least twice played the role of Ned Kelly. Jack would write for *The Bulletin* under the pen-name 'Paul Mell', recalling his early morbid meetings with Weachurch, Bondietti and Kelly and others in an article called 'Ghosts of the Gallows'.

~

Upjohn was convinced he was going to be murdered. *The Ovens and Murray Advertiser* called him 'A Social Outlaw' who lived in such a haunted state that he'd threatened to kill Inspector-General Brett and then himself. 'Serious fears are entertained that he will do something desperate, for he is now in every sense like a hunted wild beast of the wild woods.'

On the Saturday night after Castieau died, Upjohn was arrested for vagrancy. The court heard he'd been living like a dog, sleeping on vacant land behind the gaol, haunting the coffee stalls from dawn, and reduced to begging for food and asking the Salvos' boss Major Barker for the occasional sixpence. Larrikins frequently attacked Upjohn and some had threatened him with serious harm.

Upjohn spoke respectfully to the bench: 'Your worships, when I lost my situation, the Inspector-General promised me another.' Magistrate Mr Call – who'd recently attracted such ire for letting the would-be wife-killer Philip Leucy walk free – couldn't resist making fun of this bedraggled and desperate figure. 'Why don't you go up to the Mallee and frighten away the rabbits?' Then he made his ruling: 'We must send you to prison for a month. You can write then, and bring your claims forward. I think something ought to be done for you, but we cannot have you going about the streets as a vagrant.'

For Upjohn, one month in Melbourne Gaol was an act of mercy.

~

*Every Man His Own Hangman.* That was the title of the book Elijah Upjohn was reportedly writing when he was released from gaol in May 1885. Like Castieau's proposed memoir, it would have made lively reading. But, like the governor, the hangman had to live long enough to set pen to paper.

In the interim, an impresario wanted his acquaintance. An ad in *The Argus* read: 'UPJOHN, Ex-Executioner. – Drop line to James Crilly, showman; engagement, Europe, 18 Young-Street.'

Popular comic clown Jim Crilly's troupe included two dwarfs, a magnetic lady, a weightlifter and a sword swallower. *The Bulletin* was thrilled that Upjohn's fortunes were changing. He would no longer hide himself away to finish his book and keep safe from the larrikins! He'd tour the grand historic cities of Europe! To get the ball rolling, they produced text for a handbill that Crilly might use:

Sup Full Of Horrors

While you have the chance,

For —— Nights only

THE GREAT UPJOHN,

Who has with own Hand

Killed More Men

Than any other Man Living

Will be on View

And show upon a Dummy Figure

The exact manner

In which his Bloody Deeds were invariably

performed.

Admission, Threepence.

*The Bulletin* said the 'GU' – Great Upjohn – could sell souvenirs, from a knot tied in a handkerchief (6d) to a lock of his hair (2s 6d). 'Upjohn,' it joked, 'has only to resolutely put the plug in and his fortune is made.'

But Upjohn would not write his book nor be put on show. As *Bulletin* readers were having a laugh at his expense, he was the target of a murder plot by larrikins he'd flogged. Melbourne's rulers were faced with a decision. If the former hangman didn't have the decency to die already, it'd be best if he wasn't murdered in the streets. Particularly as the city was then being visited by so august a personage as the world famous George Augustus Sala, author and reporter for *The Illustrated London News*.

Unlike Harris and Gately, Upjohn couldn't pay his own way north. So, in June 1885, it was arranged that he be sent to Sydney.

So farewell Melbourne the Marvellous! city of towering warehouses, Parliament Houses – the new one as yet unfinished – law courts, free libraries, a colossal post-office, a monumental town-hall, colleges, institutes, cathedrals, churches and chapels innumerable, stately Government offices, multitudinous drinking bars ...

These were the words Sala wrote when he left Melbourne two months later. He'd loved 'thy brilliant suburbs, thy crowded omnibuses, thy splendid Botanical Garden, thy remarkable Waxworks, and Mr Coles' book arcade in Bourke Street'. Sala was a booster who focused on the heavenly and ignored the hellish – which included, during his stay, a former public official reduced to a hunted animal in mean streets ruled by murderous larrikins.

But Australia would follow Sala, celebrating the city's wonderful side while ignoring its underbelly. In much the same way that 'Ah, well, I suppose' didn't quite have the ring of 'Such is life', so too 'Melbourne the Marvellous' was discarded for a punchier expression that Sala used later in his article: 'Marvellous Melbourne.'

~

In August 1885, days after 'Marvellous Melbourne' was coined, the railway reached the town of Bourke, in north-western New South Wales. Seven hundred worthies – including future first prime minister Edmund Barton – rolled into town to celebrate the completion of this great national work, which had put 'Bourke to the Front!' A correspondent for the *Maitland Mercury and Hunter River General Advertiser* who arrived on the train described the town's outskirts: 'the floating population of navvies and camp followers are indicated by tents and "humpies" visible'.

Elijah Upjohn was living in such a tent on the outskirts. Back in June, *The Bulletin* had reported the 'thrilling news' that he'd arrived in Sydney. Why was he now living in such conditions some 500 miles north-west of the harbour city? Upjohn was an old man. But his recent flogging efforts and his very survival on the streets of Melbourne suggested he still had some strength in him. Perhaps he'd gone to Bourke to work as a navvy.

Whatever led him to the back of Bourke, Elijah Upjohn would never leave. He was found dead in his tent on 28 September 1885. He was around sixty-three.

What killed him? *The Sydney Morning Herald* reported: 'There are rumours of poisoning, and the police are investigating the case. The body was buried this afternoon, without an inquest. It is said that the man was subject to fits.'

Upjohn may have been 'subject to fits', but, if so, it'd escaped the Melbourne and Ballarat press in the past quarter of a century. Such a condition, at the very least, was something he might have used as an excuse when charged with offences or taken to task for his failings on the gallows or the triangle. In this short *Herald* notice, there was the hint of a murder mystery, coupled with the same sort of shrug that had long accompanied violence committed upon a hangman.

The man who had hanged Australia's most famous outlaw merited no further attention at the time, and his life would henceforth be reduced to a walk-on role in the death of a legend.

Yet if another attempt at mythologising had been successful, Upjohn might have been better known. In late 1906, the world's first feature film, *The Story of the Kelly Gang*, was released in Melbourne. With renewed interest in the events of a quarter-century ago, the hangman's name appeared in a few newspapers.

It was now that an imaginative writer for Melbourne's *Labor Call* claimed that after Ned Kelly said, 'Such is life,' Elijah Upjohn had pulled the bolt with a snappy retort: 'Such is death.'

# CHAPTER TWENTY-SIX

# The Hangman Is Dead, Live the Hangman

Days after 'Marvellous Melbourne' was coined, the city's new hangman, Jones, went up to Upjohn's old stamping grounds of Ballarat Gaol. Putting paid to the idea Ned Kelly could have been reprieved, Charles Bushby was to die for *wounding* a detective. Jones did his work but it was twenty to twenty-three minutes before the man's heart ceased beating. *The Age* reported:

> It is said that Jones, the hangman, had not adjusted the rope properly, and that consequently life had been cruelly prolonged. After the body had been cut down the hangman raised the dead criminal's head, and twisting it around remarked, 'Do they mean to say that his neck is not broken?'

Jones's spectacular display of callousness may also have been him doing a bit of due diligence. While the medical officer believed Bushby had strangled, the coroner later found dislocation of the neck.

~

Thomas Jones was born William Perrins in England in 1837. He came to Melbourne in 1858 as a free man, married a woman named Mary Duffy in 1864 and lived in Dunolly, in central Victoria. Jones stayed clear of the law until July 1872, when he was convicted of assault and got four months. Over the next few years, further convictions for assault and receiving stolen property saw him sentenced to another three years and three months. In October 1883, Jones accosted a little girl in the city, asked if she could show him to the railway station and then indecently assaulted her in the Treasury Gardens.

Despite the sadistic glee Jones had displayed in Ballarat when he'd bungled Bushby's execution, newspapers heralded this secretive figure as a scientific operator. In May 1885, *The Gippsland Times* said his success was the result of systematic and elaborate preparation. The office of Jack Ketch was difficult to fill, 'but in the present instance the officials seem to have been particularly fortunate in their choice'.

Jones also came with an air of mystery, because he ensured his anonymity by wearing a wig and fake beard on the gallows. Victoria's newspapers were complicit in keeping his identity secret, although their job was made easier because he wasn't causing havoc in the streets like his predecessors. In July 1885, a *Herald* reporter visited Melbourne Gaol, passed Jones in a corridor and said: 'No, no mental or physical photograph – not this time; people may meet him in the streets, in hotels and dining rooms, and sometimes it is just as well not to know one's neighbours'.

Jones's neighbours in Carlton supposedly had their suspicions about the man they knew as 'Thomas Walker'. Even so, he kept his head down and stayed out of trouble. What became of his first wife isn't known– there was a story she deserted him after learning of his new secret side-hustle as a hangman – but by 1886 Jones was married to a woman named Elizabeth and they had a son.

During his first nine years on the job, Jones was credited with hanging fourteen men. In May 1892, he was looking forward to executing serial killer Frederick Bailey Deeming, who'd been unsuccessfully defended by Alfred Deakin. Jones was sure this 'criminal of the century' was also Jack the Ripper, and he was proud that he would be the one to snuff out the monster. Puffed up at the prospect, he gave an interview to *The Herald* using his 'Walker' pseudonym, in which he explained his work.

Jones said he'd been nervous about his first hanging but since then didn't feel anything when executing men. He was paid something like £2 per week – inclusive of floggings – and when needed for a hanging, Jones allowed himself to be confined in Melbourne Gaol a week before the execution. This was to reassure Sheriff Louis Ellis, who was finally in the top job after forty years, that his hangman would be sober and rested and ready.

*The Herald*'s reporter noted that he had not looked well at Ballarat, and suggested he needed to retain 'Roberts', the helper the government had appointed to him during a period of illness. 'No fear,' he said. 'I do not want any assistants. I can do all that is wanted. I never felt better in my life.' He pounded his chest. 'I've never been unwell'. Of Deeming, he said with a hearty laugh, 'I'll turn this fellow off alright on Monday ... No fear of that.' Jones nevertheless was accompanied by Roberts – both wearing their fake beards – when it came time to hang Deeming. They did a good job; he reportedly died in an instant.

Jones enjoyed favourable press coverage as a scientific professional and gentleman hangman who kept meticulous notes and did calculations to ensure efficiency. In this he benefited from the 'Official Table of Drops', issued by the British Home Office in 1888 and revised in 1892, which set out the correct length of rope for varying body weights. Unlike the memo issued years earlier, this official advice appears to have made an impact.

Jones's public image was of a hangman like Marwood, who might one day give lectures, but in private he was a brute of the stripe suggested by his unreported prison record. Around the time Jones hanged Deeming, his wife Elizabeth gave birth to another son. But that didn't stop him from regularly beating her mercilessly. He had little to fear because she wouldn't bring charges – and even if she did, such crimes were still treated as of little consequence. Yet in her own way, Elizabeth would have her revenge.

In October 1893, Jones, after drinking for days, was trying to strangle Elizabeth when her friend and lodger Bertha Conacher returned to their Carlton house. Elizabeth called for help and Bertha slapped Jones. Then Elizabeth threw a flowerpot that hit her husband in the head.

Bruised in face and pride, but not willing to charge his wife and endure that particular scandal, Jones instead took Bertha to court for assault. During the hearing, he waved his hands around in a state of high 'excitement' and accused her of attacking him without provocation because he wouldn't let her bring male friends back to his house. Bertha's counsel, Mr Leonard, demanded to know what Jones meant by this libel, saying his client was a respectable woman who had only recently left her job because she was about to get married.

But the real sensation came when Mr Leonard forced the admission that the complainant was the public hangman, and that his 'real' name was Thomas Walker of Richardson Street, Prince's Hill. Ever more agitated, Jones now claimed he hadn't been attempting to kill his wife, just trying to get back a sovereign he'd given her. Mr Leonard asked if the sovereign was from his 'last fee'.

Jones replied: 'I didn't get it for hanging you. I haven't hung you yet.'

The magistrate threatened to send Jones to gaol for contempt.

Testifying, Bertha said she'd tried to stop Jones from choking his wife, and that he was always drunk and beating her. While Elizabeth gave evidence that he assaulted her regularly, Jones stood in the court and gesticulated wildly. It didn't help his cause.

The magistrate dismissed the charge against Bertha and ordered

Jones to pay £1/1 costs. The hangman left the court 'amidst the jeers of the spectators'.

While Jones wouldn't face legal justice for his assaults on Elizabeth, his brutality and arrogance in bringing the charge had backfired and his worst nightmare was now realised. His secret career was public – and at the worst possible time. The Brunswick 'Baby Farmer' Frances Knorr was then in custody for the murder of three infants. The following month, she was tried, found guilty and sentenced to hang. If the Executive Council didn't exercise mercy, Knorr would be the second woman executed in Victoria after Elizabeth Scott back in 1863.

Jones had raped a child and beaten and strangled his wife. But he drew the line at hanging a woman. Not because he was sensitive to Knorr's suffering. Rather, he was in a panic because his neighbours now knew the truth about him. And they'd hate him even more if he was so low as to put his rope around a woman's neck. Jones's shame was compounded by his wife saying she'd leave him if he went through with hanging Frances Knorr.

Jones drank more and more. He heard spirit voices taunting him, and the real voices of his neighbours telling him what they thought of a man who'd hang a woman. He couldn't sleep. When the Executive Council confirmed Knorr's sentence, he collapsed and moved around in a half-dazed fashion. Jones asked if Roberts, who resided in Sydney when not needed, could be recalled to do this job. He asked if he could have more money, perhaps to leave the colony after the hanging was done. A mysterious letter arrived and disturbed Jones even further. He sobbed and was hysterical.

Jones had been in the colony since 1858 and he knew the lives that the publicly identified hangmen had endured. That was why he had done his damnedest to avoid exposure for a decade.

On the morning of 6 January 1894, Jones checked himself into Melbourne Gaol to get straight and get about his preparations. The hangman told warders of the torture he'd been enduring. But after a time he seemed to brighten. Jones said he hadn't brought his fake beard with him and that one of his henchmen would bring it later. He retired to his quarters, locked the door and ran a bath.

Then Jones used a razor on his throat to make himself his last victim.

~

For fifty years, Melbourne's hangmen had been drawn from a brutalised criminal class. They'd done the dirty work so others could keep their hands clean. Despite carrying out the dread office of the law for the sheriff and the inspector-general, for the colonial governor and Queen Victoria, these men were enslaved in and damned by a cynical and cyclical system that seemed designed to make them ever more degraded, desperate and dangerous – and thus hated, hunted and haunted.

Jack Harris had been taunted by boys, and repeatedly gaoled for being drunk and for stealing. He'd disgraced the office with sadistic comments. Yet he'd been allowed to hang men for a decade.

William Bamford had been reduced to living like an animal amid the stones so he wouldn't fall prey to his larrikin predators. He'd been gaoled on the flimsiest of pretexts when he was needed to do his duties, which expanded to include reducing men's backs to bloody pulp. His bungling and sadistic relish had led to a chorus for his removal, yet he'd been allowed to reign for fifteen years.

Michael Gately had been even worse – which was predictable, given his extensive criminal record and behaviour behind bars. Yet when this snarling beast of a man tried to tame himself, he was ridiculed, demonised and thrown to the mob. Even the sight of him drunkenly biting police, choking his wife or being pursued by hundreds of larrikins wasn't enough for him to be replaced. After seven years, he'd opted out to chase his wife to Sydney.

Elijah Upjohn's relatively upstanding record promised more, and yet he quickly delivered less. By mid-1882, his behaviour was sufficiently bad to have him stripped of his salary and lodgings, which, of course, only accelerated his decline. But it'd be more than two years before he was replaced.

Jones – aka William Perrins – lasted a decade, despite it being known he was a paedophile, a drunk and a wife-beater. He had in some measure succeeded because he was allowed secrecy and benefited from a final acceptance of the 'science' of hanging. Jones likely would have continued in his role, except for his untimely exposure. Facing that life, he'd chosen death.

~

Dr Richard Youl's conclusion at the inquest was that Jones had killed himself while insane. *The Age* reported as much in its headline: 'Suicide of the Hangman – The Result of A Diseased Brain – Domestic Trouble and Excessive Drinking'. While Jones's suicide merited a lot of column inches, none was devoted to any reflection on the system that had helped kill him.

Jones's death barely caused a hiccup for the government. They had his helper, Roberts, in reserve. He was brought down from Sydney, and on 15 January thousands gathered outside Melbourne Gaol as inside Elizabeth Knorr was executed.

The *Herald*'s headline that day read: 'The Hangman Is Dead, Live The Hangman.'

# CHAPTER TWENTY-SEVEN

# Jack Ketch Is Dead

Victoria's executioners would recede into the background, though they wouldn't disappear entirely. Despite the new science of hanging, nor they or the system would enact this punishment any better. At least eight of 19 hangings between 1894 and 1922 were reportedly botched.

Roberts – real name Thomas Pauling – reigned until 1897 when he was replaced by his helper 'Smith' – real name Robert Gibbon – who in turn was assisted by a 'Brown'.

Smith was a bungler like his predecessors. When he hanged William Jones in March 1900, he mucked up his Table of Drops. The murderer weighed 159 pounds, meaning he should have been given a fall of just over five feet. Roberts gave him three feet more than that. *The Herald*'s depiction was gruesome: 'The rope cut deep into his neck and blood spattered over the stony floor as the body reached the end of the rope, giving to the usual horrible spectacle an added horror.'

Australia was federated on 1 January 1901, thanks to the leadership of Alfred Deakin, who'd soon serve the first of his three terms as prime minister.

In August that year, Smith/Gibbon – whose arms bore tattoos of skipping girls – was sentenced to four years for sexually assaulting two girls under the age of sixteen. Nevertheless, he'd keep his job, suggesting that the new state of Victoria in the federated Australia had learned nothing from the past half-century of hangman horrors. Smith performed his last execution in June 1908. This executioner was also, like the prime minister, a spiritualist. The hangman had an otherworldly mate who was a drunken ghost named 'Bob'. On one occasion, Bob beseeched him to plead leniency on behalf of a mad murderer who was set to hang at Bendigo. Perhaps it didn't come as much of a surprise when, in January 1909, Smith was declared insane and committed to Yarra Bend Asylum. His madness seemed an amalgam of his own perversions and paranoias arising from his profession, as *The Sydney Morning Herald* reported:

> For weeks past Smith been suffering the delusion that an attempt was being made to lay a criminal charge against him. He believed that the streets were full of detectives, only too ready to place him in prison. He complained that young girls were running in front of him and jeering at him, and that others were seeking to encompass his ruin. Finally he posted to Sergeant O'Donnell a long, wild letter, setting out his complaints. He intimated that if steps were not taken to prevent further persecution he would feel justified in taking the law into his own hands, and killing his tormentors.

*The Bendigo Advertiser* reported: 'Now there is a vacancy in the office of Jack Ketch.' In March 1909 – after a prisoner who'd agreed to the role changed his mind – the same paper rolled out the old headline, 'Wanted: A Hangman'.

~

Victoria found them but they remained anonymous. Some were prisoners. Others were respectable men who worked normal jobs and kept their secondary career even from friends and family.

After William Jones's horrific death – the first Melbourne execution of the 1900s – the death penalty began a steep decline. In the 20th century, there were twenty-three hangings in Victoria. To put it in perspective, this was one fewer than in the peak years of 1857–58, when victims had first packed Philemon Sohier's Chamber of Horrors.

The most infamous case was the 1922 execution of Colin Campbell Ross, convicted of child murder during a newspaper frenzy that helped change media history. Ross was sped to the gallows by Keith Murdoch, then rising to power as editor of *The Herald*, who had latched onto the advice of his mentor, Mad Lord Northcliffe, who said the key to better circulation was finding a 'good murder'.

During the investigation, Murdoch had posted his own reward, and then, when Ross was arrested by pressured police, the newspaperman had printed prejudicial photos of the accused. Ross went to the gallows, hands and feet bound, and was executed by 'the hangman, heavily masked [and] a masked assistant'. *The Herald* reported: 'Death was instantaneous'. But it wasn't. The body was screened off a second after the drop and so Ross was out of sight when he took up to twenty minutes to die, strangled in a noose fashioned from an improper rope, just as had been the case when Jack Harris executed Jeremiah Connell seventy-five years earlier. Either way, *The Herald*'s circulation soared, Keith Murdoch's star was on the rise, and the foundations of a global empire had been laid. Forty years later, his son Rupert would run the same game to make his name with the Graeme Thorne murder in Sydney.

Nearly forty years after that, thanks to the chance discovery of the physical hair evidence that had scientifically 'sealed' Colin Campbell Ross's fate, his innocence was proved beyond doubt, and he became the first and only executed person in Australian history to receive a posthumous pardon.

If there was extant physical evidence for many of the victims of Victoria's 19th-century Jack Ketches – and those of other colonies and countries – there's no doubt Ross's name would be joined by an army of other innocent men and women.

Even in their times, verdicts and punishments were often considered unsafe and unfair, for a variety of reasons: the accused had no understanding of the law; the accused had no representation or inadequate counsel; the accused had an obvious lack of premeditation; the police had corroborated each other's stories at all costs; testimony had been elicited from unreliable, motivated or hostile civilian witnesses; 'scientific' and 'medical' evidence was shaky in the extreme; severe judges like Redmond Barry were out for a guilty verdict and wouldn't concur with a jury's recommendation to mercy; and successive governments were susceptible to the guidance of such judges and further hamstrung by their own tangled-up track record on such matters. All of this said, many of the accused were no doubt guilty, but that didn't make their convictions – or their executions – fair or just. Presented with these cases today, modern juries would be unlikely to convict in many – or even most – particularly if the accused faced a mandatory death sentence.

~

Victoria – the last among the colonies to embrace capital punishment – would hang and flog people longer than the other Australian states. The horror and degradation didn't abate. What they increasingly seemed – to 20th-century society – were appallingly barbaric punishments from a medieval age. It had been a long time since an executioner dared show his face even to the journalists allowed to be present.

The last woman hanged in Australia was Jean Lee, for murder, at Pentridge in February 1951. She was carried to the scaffold barely conscious. Lee was propped in chair on the trapdoor with a hood over her face; she fainted before she was hanged by an executioner and his assistant who both wore massive steel-rimmed goggles and hats pulled low over their faces, and who stood with their backs to reporters. Lee and her two male accomplices swung from the same beam as Ned Kelly, which had been brought from Melbourne Gaol and installed at Pentridge – by a prisoner serving time for child rape.

In April 1958, William John O'Meally, convicted police killer whose death sentence had been respited, became the last man flogged in Australia. He and a fellow Pentridge prisoner were sentenced to twelve lashes each for an escape attempt in which a chief warder was shot in the thigh. The use of the cat-o'-nine-tails on both men had to be confirmed by the High Court. Facing the lash, O'Meally said he drew courage from knowing how many others had suffered worse whippings here and remained staunch. But his ordeal was terrible. 'I was very badly mauled by the flogging,' he would later tell *The Age*. 'It opened my rib cage. I don't know if it was intentional.' His suffering continued for a long time: 'I didn't get any medical attention. It took me about three months to get back on my feet again.' O'Meally was released from gaol in 1979.

In early 1967, for shooting and killing a warder during a Pentridge escape, Ronald Ryan was scheduled to hang. Seven jurors wrote to the cabinet of Premier Henry Bolte to plead for mercy. One later said: 'We didn't want the rope. If we had known Ryan would hang, I think we would have gone for manslaughter.'

Three thousand people gathered outside the prison – this time to protest against capital punishment. Some carried placards; one read 'Don't Hang a Man Who Could Be Innocent'. Others featured the hangman's noose and the word 'No'.

Such a spectacle was no longer only reported in densely typed newspaper columns. Ryan and his case were splashed across the photo-heavy tabloid papers. The issue was discussed on the radio. Patrons who still went to the newsreel theatres saw the demonstrations and the heavy police response. But people could also watch the unfolding drama in their own homes, as Pentridge was bathed in the lights of television crews.

Henry Bolte and his Executive Council refused a reprieve.

Inside Pentridge, just before 8am on 3 February 1967, were gathered fourteen male reporters. They would see Ryan noosed and see him drop, but he'd fall behind a big khaki sheet. Of this last Australian Jack Ketch, the veteran journalist Evan Whitton was to say:

> He looked, in fact, like the lanky ghost of a once-great hangman – a tall, stooped old guy with straggly grey hair and a red neck, as if he'd 'rested' between performances at some open-air task, as a carpenter maybe. But he was still nimble, cat-like even, with a sharp turn of speed over a short distance.

This man, who appeared from the cell opposite Ryan's, wore 'welder's goggles and a green Mao Zedong cap'. This ghost of hangmen past swooped on Ryan, whose last words were reported to be, 'God bless you, please make it quick.'

The hangman, according to Whitton, was rough in a blur of movement as he gave the rope a final violent jerk, wrenched the calico hood down, sprang back and pulled the bolt for Bolte. Death was reported as instantaneous. In typical Jack Ketch fashion, the hangman penned an angry, non-apology *Apologie*, writing to Whitton about his critical portrait: 'I am convinced, in view of the circumstances, that you did not witness the execution.'

When asked what he'd been doing when Ryan hanged, Premier Bolte infamously responded: 'One of the three Ss, I suppose. A shit, a shave or a shower.'

Ronald Ryan, like so many before him, had gone to the gallows protesting his innocence. More than half a century later, debate still rages over his claim. He was the last person executed in Australia.

~

Four decades after Ryan died in the noose, in the United States doctors and medical scientists began trying to determine the process of dying by hanging. By 2010 The Working Group on Human Asphyxia had analysed fourteen videos in their search for answers. Only one was a death similar to those in this book – a man who stepped off a stool and died via full-suspension hanging. He didn't move at all. The other thirteen deaths – nine autoerotic accidents and four suicides – involved victims who were standing, kneeling or lying down.

The group found that in these cases, on average, people lost consciousness in ten seconds. Victims experienced mild general convulsions from fourteen seconds and at nineteen seconds came decerebrate rigidity, which is upper-body extension and arching caused by brain stem damage. From nineteen seconds, there was also deep abdominal respiratory movement, and from thirty-eight seconds, 'decorticate rigidity', which is caused by intercranial pressure, resulting in hands clenching into fists and arms and legs flexing and extending.

The end of the body's struggle began at an average of seventy-seven seconds, with loss of muscle tone, and at 111 seconds there was an end to the abdominal respiratory movements. While the body was now flaccid, there would be isolated movements – twitches – that on average ceased after four minutes and twelve seconds. There were wide variations in the observed deaths. One victim didn't lose consciousness for eighteen seconds; another's last movement was recorded at seven minutes and thirty-five seconds.

As for how people died, other forensic evaluations at this time pointed to the suspected causes – the brain being starved of oxygen and blood, with the latter being most likely – but had to conclude, 'the exact mechanism of death has yet to be elucidated'. Brain death was believed to occur by six minutes. Heartbeats persisting up to twenty minutes were said to be due to the organ's 'sinoatrial node', which does not depend on brain impulses.

Regarding suffering, the editors of the excellent website *Capital Punishment UK*, reflecting on their Working Group's efforts and videos of short-drop judicial hangings in Iran, offered this: 'It is reasonable to assume that the conscious phase is painful due to the constriction and pressure on the neck and the panic caused by being unable to breathe'.

Of course, the Working Group's fourteen filmed deaths did not replicate long-drop hangings in which there was an attempt to break the neck. Exhumations of prisoners executed in the US between 1882 and 1945 – the era of 'modern' hangings – showed very few had broken necks. As the website explains, when such a long drop fails 'and the spinal cord remains intact, there is usually obvious physical suffering and visible struggling and this may be more intense in short drop hanging'. By contrast, in a study of 53 executed Nazi war criminals, 51 showed no movement at all after the fall.

These studies are far from definitive. But what they strongly suggest – when taken with the descriptions in this book – is that most people who were hanged in Australian were conscious and suffering a great deal for at least ten seconds – which is as long as it takes to sing 'Happy Birthday'. Many who convulsed after that would have been out of their misery. But many others clearly suffered longer because their nooses had not rendered them unconscious and had not broken their necks.

~

Somewhere in the vicinity of 1650 people were hanged in Australia between 1788 and 1967.

In 1922, Queensland became the first state to abolish capital punishment. Other states would follow, but it wouldn't be until 1975 that Victoria officially did away with the death penalty, with all states abolishing hanging by 1985.

~

As for deterrence – long cited as the 'justification' for executing culprits – the homicide rate in Australia was believed to be at its highest post-1880, when every state was still hanging malefactors, though sentences were often commuted. As late as 1915, when capital punishment was still on the books everywhere, the murder rate was 1.8 per 100,000 population. In 2019–2020, more than fifty years after Ronald Ryan, it was 1.02 per 100,000. There was never any evidence that hanging people reduced the number of serious violent offences. But, of course, this wasn't anything they didn't know then – their own detailed reports of crime and punishment made that clear.

~

In 2010, the Australian federal government prohibited any state or territory from ever reintroducing the death penalty.

Jack Ketch was dead.

# Epilogue

J ack Ketch's brutalities now seem so unspeakable that it's hard to believe they went on mostly unchallenged for most of white Australian history. It'll be the year 2147 before we've been longer without hanging that we were with it.

That raises the question: how will our descendants then look at us now?

We're civilised and progressive – as Berry and Barry and Farie and Rede and Castieau and Clarke and Vagabond and the rest believed themselves. But no matter how much we criticise, we live in a climate-change dystopia in which one woman every week is murdered by her partner, where thousands rot behind bars for minor drug offences while corporate criminals go free, where gender, sexuality, religion and ethnicity make some people targets failed by the law, where First Nations people continue to suffer police brutality and deaths in custody, and where asylum seekers created by the endless wars are endlessly detained.

Then there are forces who believe these are exaggerated or imaginary concerns.

Or that things should be more brutal.

Close to the end of the writing of this book, in November 2021, people marched the streets of Melbourne in a 'freedom rally', and took selfies and videos in front of a gallows with nooses.

It made me wonder how much they knew of what they wanted to return to their city and country.

It made me worry that while Jack Ketch may be dead, his spirit will never rest.

# Acknowledgements

A big shout-out to all *Forgotten Australia* listeners. Your support, kind reviews and generous comments helped make this book possible.

With special thanks to Clare and Ava, who make everything worthwhile, and to our wonderful families, whose love and support sustains. Mic Looby, who's always there. Martin Hughes, Kevin O'Brien, Ruby Ashby-Orr, Dana Anderson and Julian Welch for their belief in – and hard work on – on a book that turned out to be far bigger than expected. Melanie Ostell, for her guidance. Brad Argent, Jennifer Dodd and the Ancestry.com.au team, and Guy Scott-Wilson, Jordon Lott, Olivia O'Flynn and the Acast team, for their ongoing support of *Forgotten Australia*. Michael Anson, Elisabeth O'Sullivan, Anne Jones and Charles Spiteri of the Public Records Office of Victoria's North Melbourne Reading Room for all their kind assistance. Desiree Pettit-Keating of the Bendigo Regional Archives Centre for her invaluable research advice. Kathleen Toohey and all the staff and guides at Old Melbourne Gaol for making me feel welcome within those old bluestone walls. Thanks also to Stephen Davis and Madeleine Wilson, for their support.

Special acknowledgement to Trevor Poultney, late guide at Old

Melbourne Gaol, and author of *Artists in Hemp: Hangmen in Port Phillip and Victoria 1842–1967*. While I was unable to access Mr Poultney's book during the pandemic, when I eventually got to the Gaol in April 2022 and was able to purchase a copy, I was gratified to see I'd found almost all the same sources as he had in relation to hangmen from 1842 to 1909. Where I'd missed something and was able to make an inclusion, I have specifically noted Mr Poultney's work in the endnotes, which are available at: affirmpress.com.au/publishing/hanging-ned-kelly. I hope *Hanging Ned Kelly* stands as a worthwhile companion to his pioneering work. Vale.

# References

The source references accompanying this book can be found online at affirmpress.com.au/publishing/hanging-ned-kelly.